PRECISION SHEET METAL

MATHEMATICS

Precision Sheet Metal

MATHEMATICS

RICHARD S. BUDZIK

Instructor, Vocational Sheet Metal
Prosser Vocational High School
Chicago, Illinois

PRACTICAL PUBLICATIONS
6272 W. North Avenue
Chicago, IL 60639
312-237-2986

About the Author

As a professional vocational educator, with a decade of trade experience, Richard S. Budzik is exceptionally well qualified. His years in both the trade and teaching, in addition to his professional education, have provided him with an insight and knowledge of vocational precision sheet metal that is found rarely in an educator.

In his years at Prosser Vocational High School, Chicago, Illinois, Mr. Budzik has trained hundreds of students in the field of precision sheet metal, both at the secondary level and in adult education, by teaching them blueprint reading, shop mathematics, shop theory, and shop practice. He has conducted training programs for several industrial firms.

His insight into the needs of industry and the near absence of educational material in precision sheet metal led Mr. Budzik to a three-year effort in developing this material. He has also served as a curriculum consultant for the Chicago Public Schools.

THIRD EDITION

COPYRIGHT © 1993 by Practical Publications, 6272 W. North Avenue, Chicago, IL 60639. Printed in the Unites States of America.

Library of Congress Catalog Card Number 71-83129

ISBN-0-912914-49-1

FOREWORD

The enormous recent demands for skilled workers in precision sheet metal is a development that has come about in recent years due to the growth in production of the following:

Aircraft	Computers	Restaurant Equipment
Missile	Date Processing	Food processing
Spaceship	Defense	Air handling
Electronic	Military	Laboratory
Communication	Photographic	Appliances
Transportation	X-ray	Shipbuilding
	Signs	

Using these books in sheet metal courses, both public and private, will provide those who complete the training program with a readily employable skill needed in a variety of companies, both large and small, found in most geographic areas. Teaching this new sheet metal technology is more realistic for those with a sincere interest in vocational education. There are so many job classifications within precision sheet metal work that there is a place for students and trainees of all levels of ability.

The employment opportunities of our students or trainees should always remain foremost in our minds, due to our responsibility as educators in industrial subjects. This series of precision sheet metal handbooks, workbooks and instructors guides meet the need for training people for these types of employment.

Ron Fowler, Director
Metal Fabricating Institute
Rockford, IL

Ronald S Fowler, Director

Acknowledgments

Special thanks is extended to the following staff members, who contributed much to the author's overall training and background at Washburne Trade School in Chicago: Frank Wietzke, Head of the Sheet Metal Department and shop theory teacher; Fred Schumacher, drawing teacher; Claude Zinngrabe, shop mathematics teacher; and Fred Hanson, shop practice teacher. Their well-organized courses of study provided a realization of the importance of the related technical subjects, in addition to shop experiences.

While the author was working as a sheet metal apprentice and journeyman, extremely valuable training and gratifying shop experiences were provided by: Ed Lemke, shop foreman; Jake Froehlich and John McDonough, shop superintendents, all of whom are master sheet metal craftsmen. Helpful guidance and direction during both trade experience and later as a vocational teacher have been provided by Joseph Kaberlein, trade teacher, author, and union representative.

As a vocational teacher, the author has benefited much from his associations with the following professional educators: Clyde Nelson, Director of Manpower; Donald Racky, Principal of Lane Technical High School in Chicago; Joseph Sirchio, Principal of Chicago Vocational High School; Maurice Maloff, Assistant Principal of Prosser Vocational High School in Chicago; and Joseph Eckl, Supervisor of Metal Trades Teachers.

The parts illustrated in the textbook and workbook were taken from actual drawings provided by the following companies: Douglas Aircraft Co., Inc.; Hughes Aircraft Co.; Lockheed Aircraft Corp.; North American Aviation, Inc.; Northrop Corp.; Bendix Aviation Corp.; The Garrett Corporation; Control Data Corp.; International Business Machines Corp.; Smith-Corona Marchant Inc.; Litton Industries; Friden Inc.; The Magnavox Company; Beckman Instruments Inc.; Borg-Warner Corp.; Burroughs Corp.; National Cash Register Co.; McDonnell-Douglas Corp.; Westinghouse Electric Corp.; General Electric Co.; Link-Belt Co.; Zenith Radio Corp.; Stewart-Warner Corp.; Admiral Corp.; Automatic Electric Co.; Cook Electric Company; Western Electric Co.; Hotpoint Co.; Sunbeam Corporation; Bell & Howell Co.; Charles Bruning Co., Inc.; Pullman Standard; International Harvester Co.; Caterpillar Tractor Co.; Xerox Corporation; Motorola, Inc.; Eastman Kodak Co.; General Dynamics Corp.; and Radio Corporation of America.

Preface

The need for training people to become skilled precision sheet metalworkers has evolved only in recent years. Precision sheet metal parts are required in various types of products, which have grown in demand in recent years and continue in demand at an ever-increasing rate. These include the following types of products:

Aircraft	Military	Laboratory
Missile	Photographic	Appliances
Electronics	X-ray	Spaceship
Communication	Restaurant	Shipbuilding
Data processing	Food processing	Sign manufacturing
Defense	Air handling	Transportation

The general classifications of precision sheet metalworkers include:

Modelmakers	Fabricators
Inspectors	Assemblers
Setup men	Machine operators (punch press, press brake, and shear)

Some of these workers are employed by the manufacturing companies that produce the end products. Other sheet metalworkers are employed by job shops that perform the precision sheet metalwork for the manufacturers.

This textbook explains the basic principles of mathematics, and illustrates their applications to sheet metal shop problems. A step-by-step explanation and solution are provided for each type of problem. A typical shop problem is presented and solved in each unit.

The addition, subtraction, multiplication, and division of whole numbers, fractions, and decimals are reviewed. They are applied to the problems and formulas used in precision sheet metalwork. Emphasis is placed on determining bend allowances and blank sizes.

Only the principles of geometry and trigonometry that apply to precision sheet metalwork are presented in the textbook.

The textbook emphasizes technical theory, but it does not omit practical applications. The correlated units in the workbook consist of problems that provide practice in the mathematical operation emphasized and trade problems that apply to the specific mathematical operation.

This textbook is not intended to be comprehensive to the point that it includes all the information needed by the various classifications of precision sheet metalworkers. Its chief purpose is to provide familiarity with the application of mathematical principles to shop problems. Three other books in this series are combined with this book to present all the information related to precision sheet metalwork. The three textbooks are: (1) *Precision Sheet Metal—Shop Theory;* (2) *Precision Sheet Metal—Blueprint Reading;* and (3) *Precision Sheet Metal—Shop Practice.*

RICHARD S. BUDZIK

Preface to Second Edition

Throughout this Edition you will notice typical shop drawings from the precision sheet metal industry. They are at the beginning and end of most units. However, each one does not necessarily relate directly to the specific information in the chapter next to it.

The purposes of these drawings are:

1) to show actual and complete shop drawings that are used in the precision sheet metal industry.

2) wherever possible, to show a drawing at the beginning or end of each chapter that relates to the information in that chapter.

Preface to Third Edition

Added to this Edition is Unit 82 titled "Using a Hand-Held Calculator to Solve Metal Fabrication Problems."

Richard S. Budzik

Contents

CONTENTS

CONTENTS

Reading and Writing
Whole Numbers

Before proceeding with the application of mathematics to precision sheet metal problems, we must be sure that we have a thorough understanding of the arithmetic fundamentals (addition, subtraction, multiplication, and division). This means that we must be able to perform the four fundamental operations accurately with whole numbers, common fractions, decimals, and mixed numbers. The first requirement is the ability to read and write the numerals.

Two common numbering systems are used for calculations and numerals. The Arabic numerals (1, 2, 3) are usually used for calculations. The Roman numerals

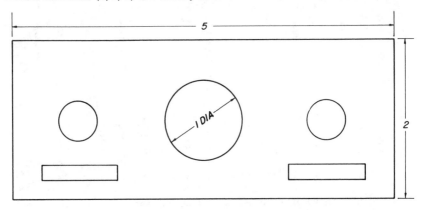

Fig. 1-1. Part dimensions in whole numbers.

15

(I, II, III) are usually used to number the chapters in books and other publications. The Arabic numerals, of course, are used in precision sheet metalwork (Fig. 1-1).

In the Arabic system, 10 numerals are used as the symbols. These 10 numerals, or digits can be used in any combination of one or more of them. The numerals are written as follows:

0	1	2	3	4	5	6	7	8	9
zero	one	two	three	four	five	six	seven	eight	nine

All numbers are expressed by means of the 10 numerals or digits. This includes the zero, which is sometimes called a "naught" or "cipher." When used alone, it has no value; but it is used in unoccupied places in a combination of numerals. A numeral or digit varies in value, depending on its location or place in a number. A number consists of one or more digits that are used to express a quantity.

The word *place* in numbers has a special meaning, as indicated in Table 1. Each group of three digits is referred to as a "period," and is separated from the other periods by a comma. This makes reading the larger numbers less difficult.

As you will note within each period, the numbers are read the same; then the name of that period is inserted before moving to the next period. Reading of the numbers begins at the extreme left-hand side. The word *and* is not inserted when reading the whole numbers. If a period consists of all zeros, that period is not mentioned.

Table 1-1. How to Read Whole Numbers

Trillions Group			Billions Group			Millions Group			Thousands Group			Units Group		
hundred trillions	ten trillions	trillions	hundred billions	ten billions	billions	hundred millions	ten millions	millions	hundred thousands	ten thousands	thousands	hundreds	tens	units
3	2	5	5	3	8	6	2	9	2	1	4	6	2	4

The number shown in Table 1-1 is read, as follows: "Three hundred twenty-five trillion, five hundred thirty-eight billion, six hundred twenty-nine million, two hundred fourteen thousand, six hundred twenty-four.

The following numbers are read as shown:

122	One hundred twenty-two.
4000	Four thousand.
69,461	Sixty-nine thousand, four hundred sixty-one.
400,006	Four hundred thousand, six.
136,018	One hundred thirty-six thousand, eighteen.
3,000,437	Three million, four hundred thirty-seven.
79,857,385	Seventy-nine million, eight hundred fifty-seven thousand, three hundred eighty-five.
201,003,124	Two hundred one million, three thousand, one hundred twenty-four.
30,111	Thirty thousand, one hundred eleven.
4,306	Four thousand, three hundred six.
806	Eight hundred six.
70	Seventy.
34	Thirty-four.

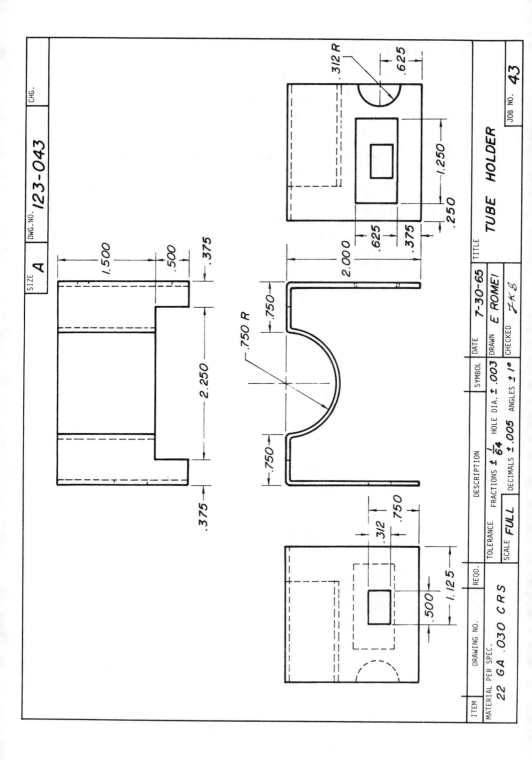

SIZE **A** DWG. NO. **123-043** CHG.

1.500
.500
.375
2.250
.375

.750 R
.750
.750

.312 R
.625
2.000
.625
.375
1.250
.250

.312
.750
.500
1.125

TITLE **TUBE HOLDER**
JOB NO. **43**

ITEM	DRAWING NO.	REQD.	DESCRIPTION	SYMBOL

MATERIAL PER SPEC.
22 GA .030 CRS

TOLERANCE FRACTIONS ± 1/64 HOLE DIA. ± .003
DECIMALS ± .005 ANGLES ± 1°

SCALE **FULL**

DATE **7-30-65**
DRAWN **E ROME!**
CHECKED **℈KB**

Addition of
Whole Numbers

Although the precision sheet metalworker rarely uses only whole numbers, he must know how to add them before he can add fractions and decimals (Fig. 2-1).

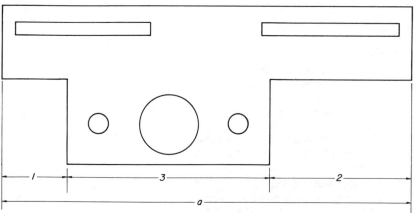

Fig. 2-1

Combining two or more numbers into a single number is called *addition*. The *sum* is the result obtained from adding two or more numbers. The plus (+) sign is used to indicate addition, and it is read "plus."

19

Only identical terms can be added. You cannot add inches to feet. The dimension *2 feet and 7 inches* is not a number that consists of $2 + 7 = 9$. Each number must retain its own terms *2 feet + 7 inches*.

Numbers that are to be added must be placed with the 1's or units digits in a single column, the 10's digits in another column, etc. When you add real quantities, the total should contain the name of the quantities that have been added.

When an addition, subtraction, multiplication, or division sign is not present, addition is understood.

Definition of Terms

1. *Addends.* The numbers being added.
2. *Sum.* The result of addition.

Adding Whole Numbers

1. Place the numbers in vertical columns with the 1's or units digits in the units column, the 10's in another column, etc.
2. Add each column, beginning with the right-hand column, placing the total of the column below the column. When the total is a two-digit number, write the units digit at the bottom of the column and "carry" or add the 10's digit to the next column. The number that is "carried over" can be written at the top of the next column if helpful. Add each column, always working from the right-hand column toward the left-hand column.

Problem: $3 + 57 + 42$

Solution:

1. Arrange the numbers in vertical columns—units below the units, etc.

   $$\begin{array}{r} 3 \\ 57 \\ \underline{42} \end{array}$$

2. Add the column at the extreme right: $3 + 7 + 2 = 12$. Write the units digit (2) beneath this column; and add the 10's digit (1) to the next column.

   $$\begin{array}{r} 1 \\ 3 \\ 57 \\ \underline{42} \\ 2 \end{array}$$

3. Add the next column: $1 + 5 + 4 = 10$. Since there is no third column, write the complete total (10) at the left of the units digit.

   $$\begin{array}{r} 1 \\ 3 \\ 57 \\ \underline{42} \\ 102 \end{array}$$

4. The *sum* is *102.*

To check your addition, add the columns upward; then you are not adding the numbers in the same sequence.

Units of Measure in Addition

When inches or other units of measure are added, the sum will be in a like unit. Only like units can be added; for example, inches cannot be added to feet—without first converting the feet to inches.

Trade Problem

Problem: Find the total length a of the part in the diagram in Fig. 2-1.

Solution:

1. Add the dimensions.

2. The total length a of the part is *6* in.

$$a = 1 \text{ in.} + 3 \text{ in.} + 2 \text{ in.}$$
$$= 6 \text{ in.}$$

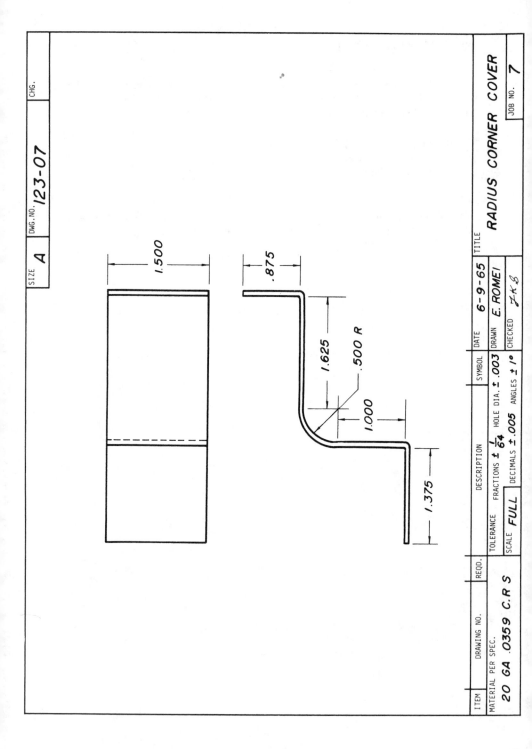

1.500

.875

1.625

.500 R

1.000

1.375

SIZE **A**   DWG. NO. **123-07**   CHG.

ITEM	DRAWING NO.	REQD.	DESCRIPTION	SYMBOL	DATE **6-9-65**	TITLE

MATERIAL PER SPEC.
20 GA .0359 C.R S

TOLERANCE   FRACTIONS ± $\frac{1}{64}$ HOLE DIA. ± **.003**
DECIMALS ± **.005**   ANGLES ± **1°**

SCALE **FULL**

DRAWN **E. ROMEI**

CHECKED **J.K.B**

RADIUS CORNER COVER

JOB NO. **7**

Subtraction of
Whole Numbers

Although the precision sheet metalworker rarely deals with only whole numbers, he must know how to subtract the whole numbers before he can use the fractions and decimals (Fig. 3-1).

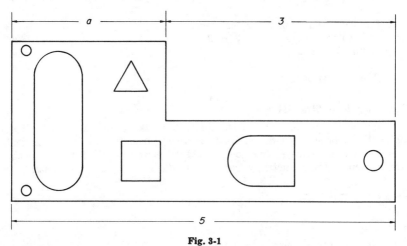

Fig. 3-1

Subtraction is the direct opposite of addition. In addition, you combine two or more numbers. In subtraction, you take one number from another number. The

23

quantities or numbers to be subtracted must, however, still be in the same or identical terms.

Definition of Terms

1. *Subtraction*. Process of taking one number from another; or of finding the difference between two numbers.
2. *Minuend*. The number from which you subtract a number.
3. *Subtrahend*. The number that is to be subtracted.
4. *Difference*. The result or answer.
5. *Remainder*. The result or answer.
6. *Sign*. The minus (−) sign is read as "minus."

Subtracting Whole Numbers

Place the number to be subtracted (subtrahend) beneath the number from which it is to be subtracted (minuend). Draw a line and subtract. Always begin with the right-hand column (units) and work toward the left-hand side.

Problem: 379 − 134

Solution:

1. Arrange the problem in columns.
2. Subtract the units column: 9 − 4 = 5.
3. Subtract the remaining columns, each column individually: 7 − 3 = 4; and 3 − 1 = 2.

$$
\begin{array}{r}
379 \\
-134 \\
\hline
5
\end{array}
$$

$$
\begin{array}{r}
379 \\
-134 \\
\hline
245
\end{array}
$$

4. The *difference* is *245*.

Borrowing in Subtraction

In any column, if the number to be subtracted is larger than the number from which it is to be subtracted, you must "borrow" *1* from the next column and add it to the number. Always remember to add "0" first, since it is from the next larger column. You are actually adding 10 to the number that is too small.

Problem: 371 − 134

Solution:

1. Arrange the problem in columns.
2. Subtract the units column (1 − 4). Since *4* is larger than *1*, it is necessary to "borrow" 1 from the next column. The 10's column is now *6*;

$$
\begin{array}{r}
371 \\
-134 \\
\hline
\end{array}
$$

make a notation of this, so that you
do not forget when you get to this
column. Add 10 to the 1 in the units
column $(10 + 1 = 11)$. Now subtract: $11 - 4 = 7$.

3. Subtract the 10's column: $6 - 3 =$
3.

4. Subtract the 100's column: $3 - 1 =$
2.

5. The *difference* is *237*.

$$\begin{array}{r} 6 \\ 3\!\!\!/1 \\ -134 \\ \hline 7 \end{array}$$

$$\begin{array}{r} 6 \\ 3\!\!\!/1 \\ -134 \\ \hline 237 \end{array}$$

Units of Measurement

When inches or other units of measurement are subtracted, the difference will
be in the same unit. Only like units can be subtracted. For example, inches cannot be subtracted from feet, without first changing the feet to inches.

Trade Problem

Problem: Determine the correct label of
the dimension a in Fig. 3-1.

Solution: The dimension a can be found
by subtracting that length of the
known part (3 in.) from the total
length (5 in.) :

1. Subtract the known dimension (3
in.) from the total length (5 in.).

2. The dimension a is *2 in.*

$a = 5$ in. $- 3$ in.
$= 2$ in.

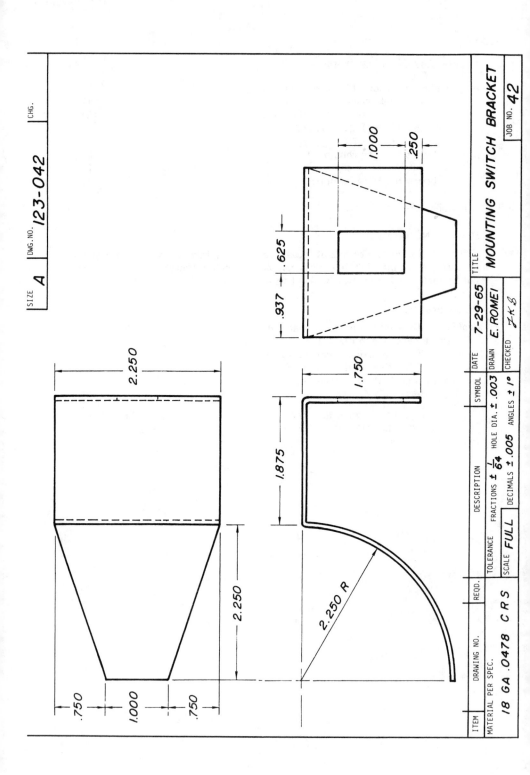

SIZE **A** | DWG. NO. **123-042** | CHG.

2.250

.750 | 1.000 | .750

2.250

1.000

.250

.937 | .625

1.750

1.875

2.250 R

ITEM	DRAWING NO.	REQD.	DESCRIPTION	SYMBOL	DATE **7-29-65**	TITLE

MATERIAL PER SPEC.
18 GA .0478 C R S

TOLERANCE
FRACTIONS **± $\frac{1}{64}$** HOLE DIA. **± .003**

SCALE **FULL** DECIMALS **± .005** ANGLES **± 1°**

DRAWN **E. ROMEI**

CHECKED **$\mathcal{JKB}$**

TITLE **MOUNTING SWITCH BRACKET**

JOB NO. **42**

Multiplication of
Whole Numbers

Although the precision sheet metalworker rarely deals with only whole numbers, he must know how to multiply the whole numbers before using the fractions and decimals. Multiplication is the process of increasing a number by its own value a specified number of times. In reality, it is a short method of adding (Fig. 4-1).

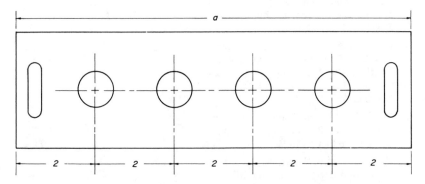

Fig. 4-1

Definition of Terms

    1. *Multiplicand.* The number that is to be increased.

27

2. *Multiplier*. The number indicating the number of times that the multiplicand is to be increased.

3. *Product*. The result of multiplying.

4. *Times Sign (×)*. The sign of muplication is read *times*. It is written between the numbers: *3 × 2*.

Multiplying the Whole Numbers

If a number contains more digits than another number, the number with more digits is usually used as the multiplicand. This makes the process easier and shorter. The steps in multiplying are as follows:

1. Place the multiplier below the multiplicand.

$$\begin{array}{r} 725 \\ \times\ 35 \\ \hline \end{array}$$

2. Begin by multiplying the multiplicand (725) by the units digit (5) in the multiplier for the first partial product: $5 \times 5 = 25$.

3. Place the *5* in the units column, directly below the number by which we are multiplying (5).

$$\begin{array}{r} 725 \\ \times\ 35 \\ \hline 5 \end{array}$$

4. The second digit (2) represents 10's, and must be placed in the next column. Still using the units digit (5) in the multiplier, multiply this number (5) by the 10's digit (2) in the multiplicand, and add the *2* of the first partial product to this number: $5 \times 2 = 10 + 2 = 12$.

5. Place the *2* in the 10's column; the *1* will be added to the next column. Multiply the 100's digit (7) in the multicand by *5;* then add *1:* $7 \times 5 = 35 + 1 = 36$.

$$\begin{array}{r} 725 \\ \times\ 35 \\ \hline 25 \end{array}$$

6. Place the *6* in the 100's column and the *3* in the 1000's column. The first partial product is *3625*.

$$\begin{array}{r} 725 \\ \times\ 35 \\ \hline 3625 \end{array}$$

7. Next, multiply the multiplicand by the second digit (3) in the 10's column of the multiplier. The first number (5) is placed in the 10's column, since we are multiplying by a number in the 10's position. Multiply in the same manner as above. The second partial product is *2175*.

$$\begin{array}{r} 725 \\ \times\ 35 \\ \hline 3625 \\ 2175 \end{array}$$

8. Add the partial product to obtain the
total product.

9. The *product* is *25,375*.

```
    725
×    35
   3625
   2175
  25375
```

Checking the Multiplication Problem

The best method for checking a multiplication problem is to invert the multiplier and the multiplicand, and multiply. If you do not invert the numbers, you may repeat the error, if an error has been made.

Zeros in Multiplication

Since zero has no value, zero times *any* number is always zero: For examples, $0 \times 0 = 0$; and $0 \times 5 = 0$.

Problem: 323×300

Solution:

1. Note that the zeros are set at the right of the units column.
2. Place the zeros beneath the zeros; then multiply by the digit (3).

```
    323
×   300
  96900
```

If there is a zero inside the multiplier:

Problem: 321×201

Solution:

1. Arrange the problem.
2. When you arrive at the zero, merely place one zero in the 10's place, and proceed with the next digit.

```
    321
×   201
    321
   6420
  64521
```

3. Add the partial products, as before.

Always place the first digit of a new partial product directly below the number being used in the multiplier. Be extremely careful with the zeros, as shown above.

Units of Measurement

When inches or other units of measurement are multiplied by a number with no dimension, the product will be in terms of the unit of measurement:

$$3 \times 2 \text{ in.} = 6 \text{ in.}$$

A linear unit of measurement times another linear unit results in an area measurement, not in a linear measurement: For example, 3 in. $\times$ 2 in. = 6 sq in., which will be explained fully later.

Trade Problem

Problem: Find the total length a of the metal part in Fig. 4-1.

Solution:

1. Since each of the five dimensions is 2 in., multiply to obtain the total length.
2. The total length a of the part is *10 in.*

$$a = 2 \text{ in.} \times 5$$
$$= 10 \text{ in.}$$

Division of
Whole Numbers

Although the precision sheet metalworker rarely deals with only whole numbers, he must know how to divide the whole numbers, before he can divide fractions and decimals (Fig. 5-1). Division is the process of finding the number of times one number contains another number. It is the reverse process of multiplication.

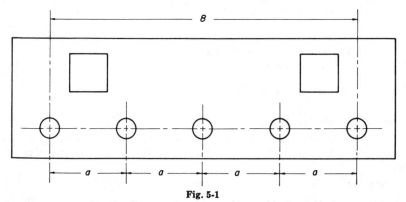

Fig. 5-1

Definition of Terms

1. *Dividend.*   The number to be divided.
2. *Divisor.*   The number which you divide by.

31

3. *Quotient.* The result of division.

4. *Remainder.* The portion of the dividend left when the quotient is not a whole number.

5. *Division ($\div$) Sign.* The sign of division is read "divided by."

Dividing Whole Numbers (Short Division)

Short division is usually used when the divisor has only one digit other than the zeros.

Problem: 558 $\div$ 6

Solution:

1. Arrange as a division problem. $6\,\overline{\smash{\big)}\,558}$

2. Attempt to divide 6 into the first digit (5) at the left under the bracket. This is impossible.

   $$6\,\overline{\smash{\big)}\,558}\quad\overset{9}{}$$

3. Attempt to divide 6 into the first two digits (55) to the left under the bracket. Thus, 55 $\div$ 6 = 9 with a remainder of *1*. Write the *9* above the last digit to the right which was used (the second *5*).

   $$\begin{array}{r} 9 \\ 6\,\overline{\smash{\big)}\,558} \\ 54 \\ \hline 18 \end{array}$$

4. "Carry" the remainder *1*, which was in the 10's place, to the next digit; then, the digit *8* becomes (8 + 10), or *18*.

5. Attempt to divide 6 into 18: then 18 $\div$ 6 = 3. Write the *3* at the right of the *9* in the quotient.

   $$\begin{array}{r} 93 \\ 6\,\overline{\smash{\big)}\,558} \\ 54 \\ \hline 18 \\ 18 \\ \hline \end{array}$$

6. The result or *quotient* is *93*.

Checking the Division Problem

A division problem can be checked by multiplying the quotient by the divisor to obtain the dividend. If there is a remainder, add it to the product.

Dividing Whole Numbers (Long Division)

Long division is used when the divisor is a larger number, consisting of more than one digit. This process is identical to short division, except for writing the partial products below the proper digit in the dividend. This is done to find the remainder that is to be used with the next digit.

Problem: 97,453 $\div$ 132

Solution:

1. Arrange the problem as a division problem.

$$132 \,/\overline{97453}$$

2. The smallest number into which we can divide *132* is *974*. We cannot readily determine the number of times that 132 can be divided into *974;* therefore, we try a number that seems to be nearly correct. We try the number *8*. Multiply the divisor by *8*, placing the first number (6) at the right, directly below the farthest number to the right (4) being considered in the dividend.

$$\begin{array}{r} 8 \\ 132 \,/\overline{97453} \\ 1056 \end{array}$$

$$\begin{array}{r} 132 \,/\overline{97453} \\ 1056 \end{array}$$

3. The number (8) is too large, so we erase and try the next smaller number (7). Subtract for the remainder, and bring down the next number (5). A quicker method of obtaining the "trial divisor" is to consider all but the last number in each part: $97 \div 13 = 7$.

$$\begin{array}{r} 7 \\ 132 \,/\overline{97453} \\ 924 \\ \hline 505 \end{array}$$

4. Repeat this procedure.

5. The number remaining at the end is the "remainder."

$$\begin{array}{r} 738 \\ 132 \,/\overline{97453} \\ 924 \\ \hline 505 \\ 396 \\ \hline 1093 \\ 1056 \\ \hline r. = 37 \end{array}$$

6. The *quotient* is *738* with a remainder (r.) of *37*.

Units of Measurement

When inches or other units of measurement are divided by another number with *no* dimension, the quotient will be in the same unit of measurement:

$$6 \text{ in.} \div 2 = 3 \text{ in.}$$

When either inches or other units of measurement are divided by inches or a like unit, the quotient will be merely a number—without units of measurement. Thus the units *cancel* themselves:

$$6 \text{ in.} \div 2 \text{ in.} = 3$$

Trade Problem

Problem: Find the dimension *a* between the centers of each pair of holes in the part in Fig. 5-1.

Solution:

1. Divide the overall dimension (8 in.)
   by the number of spaces (4).
2. The dimension a between each pair
   of holes is *2 in.*

$$a = 8 \text{ in.} \div 4$$
$$= 2 \text{ in.}$$

Common Fractions

It is impossible for the precision sheet metalworker to solve all the problems of his work by the sole use of whole numbers. In fact, he rarely uses only whole numbers. He frequently must use fractional divisions of an inch, such as $\frac{1}{2}''$, $\frac{1}{4}''$, $\frac{1}{8}''$, $\frac{1}{16}''$, $\frac{1}{32}''$, and $\frac{1}{64}''$. These divisions can be found on the steel rule (Fig. 6-1).

Fig. 6-1. Fractional divisions of an inch.

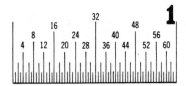

Symbols

The symbols used with fractions are identical to those used with the whole numbers:

1. Addition (+) means:
   a. Plus.
   b. Sum of.
   c. Added to.
   d. Increased by.
2. Subtraction (−) means:
   a. Minus.
   b. Subtracted from.
   c. Difference between.
   d. Decreased by.

3. Multiplication (×) means:
   a. Multiplied by.
   b. Times.
   c. Product of.
4. Division (÷) means:
   a. Divided by.
   b. Fractional part of.
   c. Quotient of.

Definition of Terms

1. *Fraction.* A fraction indicates one or more of the equal parts into which a unit is divided; it is always written in a form that indicates division.
   Example: The dimension *1/2″* means that 1 inch is being divided into two equal parts and that one of the two parts is being referred to here. We can also write the fraction as (1 ÷ 2) to indicate that the fraction *1/2* indicates division.

2. *Numerator.* The numeral written above the line of the fraction is the denominator. It indicates the number of equal parts into which the whole quantity is being divided.
   Example: In the fraction *1/6*, the numerator is *1*; therefore, one part of six parts is being considered.

3. *Denominator.* The numeral written below the line in the fraction is the denominator. It indicates the number of equal parts into which the whole quantity is being divided.
   Example: In the fraction *1/6*, the denominator is *6*, meaning that the whole quantity is being divided into six equal parts.

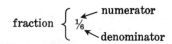

4. *Terms.* The numerator and denominator are the terms of the fraction.

5. *Common fraction.* A fraction in which *both terms are expressed* is a common fraction.

6. *Proper fraction.* A fraction in which the *numerator is less than its denominator* is a proper fraction.
   Examples: ½, ⅞, and 9/16.

7. *Improper fraction.* A fraction in which the *numerator is a larger number than its denominator* is an improper fraction.
   Examples: 5/2, 9/8, and 30/16.

8. *Unit fraction.* A fraction in which the *numerator is 1* is considered to be a unit fraction.
   Examples: ½, ⅛, and 1/64.

9. *Mixed number.* A number that consists of *both a whole number and a fraction* is a mixed number.
   Examples: 3½ and 7¾4.

10. *Complex fraction.* A fraction in which *either or both terms is a fraction or mixed number* is a complex fraction.

$$\frac{7/8}{4} \qquad \frac{9}{7/64} \qquad \frac{3 1/8}{4 1/2}$$

Deriving a Fraction

If a line is divided into four equal parts, one of these parts is:

$$\frac{\text{one part}}{\text{all parts}}$$

or one-fourth the total length of the line.

One part is equal to *1/4* the total length.
Two parts are equal to *2/4* the total length.
Three parts are equal to *3/4* the total length.
Four parts are equal to *4/4* the total length.

Reducing a Fraction to its Lowest Terms

When both the numerator and denominator of a fraction are multiplied by the same number, the value of the fraction is not changed.

$$\frac{1}{2} = \frac{1 \times 2}{2 \times 2} = \frac{2}{4}$$

When both the numerator and denominator of a fraction are divided by the same number, the value of the fraction is not changed. Therefore, fractions are reduced to their lowest terms in this manner.

$$\frac{2}{4} = \frac{2 \div 2}{4 \div 2} = \frac{1}{2} \qquad\qquad \frac{6}{8} = \frac{6 \div 2}{8 \div 2} = \frac{3}{4}$$

Changing a Mixed Number to an Improper Fraction

A mixed number is changed to an improper fraction by multiplying the whole number by the denominator and then adding the numerator, placing the result above the denominator.

Problem: Change the mixed number 3½
    to an improper fraction.

Solution:

1. Multiply the whole number (3) by $3 \times 2 = 6$
   the denominator of the fraction (2).
2. Add the numerator of the fraction $6 + 1 = 7$
   (1).
3. Place the result over the denomina- $\frac{7}{2}$
   tor (2).
4. The *improper fraction* is ⅞.
5. Combining the above steps, the problem is:

$$3\frac{1}{2} = \frac{3 \times 2 + 1}{2} = \frac{7}{2}$$

Changing an Improper Fraction to a Mixed Number

An improper fraction is changed to a mixed number by dividing the numerator by the denominator and then placing the remainder over the denominator.

Problem: Change the improper fraction
$13/4$ to a mixed number.

Solution:

1. Divide the numerator (13) by the denominator of the fraction (4).

$$13 \div 4 = 3$$
$$r. = 1$$

2. The remainder (1) is placed over the denominator (4) to form the fraction ($\frac{1}{4}$).

$$\frac{1}{4}$$

3. Combining the whole number (3) and the fraction ($\frac{1}{4}$) results in the *mixed number* $3\frac{1}{4}$.

$$3\frac{1}{4}$$

Fractional Divisions
of the Steel Rule

The steel rule is used to measure lengths in inches and in fractional parts of an inch. They can be purchased in various lengths and graduations (8ths, 16ths, 32nds, 64ths), depending on the needs of the worker. The precision sheet metalworker uses the fractional steel rule with 64ths graduations (Fig. 7-1).

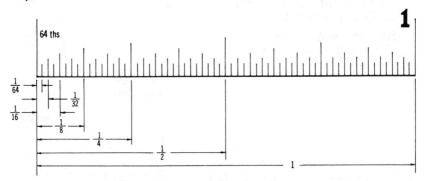

Fig. 7-1. Fractional divisions of the 64ths scale.

The fractional divisions of an inch are determined by dividing the inch into equal parts. There are eight $\frac{1}{8}$" divisions and sixteen $\frac{1}{16}$" divisions an inch, etc. The abbreviation for the words *inch* and *inches* is *in.* or the symbol (").

Using the rule: "When both the numerator and the denominator are multiplied by the same number, the value of the fraction is not changed," we arrive at the following useful equivalents:

$$\frac{1}{2} = \frac{2}{4} \qquad \frac{1}{4} = \frac{2}{8} \qquad \frac{1}{8} = \frac{2}{16} \qquad \frac{1}{16} = \frac{2}{32}$$
$$= \frac{4}{8} \qquad\quad = \frac{4}{16} \qquad\quad = \frac{4}{32} \qquad\quad = \frac{4}{64}$$
$$= \frac{16}{32} \qquad\quad = \frac{8}{32} \qquad\quad = \frac{8}{64}$$
$$= \frac{32}{64} \qquad\quad = \frac{16}{64}$$

Reading the Common Divisions on the Steel Rule

The common divisions of the steel rule are:

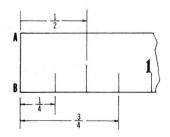

1. *Half-inch* (½″). To find ½″, count one ½″ division on the scale A.

2. *Fourth-inch* (¼″). To find *3/4″*, count three ¼″ divisions on the scale **B**.

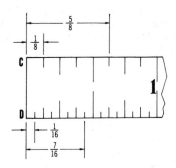

3. *Eighth-inch* (⅛″). To find *5/8″*, count five divisions, or one mark beyond the ½″ division C.

4. *Sixteenth-inch* (1⁄16″). To find *7/16″*, count seven 1⁄16″ divisions or one mark before the ½″ division D.

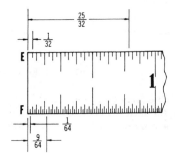

5. *Thirty-Seconds* (1⁄32″). To find ²⁵⁄₃₂″, county twenty-five 1⁄32″ divisions, or one mark beyond the ¾″ division E.

6. *Sixty-fourths* (1⁄64″). To find ⁹⁄₆₄″, count nine 1⁄64″ divisions, or one 1⁄64″ division beyond the ⅛″ division F.

Measuring

The following steps should be observed in measuring with the steel rule:

1. Turn the steel rule until the proper scale is in contact with the work to be measured. It is more accurate to begin measuring at the 1-inch division.
2. Read the rule graduations to determine the correct length. Subtract 1 inch from the reading if the measurement begins at the 1-inch division.

Fig. 7-2

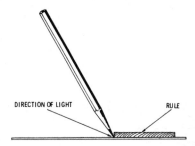

DIRECTION OF LIGHT   RULE

Laying Out

Observe the following points in laying out with the steel rule:

1. Turn the rule to obtain accurate measurement with the proper scale.
2. When drawing a line, tilt the pencil; then the line being drawn will be as close to the rule as possible (Fig. 7-2).
3. Be sure to position the rule and pencil so that the line to be drawn will pass through the required points, not just near them.

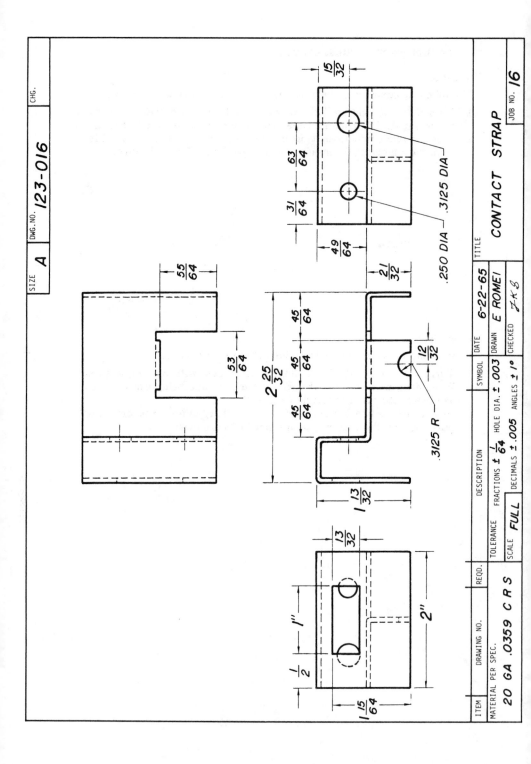

SIZE **A** | DWG. NO. **123-016** | CHG.

15/32

63/64

31/64

49/64

.3125 DIA

.250 DIA

21/32

55/64

53/64

45/64

45/64

2 25/32

45/64

12/32

.3125 R

1 13/32

13/32

1"

1/2

1 15/64

2"

TITLE **CONTACT STRAP**

DATE **6-22-65**

DRAWN **E ROME!**

CHECKED **J K B**

SYMBOL

DESCRIPTION

TOLERANCE FRACTIONS ± 1/64 HOLE DIA. ± .003

DECIMALS ± .005 ANGLES ± 1°

SCALE **FULL**

ITEM | DRAWING NO. | REQD.

MATERIAL PER SPEC. **20 GA .0359 C R S**

JOB NO. **16**

Addition of
Common Fractions

The precision sheet metalworker is required to add fractions when working from a drawing on which the draftsman has indicated the dimensions in fractional form (Fig. 8-1).

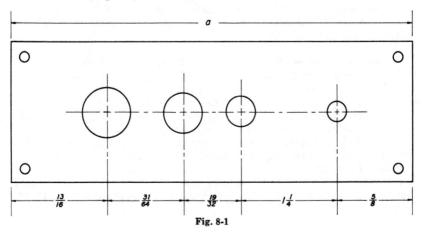

Fig. 8-1

Adding Fractions With the Same Denominator

To add fractions with identical denominators:

43

1. Place the numbers in columnar form
   and add the numerators, leaving the
   denominator alone.

$$\begin{array}{r} \frac{1}{6} \\ \frac{3}{6} \\ \hline \frac{4}{6} \end{array}$$

2. If the *sum* of the fractions is an improper fraction, change it to a mixed
   number.

$$\begin{array}{r} \frac{5}{6} \\ \frac{5}{6} \\ \hline \frac{10}{6} \end{array}$$

or $1\frac{4}{6}$

3. If the *sum* of the fractions is not in
   its lowest terms, reduce it to its lowest terms.

$$\begin{array}{r} \frac{1}{8} \\ \frac{3}{8} \\ \hline \frac{4}{8} \end{array}$$

or $\frac{1}{2}$

Finding the Least Common Denominator

Occasionally, it is necessary to add fractions, such as $\frac{1}{4}$ and $\frac{7}{10}$. You cannot change the fraction *1/4* to an equivalent fraction with the denominator *10*, and you cannot change the fraction *7/10* to an equivalent fraction with the denominator *4*. You are required to change both fractions to equivalent fractions with the same denominators. This denominator is called the *common denominator*.

The common denominator of a list of several fractions is any number that can be divided evenly by each of the denominators.

Example: The number *60* is a common denominator of the fractions *1/4* and *7/10*, because both *4* and *10* can be divided evenly into *60;* the number *40* is also a common denominator of the fractions, and the number *20* is still another common denominator.

It is always best to use the smallest number that can be divided evenly by the denominators of the fractions you are adding. This number is called the *smallest common denominator* or the *least common denominator*. To find the least common denominator, begin with the largest denominator.

Example: The largest denominator of the fractions *1/6, 1/2, and 7/10* is 10. Then count by 10's until you find the smallest number that is also divisible by both 2 and 6, as follows: 10 (not by 6) ; 20 (not by 6) ; and 30 (divisible by both 2 and 6). Therefore, the number *30* is the least common denominator for these fractions.

For the fractions *2/5, 5/7, and 5/14,* count by 14's until you arrive at a number that is also divisible by both 5 and 7—for example: 14, 28, 42, 56, and *70.*

Adding Mixed Numbers

It is easier to add the mixed numbers if the numbers are placed in columns with the whole numbers and the fractions directly below each other. Then add separately the columns of fractions and the columns of whole numbers. Combine the two sums for the final total.

Problem 1: Find the sum of $8\frac{3}{8}$ + $9\frac{1}{8}$

Solution:

1. Arrange the mixed numbers in columns.
2. Add the fractions; then add the whole numbers.
3. Reduce to the lowest terms.
4. The *sum* is $17\frac{1}{2}$.

$$8\frac{3}{8}$$
$$+\ 9\frac{1}{8}$$
$$17\frac{4}{8}$$

$$17\frac{1}{2}$$

Problem 2: Find the sum of $5\frac{2}{5}$ + $2\frac{1}{5}$ $+1\frac{4}{5}$

Solution:

1. Arrange the mixed numbers in columns.

$$5\frac{2}{5}$$
$$2\frac{1}{5}$$
$$1\frac{4}{5}$$

2. Add the fractions; then add the whole numbers.

$$5\frac{2}{5}$$
$$2\frac{1}{5}$$
$$1\frac{4}{5}$$
$$8\frac{7}{5}$$

3. Change the fraction to a mixed number.

$$\frac{7}{5} = 1\frac{2}{5}$$

4. Add the mixed number to the whole number obtained previously.

$$8 + 1\frac{2}{5} = 9\frac{2}{5}$$

5. The *sum* is $9\frac{2}{5}$.

Trade Problem

Find the total length a of the part in Fig. 8-1.

Problem: Total length = $\frac{13}{16}$ + $\frac{31}{64}$ + $\frac{19}{32}$ + $1\frac{1}{4}$ + $\frac{5}{8}$

Solution:

1. Determine the *least* common denominator (64), and change all the fractions.

$$\frac{13}{16} = \frac{52}{64}$$
$$\frac{31}{64} = \frac{31}{64}$$
$$\frac{19}{32} = \frac{38}{64}$$
$$\frac{1}{4} = \frac{16}{64}$$
$$\frac{5}{8} = \frac{40}{64}$$

2. Arrange the numbers in columns; then add the columns of fractions and the whole numbers separately.

$$\frac{5}{64}$$
$$\frac{31}{64}$$
$$\frac{38}{64}$$
$$1\frac{16}{64}$$
$$\frac{40}{64}$$
$$\overline{1\frac{177}{64}}$$

3. Change the fraction to a mixed number.

$$\frac{177}{64} = 2\frac{49}{64}$$

4. Add the whole number and the fraction changed to a mixed number.

$$1 + 2\frac{49}{64} = 3\frac{49}{64}$$

5. The *sum* or total length a is $3\frac{49}{64}$ in.

Subtraction of
Common Fractions

The precision sheet metalworker often finds that there is an unmarked dimension, which he needs, on the drawing. It may be necessary for him to subtract fractional dimensions to obtain the unmarked dimension (Fig. 9-1).

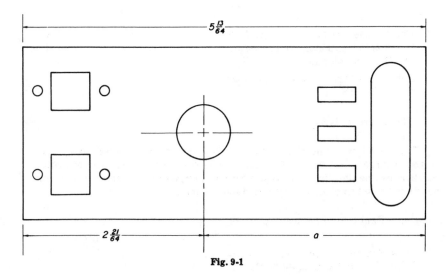

Fig. 9-1

Subtracting Fractions With Identical Denominators

To subtract fractions with identical denominators, place the fractions in columns; then subtract the numerators, leaving the denominator the same.

$$\begin{array}{r} \tfrac{3}{5} \\ -\tfrac{1}{5} \\ \hline \tfrac{2}{5} \end{array}$$

If the resulting total is not in its lowest terms, it can be reduced to its lowest terms if this is helpful.

$$\begin{array}{r} \tfrac{5}{8} \\ -\tfrac{3}{8} \\ \hline \tfrac{2}{8} \\ \text{or } \tfrac{1}{4} \end{array}$$

Subtracting Fractions With Different Denominators

Frequently, it is necessary to subtract fractions with different denominators, such as $\tfrac{5}{8}$ from $\tfrac{13}{16}$. Change the fractions to their least common denominator; then subtract only the numerators.

$$\begin{array}{r} \tfrac{13}{16} \\ -\tfrac{5}{8} = \tfrac{10}{16} \\ \hline \tfrac{3}{16} \end{array}$$

Subtracting Mixed Numbers

Subtract the fractions after they have been reduced to their least common denominator; then subtract the whole numbers, combining the two for the difference.

Problem: Find the difference: $8\tfrac{3}{8} - 5\tfrac{1}{4}$

Solution:

1. Change the fractions to their least common denominator, and place the fractions in columns.

$$\begin{array}{r} 8\tfrac{3}{8} \\ -5\tfrac{2}{8} \\ \hline 3\tfrac{1}{8} \end{array}$$

2. Subtract the fractions; then subtract the whole numbers.

3. The *difference* is $3\tfrac{1}{8}$

To subtract mixed numbers when the fraction of the number being subtracted is larger, first reduce the fractions to the least common denominator; then borrow one unit from the whole number to make up a fraction larger than the one being subtracted. Subtract in the usual manner.

Problem: Find the difference: $8\tfrac{3}{8} - 5\tfrac{5}{8}$

Solution:

1. Place fractions in columns; borrow *1* from *8* to make $\tfrac{3}{8}$ equal to $1\tfrac{3}{8}$, but changed to an improper fraction.

$$\begin{array}{r} 8\tfrac{3}{8} = 7\tfrac{11}{8} \\ -5\tfrac{5}{8} = 5\ \tfrac{5}{8} \end{array}$$

2. Subtract the columns.
3. Reduce to the lowest terms.

$$7^{11}\!/_8$$
$$-5\ ^5\!/_8$$
$$\overline{\ \ \ 2\ ^6\!/_8\ \ }$$
or $2\ ^3\!/_4$

4. The *difference* is $2^3\!/_4$

Trade Problem

Find the dimension a in the part in Fig. 9-1.

Problem: Find the difference: $5^{13}\!/_{64}{''}\ -$
   $2^{21}\!/_{64}{''}$

Solution:

1. Place the problem in columns, and
   borrow to subtract.

$$5^{13}\!/_{64} = 4^{77}\!/_{64}{''}$$
$$-2^{21}\!/_{64} = 2^{21}\!/_{64}{''}$$
$$\overline{\ \ \ \ \ 2^{56}\!/_{64}{''}\ \ }$$
or $2^7\!/_8{''}$

2. The dimension a is $2^7\!/_8$ *in.*

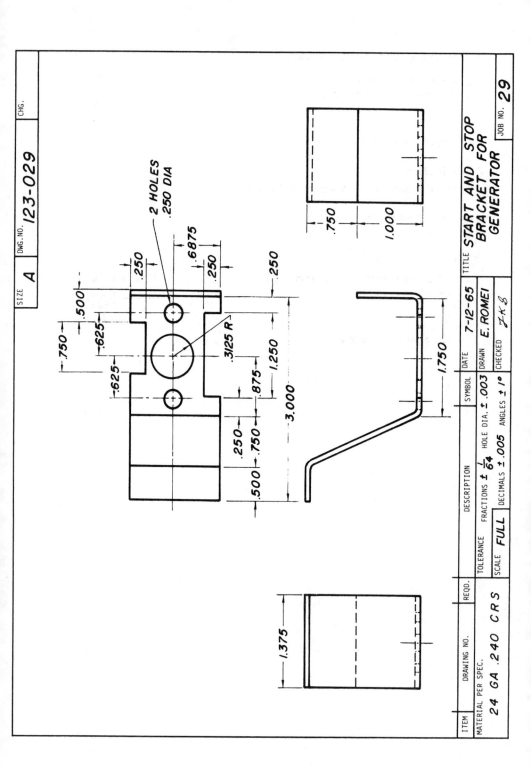

SIZE **A** | DWG. NO. **123-029** | CHG.

2 HOLES .250 DIA

.3125 R

TITLE START AND STOP BRACKET FOR GENERATOR | JOB NO. **29**

DATE **7-12-65** | DRAWN **E. ROMEI** | SYMBOL | DESCRIPTION

CHECKED ℐ𝒦ℬ

TOLERANCE
FRACTIONS ± 1/64
DECIMALS ± .005
HOLE DIA. ± .003
ANGLES ± 1°

SCALE **FULL**

ITEM | DRAWING NO. | REQD.

MATERIAL PER SPEC.
24 GA .240 CRS

Multiplication of Common Fractions

The precision sheet metalworker is often required to multiply fractions in working from a drawing on which the draftsman has indicated the dimensions in fractions (Fig. 10-1).

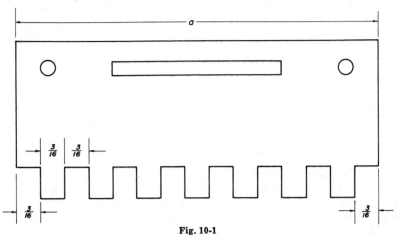

Fig. 10-1

Multiplying a Fraction by a Whole Number

To multiply either a proper or an improper fraction by a whole number,

51

multiply the numerator of the fraction by the whole number; then place the product above the denominator. Convert the resulting fraction to a mixed number or reduce it to its lowest terms, if necessary.

Problem: Multiply $5 \times \frac{3}{4}$

Solution:

1. Multiply the numerator of the fraction by the whole number. $5 \times 3 = 15$

2. Use this product for the numerator. $\dfrac{15}{4}$

3. If necessary, convert the improper fraction to a mixed number. $3\frac{3}{4}$

4. The *product* is $3\frac{3}{4}$

Multiplying a Fraction by a Fraction

To find the product of two fractions, multiply the two numerators and the two denominators. Write the product of the numerators over the product of the denominators. If necessary, reduce the resulting fraction to its lowest terms.

Problem: Multiply $\frac{2}{3} \times \frac{7}{8}$

Solution:

1. Arrange the problem in either of two forms.

$$\frac{2}{3} \times \frac{7}{8}$$

or

$$\frac{2 \times 7}{3 \times 8}$$

2. Multiply the numerators and the denominators.

$$\frac{2}{3} \times \frac{7}{8} = \frac{14}{24}$$

3. Reduce the fraction to its lowest terms.

$$\frac{14}{24} = \frac{7}{12}$$

4. The *product* is $\frac{7}{12}$

Multiplying Three or More Fractions

In the same manner that two fractions are multiplied, multiply all the numerators and all the denominators. Write the product of the numerators over the product of the denominators. Reduce to lowest terms or change to a mixed number, if necessary.

Problem: Multiply $\frac{3}{4} \times \frac{1}{2} \times \frac{7}{8}$
Solution:

1. Write the problem in the proper form.

$$\frac{3}{4} \times \frac{1}{2} \times \frac{7}{8}$$

2. Multiply the numerators and the denominators.

$$\frac{3}{4} \times \frac{1}{2} \times \frac{7}{8} = \frac{21}{64}$$

3. The *product* is the common fraction
$^{21}\!/_{64}$

Multiplying Mixed Numbers

To multiply mixed numbers, change the mixed numbers to improper fractions, and multiply in the usual manner.

Problem 1: Multiply $3\frac{1}{2} \times 7$

Solution:

1. Change the mixed number to an improper fraction.

2. Multiply the numerator of the fraction by the whole number; place this over the denominator of the fraction.

$$3\frac{1}{2} = \frac{7}{2}$$

$$7 \times 7 = \frac{49}{2}$$

3. Change the improper fraction to a mixed number.

$$\frac{49}{2} = 24\frac{1}{2}$$

4. The *product* is $24\frac{1}{2}$

Problem 2: $2\frac{1}{5} \times 5\frac{1}{2}$

Solution:

1. Change the mixed numbers to improper fractions.

$$2\frac{1}{5} = \frac{11}{5}$$

$$5\frac{1}{2} = \frac{11}{2}$$

2. Arrange the problem for multiplying two fractions. Multiply the numerators and the denominators.

$$\frac{11}{5} \times \frac{11}{2} = \frac{121}{10}$$

3. Change the improper fraction to a mixed number.

$$\frac{121}{10} = 12\frac{1}{10}$$

4. The *product* is $12\frac{1}{10}$

Short-Cut Method of Multiplying

When multiplying fractions, you sometimes deal with large numbers or with several numbers. A short-cut method that can often be used is known as cancellation.

Factors are parts of numbers which, when multiplied together, will give that number.

Examples:

1. The factors of *6* are *3* and *2*, because 3 × 2 = 6.
2. The factors of *8* are *2* and *4*, because 2 × 4 = 8.
3. The factors of *8* are also *2*, *2*, and *2*, because 2 × 2 × 2 = 8.

Cancellation consists of reducing the fraction before multiplying, thus avoiding larger numbers. It consists of dividing the factors that are common to the numerators and the denominators of the fraction.

Problem 1: Multiply, using cancellation,
$\frac{3}{4} \times \frac{4}{7}$

Solution:

1. Arrange the problem with the line extended.

$$\frac{3 \times 4}{4 \times 7}$$

2. Cancel each number that is above the line with a corresponding number below the line.
3. Then multiply.

$$\frac{3 \times \overset{1}{\cancel{4}}}{\cancel{4} \times 7}$$
$$_{1}$$

$$\frac{\overset{1}{3} \times \overset{1}{\cancel{4}}}{\underset{1}{\cancel{4}} \times 7}$$

4. The *product* is $\frac{3}{7}$
   Without cancellation, the problem would be:

$$\frac{3 \times 4}{4 \times 7} = \frac{12}{28} = \frac{3}{7}$$

Example 2: Multiply, using cancellation,
$\frac{2}{3} \times \frac{7}{8} \times \frac{3}{7}$

Solution:

1. Arrange the problem in the convenient manner.

$$\frac{2 \times 7 \times 3}{3 \times 8 \times 7}$$

2. Cancel and multiply.

$$\frac{\overset{1}{\cancel{2}} \times \overset{1}{\cancel{7}} \times \overset{1}{\cancel{8}}}{\underset{1}{\cancel{8}} \times \underset{4}{\cancel{8}} \times \underset{1}{\cancel{7}}} = \frac{1}{4}$$

3. The *product* is the common fraction $\frac{1}{4}$. Solved by the long method, this problem would be:

$$\frac{2 \times 7 \times 3}{3 \times 8 \times 7} = \frac{42}{168} = \frac{1}{4}$$

Note: In Step 2, the number *8* is divided into its factors *2* and *4*; the *2* is canceled and the *4* remains.

Trade Problem

Find the total length a of the part in Fig. 10-1.

Problem: Multiply ³⁄₁₆ in. × 15

Solution:

1. Multiply the numerator of the fraction by the whole number; place this result over the denominator of the fraction.

$$15 \times 3 = 45$$
$$= \frac{45}{16}$$

2. Change the improper fraction to a mixed number.

$$\frac{45}{16} = 2\frac{13}{16}$$

3. The total length a of the part is 2¹³⁄₁₆ in.

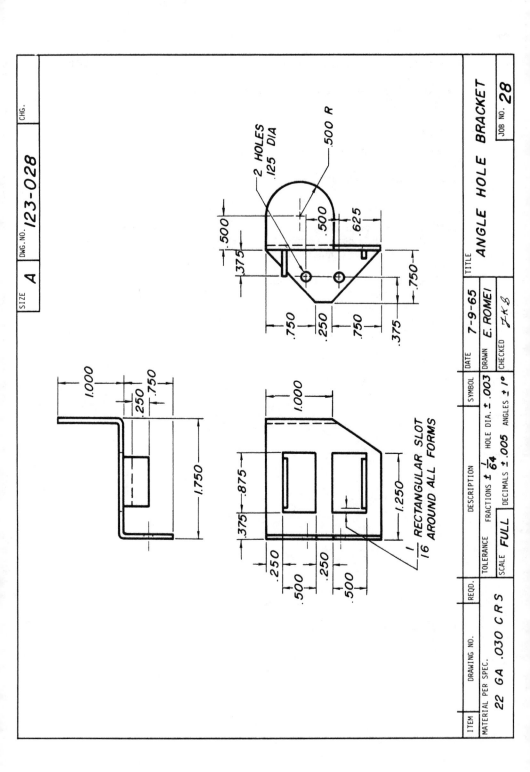

2 HOLES
.125 DIA

.500 R

.500

.625

.500

.375

.750

.750

.375

.250

.750

1.000

.250

.750

1.750

1.000

.375

.875

.250

.500

.250

.500

1.250

1/16 RECTANGULAR SLOT
AROUND ALL FORMS

SIZE A DWG. NO. 123-028 CHG.

TITLE ANGLE HOLE BRACKET

JOB NO. 28

ITEM | DRAWING NO. | REQD. | DESCRIPTION | SYMBOL | DATE 7-9-65

TOLERANCE FRACTIONS ± 1/64 HOLE DIA. ± .003
DECIMALS ± .005 ANGLES ± 1°

SCALE FULL

MATERIAL PER SPEC.
22 GA .030 C R S

DRAWN E. ROMEI
CHECKED J K B

Division of
Common Fractions

Division of fractions is used by the precision sheet metalworker when it is necessary to divide a line or a length of material into equal parts, when it is necessary to find the number of pieces that can be obtained from a length of metal, and when it is necessary to locate a series of holes in a part. (Fig. 11-1).

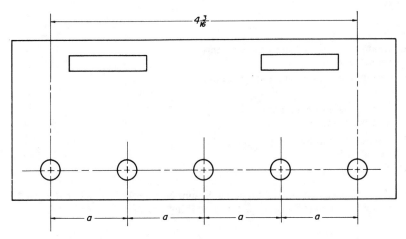

Fig. 11-1

57

Dividing a Fraction by a Fraction

To divide fractions, invert the divisor (second fraction), and then multiply the fractions.

Problem: Divide $\frac{7}{8}$ by $\frac{1}{4}$

Solution:

1. Arrange the problem in the form of a division problem.

$$\frac{7}{8} \div \frac{1}{4}$$

2. Invert the divisor, changing the division sign to a multiplication sign.

$$\frac{7}{8} \times \frac{4}{1}$$

3. Multiply, canceling as before.
4. Change the improper fraction to a mixed number.

$$\frac{7}{\cancel{8}_2} \times \frac{\cancel{4}^1}{1} = \frac{7}{2}$$

$$\frac{7}{2} = 3\frac{1}{2}$$

5. The *quotient* is $3\frac{1}{2}$

Dividing a Mixed Number by a Whole Number

Change mixed numbers to improper fractions before dividing. Then divide in the usual manner.

Problem 1:   Divide $4\frac{1}{2}$ by 2

Solution:

1. Change the mixed number to an improper fraction.

$$4\frac{1}{2} = \frac{9}{2}$$

2. Arrange in the form of a division problem.

$$\frac{9}{2} \div \frac{2}{1}$$

3. Invert the second fraction, and then multiply.

$$\frac{9}{2} \times \frac{1}{2} = \frac{9}{4}$$

4. Change the improper fraction to a mixed number.

$$\frac{9}{4} = 2\frac{1}{4}$$

5. The *quotient* is $2\frac{1}{4}$

Note: A fraction can be made from a whole number, merely by using the whole number for the numerator and the number *1* for the denominator, as:

$$1 = \frac{1}{1} \qquad\qquad 3 = \frac{3}{1} \qquad\qquad 16 = \frac{16}{1}$$

Problem 2: Divide $7\frac{1}{3}$ by $1\frac{1}{3}$

Solution:

1. Change the mixed numbers to fractions.

$$7\frac{1}{3} = \frac{22}{3}$$

$$1\frac{1}{3} = \frac{4}{3}$$

2. Arrange in the form of a division problem.

$$\frac{22}{3} \div \frac{4}{3}$$

3. Invert the second fraction, and multiply.

$$\frac{22}{3} \times \frac{3}{4} = \frac{66}{12}$$

4. Change the improper fraction to a mixed number.

$$\frac{66}{12} = 5\frac{1}{2}$$

5. The *quotient* is $5\frac{1}{2}$

Trade Problem

Find the dimension a between the centers of each pair of holes in the part in Fig. 11-1.

Problem: Divide $4\frac{3}{16}''$ by 4

Solution:

1. Arrange in the form of a division problem and solve.

$$\frac{67}{16} \div \frac{4}{1} = \frac{67}{16} \times \frac{1}{4} = \frac{67}{64}$$

2. The dimension is $1\frac{3}{64}$ in.

$$\frac{67}{64} = 1\frac{3}{64}$$

3. The dimension a between centers is $1\frac{3}{64}$ in.

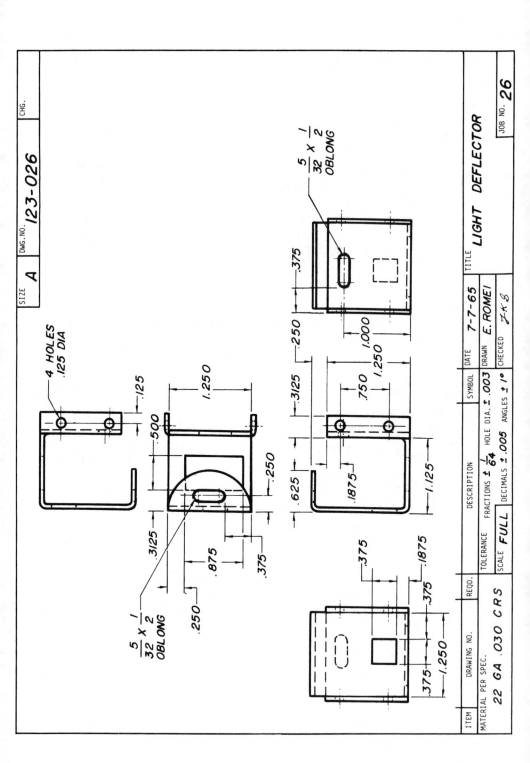

4 HOLES
.125 DIA

.125

1.250

.500

.250

3125

.875

.250

.375

5/32 x 1/2
OBLONG

.375

.250

1.000

.3125

.625

.1875

.750

1.250

1.125

5/32 x 1/2
OBLONG

.375

.1875

.375

.375

1.250

Decimals

Rather than express the parts of an inch in the form of a fraction, it is often more convenient or necessary for the precision sheet metalworker to express these fractions as decimals. A thorough knowledge of decimals is essential in performing measurements with the decimal steel rule, micrometer, vernier caliper, and other precision measuring instruments that are used by the precision sheet metalworker (Fig. 12-1).

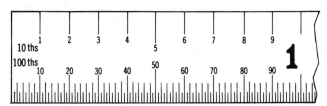

Fig. 12-1. Steel rule graduated in tenths and hundredths.

A decimal number is, in reality, a fraction in which the denominator is omitted. The denominator is understood to be 10, 100, 1000, etc. The "period" in a decimal fraction is called the decimal point.

There are as many digits on the right-hand side of the decimal point as there are zeros in the denominator (which is understood). Examples of decimal fractions are:

$$\frac{3}{10} = .3; \text{ read as: } \textit{three tenths}$$

$$\frac{3}{100} = .03; \text{ read as: } \textit{three hundredths}$$

61

$$\frac{3}{1000} = .003; \text{ read as: } three \ thousandths$$

$$\frac{3}{10,000} = .0003; \text{ read as: } three \ ten\text{-}thousandths$$

$$\frac{3}{100,000} = .00003; \text{ read as: } three \ hundred\text{-}thousandths$$

Zeros on the right-hand side of the last digit in a decimal have no meaning, and they can be omitted; this is also true for the zeros on the left-hand side of a whole number:

$$079.800 = 79.8$$

In reading a number that includes both a whole number and a decimal fraction, read the decimal point as "and"; therefore, read 3.25 as: *three and twenty-five hundredths.*

Converting a Common Fraction to a Decimal Fraction

When the *denominator is less than 100,* divide 100 by the denominator; then multiply both the numerator and the denominator by this result. The answer will have a denominator of 100 and can be converted into a decimal. Remember to count the number of zeros in the denominator to determine the position of the decimal point. Count from the right-hand side when placing the decimal point. If there are not enough digits, place one or more zeros on the left-hand side of the number preceding the decimal point.

Problem: Convert the common fraction
         7/25 to 100ths

Solution:

1. Divide 100 by the denominator of the fraction. $25\overline{\smash{\big)}100}^{\,4}$

2. Multiply both the numerator (7) and the denominator (25) by the result (4). $\dfrac{7 \times 4}{25 \times 4} = \dfrac{28}{100}$

3. Convert the fraction to a decimal fraction. $\dfrac{28}{100} = .28$

4. The *decimal fraction* is *.28*

When the *denominator is more than 100,* divide the denominator and the numerator by the number needed to have 100 in the denominator.

Problem: Convert the fraction *18/600* to
         100ths

Solution:

1. Divide both the denominator (600) and the numerator (18) by a number (6) that will make the denominator 100.

$$\frac{18 \div 6}{600 \div 6} = \frac{3}{100}$$

2. There are two zeros in the denominator; therefore, there must be two places on the right-hand side of the decimal point.

$$\frac{3}{100} = .03$$

3. The *decimal fraction* is *.03*

Converting a Decimal Fraction to a Common Fraction

To change a decimal fraction to a common fraction, use the number which appears on the right-hand side of the decimal point as the numerator. As in the denominator, write the number *1* with as many zeros added to it as there are digits in the numerator.

Problem: Convert the decimal fraction .75 to a common fraction.

Solution:

1. Place the digits on the right-hand side of the decimal point in the numerator of a fraction, eliminating the decimal point.

$$\frac{75}{}$$

2. For the denominator, use the number *1* with two zeros added, since there are two digits in the numerator.

$$\frac{75}{100}$$

3. Reduce the fraction to its lowest terms.

$$75/100 = \frac{3}{4}$$

4. The result is the *common fraction* ¾

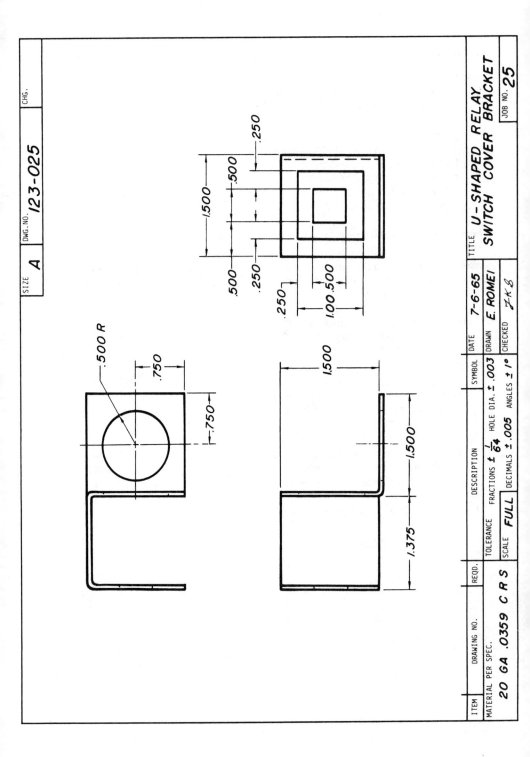

SIZE **A** | DWG. NO. **123-025** | CHG.

.500 R

.750

.750

.500

1.500

1.500

1.375

1.500

.250

.500

.250

.250

.500

.250

1.00

.500

| ITEM | DRAWING NO. | REQD. | DESCRIPTION | SYMBOL | DATE 7-6-65 | TITLE **U - SHAPED RELAY** |
| | | | | | | **SWITCH COVER BRACKET** |

MATERIAL PER SPEC.
20 GA .0359 CRS

TOLERANCE — FRACTIONS ± $\frac{1}{64}$ HOLE DIA. ±.003   DRAWN **E. ROMEI**

DECIMALS ±.005   ANGLES ± 1°   CHECKED *J·K·B*

SCALE **FULL**

JOB NO. **25**

Unit **13**

Decimal Divisions
of the Steel Rule

Some of the steel rules used by the precision sheet metalworker are divided into decimal divisions, such as 10ths, 50ths, and 100ths (Fig. 13-1). If greater accuracy is required than 1/100, other measuring instruments are used.

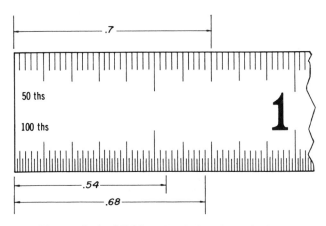

Fig. 13-1. Decimal divisions of an inch on the steel rule.

The possible divisions of an inch using decimals include:

$$\frac{1''}{10} = .1'' = \text{one 10th of an inch.}$$

$$\frac{1''}{50} = .02'' = \begin{array}{l}\text{one 50th of an inch.}\\ \text{(or two 100ths of an inch.)}\end{array}$$

$$\frac{1''}{100} = .01'' = \text{one 100th of an inch.}$$

$$\frac{1''}{1000} = .001'' = \text{one 1000th of an inch.}$$

The distances marked on the rule in Fig. 13-1 are read as follows:

1. For .7″, count seven $\frac{1}{10}$″ divisions.
2. For .5″ + .04″ = .54″, count five $\frac{1}{10}$″ divisions; then add four $\frac{1}{100}$″ divisions.
3. For .6″ + .08″ = .68″, count six $\frac{1}{10}$″ divisions; then add eight $\frac{1}{100}$″ divisions (or subtract two $\frac{1}{100}$″ divisions from seven $\frac{1}{10}$″ divisions.

Addition of Decimals

If the dimensions of a part are given as a decimal fraction on the drawing, it is often necessary for the precision sheet metalworker to add decimals (Fig. 14-1).

Fig. 14-1

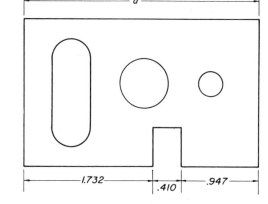

Adding the Decimals

To add either pure or mixed decimals, write the numbers with the decimal points directly below each other. Therefore, units will be added to units, 10's to 10's, and 100's to 100's. To avoid confusion, add zeros to the numbers with fewer decimal places than the longest number. Then, all the numbers will have the same number of places after the decimal point. Then, add as with whole numbers. After adding, place the decimal point of the sum directly below the other decimal points.

Problem: Add 3.79 + 27.8 + 9.487

Solution:

1. Arrange the numbers with the deci-   3.79
   mal points directly below each other.   27.8
                                                9.487

2. To reduce the possibility of error,   3.790
   add zeros to the numbers with fewer   27.800
   places than the longest number.   9.487
3. Add, as in adding whole numbers.   41 077

4. Place the decimal point below the
   other decimal points; the *sum* is   41.077
   41.077

Checking the Addition of Decimals

As in checking the addition of whole numbers, merely add again, reading upward on the columns.

Trade Problem

Find the total length *a* of the part in Fig. 14-1.

Problem: Add the dimensions: 1.732″ +
   .410″ + .947″

Solution:

1. Arrange the numbers with the deci-   1.732
   mal points directly below each other.   .410
                                                 .947

2. It is not necessary to add zeros, since
   this has been indicated on the drawing.
3. Add, as in adding whole numbers.   1.732
                                                 .410
                                                 .947
                                                3.089

4. The total length *a* is *3.089 in.*

Unit **15**

Subtraction of Decimals

If the dimensions of a part are in decimals on the drawing, it is often necessary for the precision sheet metalworker to subtract decimals (Fig. 15-1).

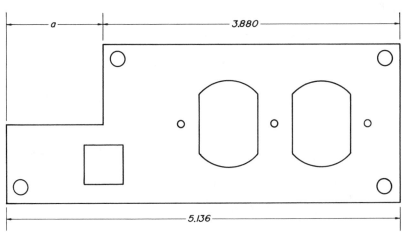

Fig. 15-1

Subtracting Decimals

To subtract either pure or mixed decimals, arrange the numbers with the decimal points directly below each other. Therefore, the units will be in line. To avoid confusion, add zeros to the number with fewer places. Thus, both numbers will have the same number of places on the right-hand side of the decimal point. Then, subtract as in subtracting whole numbers. After subtracting, place the decimal point of the remainder directly below the other decimal points.

Problem: Subtract: 3.27 − 1.843

Solution:

1. Arrange the numbers with the decimal points directly below each other.

$$\begin{array}{r} 3.27 \\ -\ 1.843 \\ \hline \end{array}$$

2. Add zeros to the number with less decimal places.

$$\begin{array}{r} 3.270 \\ -\ 1.843 \\ \hline \end{array}$$

3. Subtract, as in subtracting whole numbers.

$$1\ 427$$

4. Place the decimal point of the remainder directly below the other decimal points.

$$1.427$$

5. The *difference* is 1.427

Checking Subtraction of the Decimals

The minuend should be equal to the sum of the subtrahend and the remainder. The steps in checking are as follows:

1. Inspect the completed problem:

$$\begin{array}{r} 3.270 \\ -\ 1.843 \\ \hline 1.427 \end{array} \begin{array}{l} \text{(minuend)} \\ \text{(subtrahend)} \\ \text{(difference)} \end{array}$$

2. Cover the upper number, and add the subtrahend and the difference.

$$\begin{array}{r} 1.843 \\ \hline 1.427 \end{array} \begin{array}{l} \text{(subtrahend)} \\ \text{(difference)} \end{array}$$

3. The sum of the subtrahend and difference should be equal to the minuend.

$$\begin{array}{r} 1.843 \\ +\ 1.427 \\ \hline 3.270 \end{array} \begin{array}{l} \text{(subtrahend)} \\ \text{(difference)} \\ \text{(minuend)} \end{array}$$

4. Compare the sum obtained and the number that was covered (minuend). If they are not identical, the subtraction is incorrect.

Trade Problem

Find the dimension *a* in the part in Fig. 15-1.

Problem: a = 5.136″ − 3.880″

Solution:

1. Arrange the numbers with the decimal points directly below each other.

$$\begin{array}{r} 5.136 \\ -\ 3.880 \\ \hline \end{array}$$

2. Subtract, as in subtracting whole numbers.

$$\begin{array}{r} 5.136 \\ -\ 3.880 \\ \hline 1.256 \end{array}$$

3. The *difference* or dimension a is *1.256 in.*

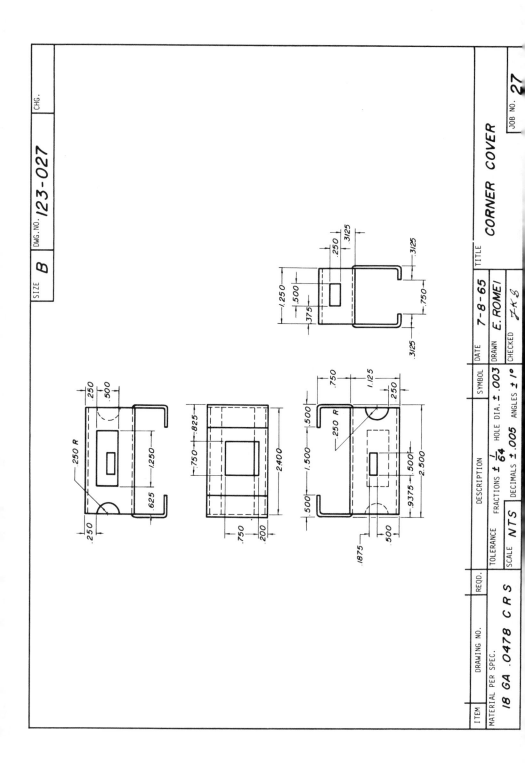

SIZE **B** DWG. NO. **123-027** CHG.

ITEM	DRAWING NO.	REQD.	DESCRIPTION		SYMBOL	DATE 7-8-65	TITLE

CORNER COVER

MATERIAL PER SPEC.
18 GA .0478 C R S

TOLERANCE FRACTIONS ± 1/64   HOLE DIA. ± .003
SCALE **NTS**   DECIMALS ± .005   ANGLES ± 1°

DRAWN E. ROMEI
CHECKED Z.K.B.

JOB NO. **27**

Multiplication of Decimals

If the dimensions of a part are in decimals on the drawing, it is often necessary for the precision sheet metalworker to multiply decimals (Fig. 16-1).

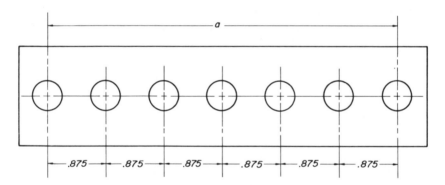

a

.875 — .875 — .875 — .875 — .875 — .875

Fig. 16-1

Multiplying the Decimals

To multiply decimals, it is not necessary to place the decimals below each other. Multiply, as in multiplying whole numbers. Find the sum of the number of decimal places in the two quantities being multiplied. Using this sum, begin at the right-hand side of the product; then count toward the left a number of places equal to the sum. Immediately to the left of the last number counted, place the decimal point in the product. If there are not enough numbers, add zeros to the *left* before placing the decimal point.

Problem: Multiply: 1.27 × .583

Solution:

1. Multiply, as in multiplying whole numbers.

2. Find the sum of the number of decimal places in the two quantities being multiplied:
2 places (1.27) + 3 places (.583) = 5 places

3. Since there are five decimal places in the numbers being multiplied, count five numbers from the right in the product.

4. Directly to the left of the fifth number counted (7), place the decimal point.

5. The *product* is *.74041*

```
          1.27
          .583
          ───
          381
         1016
          635
         ─────
         74041

         ←────
         54321
product = 74041

         .74041
```

Checking Multiplication of Decimals

To check your multiplication, repeat the operation; or interchange the multiplier and multiplicand, and rework the problem.

Trade Problem

Find the dimension *a* on the part in Fig. 16-1.

Problem: a = .875″ × 6

Solution:

1. Multiply, as in multiplying whole numbers.

```
          .875
             6
          ────
          5250
```

2. Count the number of decimal places in the numbers being multiplied.

3 places (.875) + 0 places (6) = 3 places

3. Count three places from the right.

```
          ←──
          321
          ────
          5250
```

4. Immediately to the left of the third number counted (2), place the decimal point.

```
          5.250
```

5. The *product* or dimension *a* is *5.250 in.*

Division of Decimals

If the dimensions of a part are in decimals on the drawing, it is often necessary for the precision sheet metalworker to divide decimals (Fig. 17-1).

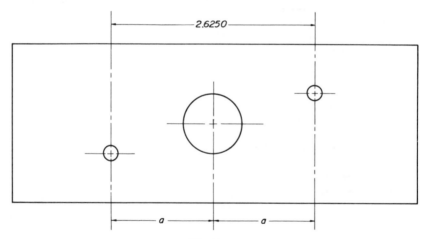

Fig. 17-1

Dividing Decimals

Divide as though both the dividend and the divisor were whole numbers.
Then count the number of places which the decimal must be moved to the
right to make the divisor a whole number. Place a carat ∧ at this point. From
the decimal point in the dividend, count to the right an equal number of places
that the decimal point was moved in the divisor. Place a carat here. Directly

75

above the carat, place the decimal point in the quotient. Add zeros when necessary.

Problem: Divide: 2.884 ÷ .14

Solution:

1. Arrange as a division problem; divide as though it involved only whole numbers.

$$\begin{array}{r} 206 \\ .14\,\overline{)\,2.884} \\ 2\,8 \\ \hline 84 \\ 84 \\ \hline 0 \end{array}$$

2. Count the number of places that the decimal point must be moved to the right to make the divisor (.14) a whole number (14); then place a carat at the right of this numeral (4). This is *two* places.

$$.14\,\overline{)\,2.884}$$

3. From the location of the decimal point in the dividend, count to the right an equal number of places that the decimal point was moved in the divisor (two). Place a carat at this point.

$$.14\,\overline{)\,2.884}$$

4. Immediately above the carat in the dividend, place the decimal point in the quotient.

$$\begin{array}{r} 20.6 \\ .14\,\overline{)\,2.884} \end{array}$$

5. The *quotient* is *20.6*

Checking the Division Problem

Multiply the quotient by the divisor; then add the remainder. The product should be equal to the dividend.

$$\begin{array}{r} 20.6 \\ .14 \\ \hline 824 \\ 206 \\ \hline 2.884 \end{array}$$

Trade Problem

Find the equal dimensions *a* of the part in Fig. 17-1.

Problem: a = 2.6250 in. ÷ 2

Solution:

1. Arrange as a division problem; divide as though it involved only whole numbers.

$$\begin{array}{r} 1.3125 \\ 2\,\overline{)\,2.6250} \end{array}$$

2. The decimal point is not moved, since the divisor is a whole number. In the quotient, place the decimal point directly above the decimal point in the dividend.

3. The *quotient* or dimension *a* is *1.3125 in.*

$$2 \overline{)\ 2.6250}^{1.3125}$$

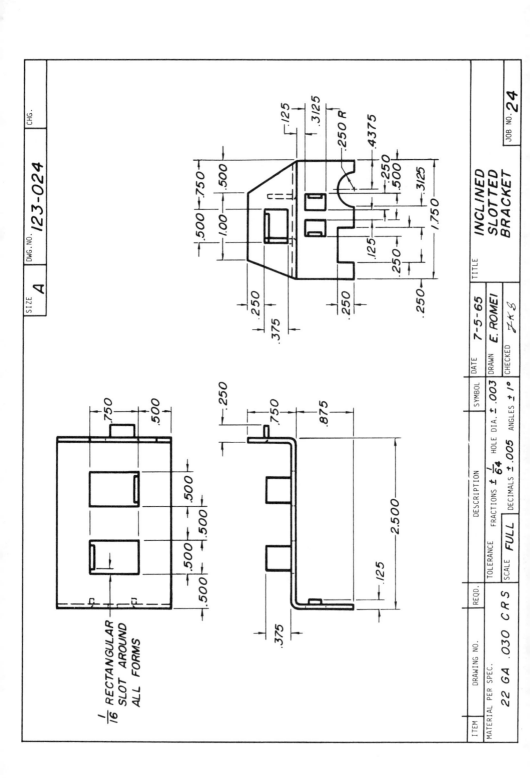

SIZE A   DWG. NO. 123-024   CHG.

ITEM | DRAWING NO. | REQD. | DESCRIPTION | SYMBOL | DATE 7-5-65 | TITLE *INCLINED SLOTTED BRACKET*

MATERIAL PER SPEC.

22 GA .030 CRS

TOLERANCE FRACTIONS ± 1/64 HOLE DIA. ± .003
DECIMALS ± .005   ANGLES ± 1°
SCALE *FULL*

DRAWN E. ROMEI
CHECKED I.K.B.

JOB NO. 24

1/16 RECTANGULAR SLOT AROUND ALL FORMS

Rounding Off the Decimals

To save time in solving a problem, the precision sheet metalworker should use only the number of decimal places indicated by the accuracy or tolerance requirement of the measurement. Normally, accuracy to not more than 1/1000 of an inch or three decimal places is required in precision sheet metalwork (Fig. 18-1).

A decimal must be "rounded off" to reduce it to the required number of decimal places. "Rounding off" involves changing the number to a smaller number of decimal places.

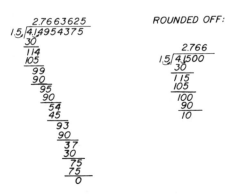

Fig. 18-1. Locating the decimal point (left), and rounding off the decimal (right).

Rounding Off

Determine the number of decimal places required in the answer. All **extra** numbers must be dropped. If the numeral following the last decimal place required is *less than 5* (1, 2, 3, or 4), merely drop the extra numerals. A zero (0) is also less than five.

However, if the numeral following the last decimal place required is *5 or more* (5, 6, 7, 8, or 9), add *1* to the last decimal place required. Then drop all the numerals following the last decimal place required.

Problem: Round off the decimal .78449
      to three decimal places.

Solution:

1. Count three places to the right from the decimal point; examine the numeral *4* following the last decimal required (4).

    $\overrightarrow{123}$
    .78449

2. The first numeral to be dropped is "4," since it is less than *5*; also drop the extra numeral (9).

    .78449

3. The *decimal,* rounded off to three decimal places, is *.784*

Problem 2: Round off the decimal *.78495*
      to three places.

Solution:

1. Count three places to the right from the decimal point; examine the numeral *9* following the last decimal required.

    $\overrightarrow{123}$
    .78495

2. The first numeral to be dropped is "9"; since it is more than *5*, add *1* to the last numeral (4) that remains (4 + 1 = 5). Then also drop the extra numeral (5).

    .78495
    <u>+1</u>
    .785

3. The *decimal,* rounded off to three decimal places, is *0.785*

Number of Decimal Places Required in Computations

During computations, retain one more decimal place than is required. This permits more accuracy.

Problem: Multiply: 3.25 × 2.19 × 3.12;
      two decimal places are required.

Solution:

1. Multiply the first two numbers (3.25
    × 2.19).

$$
\begin{array}{r}
3.25 \\
\times\ 2.19 \\
\hline
2925 \\
325 \\
650 \\
\hline
7.1175
\end{array}
$$

2. Round off this product to one extra
    decimal place (2 places + 1 = 3
    places).

$7.1175 = 7.118$

3. Multiply by the third number (3.12).

$$
\begin{array}{r}
7.118 \\
\times\ 3.12 \\
\hline
14236 \\
7118 \\
21354 \\
\hline
22.20816
\end{array}
$$

4. Round the final product to the re-
    quired number of decimal places
    (two places).

$22.20816 = 22.21$

5. The *product* of the three numbers
    is *22.21*.

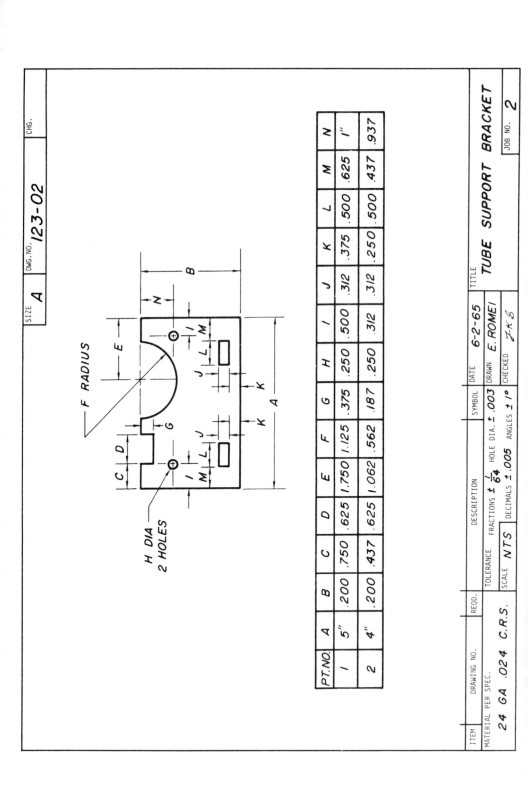

F RADIUS

H DIA
2 HOLES

PT.NO	A	B	C	D	E	F	G	H	I	J	K	L	M	N
1	5"	.200	.750	.625	1.750	1.125	.375	.250	.500	.312	.375	.500	.625	1"
2	4"	.200	.437	.625	1.062	.562	.187	.250	.312	.312	.250	.500	.437	.937

ITEM	DRAWING NO.	REQD.	DESCRIPTION	SYMBOL	DATE 6-2-65	SIZE A	DWG. NO. 123-02	CHG.

MATERIAL PER SPEC.
24 GA .024 C.R.S.

TOLERANCE FRACTIONS ± $\frac{1}{64}$ HOLE DIA. ± .003
SCALE NTS DECIMALS ± .005 ANGLES ± 1°

DRAWN E. ROME!
CHECKED J.K.B.

TITLE TUBE SUPPORT BRACKET

JOB NO. 2

Converting Common Fractions to Decimals

It is common practice for the precision sheet metalworker to change fractional dimensions on drawings to decimal dimensions to obtain more accuracy (Fig. 19-1). This is a simple matter by division, because the numerator in a fraction is the dividend and the denominator is the divisor:

$$\frac{3}{4} = \frac{\text{numerator}}{\text{denominator}} = \frac{\text{dividend}}{\text{divisor}} = 4\,\overline{)\,3}$$

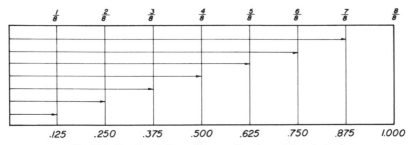

Fig. 19-1. Fractional dimensions are often converted to decimals.

Changing a Common Fraction to a Decimal Fraction

Divide the numerator of the common fraction by the denominator of the common fraction. Place zeros after the decimal point, if necessary.

Problem: Convert the common fraction
   ¾ to a decimal fraction.

Solution:

1. Arrange the common fraction in the
   form of a division problem.

   $$4\,/\overline{3}$$

2. Since the divisor *4* will not go into
   3, place a decimal point after the *3*
   and add several zeros. Then divide,
   continuing the division until there is
   no remainder.

   $$\begin{array}{r} .75 \\ 4\,/\overline{3.00} \\ 2\,8 \\ \hline 20 \\ 20 \\ \hline 0 \end{array}$$

3. The *decimal fraction* is *.75*

Uneven Numbers

With some numbers, it is impossible to reach the point at which there is no remainder; or it may not be necessary to continue to this point. If this occurs, carry the answer to one decimal place beyond the required number of places; then round it off.

Problem: Change the common fraction
   ⅓ to a decimal fraction, correct to
   three decimal places.

Solution:

1. Arrange the common fraction in the
   form of a division problem.

   $$3\,/\overline{1}$$

2. Add the necessary zeros and divide;
   since the quotient must be correct to
   three decimal places, carry the division to four places.

   $$\begin{array}{r} .333 \\ 3\,/\overline{1.0000} \\ 9 \\ \hline 10 \\ 9 \\ \hline 10 \\ 9 \\ \hline 10 \\ 9 \\ \hline 1 \end{array}$$

3. Round off the quotient.

   $$.3333 = .333$$

4. The *decimal fraction* is *.333*

Converting Decimals to Common Fractions

For the sake of convenience, the precision sheet metalworker occasionally changes decimal dimensions to fractions (Fig. 20-1). This is done easily by multiplication.

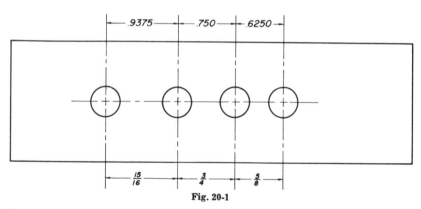

Fig. 20-1

Changing a Decimal Fraction to a Common Fraction

Multiply the decimal by the denominator of the fraction required. This rounded-off result is used as the numerator, and forms a fraction with the required denominator.

Problem: Convert the decimal dimension
        .479 in. to a common fraction, to
        the nearest 32nd of an inch.

Solution:

1. Multiply the decimal by the denom-
    inator of the fraction required
    (32nd).

    $$\begin{array}{r} .479 \\ 32 \\ \hline 958 \\ 1437 \\ \hline 15.328 \end{array}$$

2. Round off this number to a whole
    number.

    $$15.328 = 15$$

3. For the common fraction, place the
    whole number over the denomina-
    tor *32*.

    $$\frac{15}{32}$$

4. The *common fraction* is $^{15}/_{32}$ in.

The Decimal
Equivalent Table

To save valuable time the precision sheet metalworker uses the decimal equivalent table (Table 21-1) to convert common fractions to decimals and to convert decimals to common fractions (Fig. 21-1).

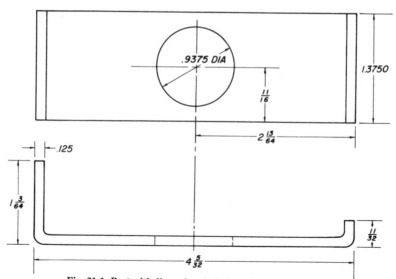

Fig. 21-1. Part with dimensions in both decimals and fractions.

87

Converting a Fraction to a Decimal

Find the specified fraction in the proper column of the decimal equivalent table (Table 21-1); then read its corresponding decimal equivalent.

Table 21-1. Decimal Equivalent Table

Fraction	Decimal	Fraction	Decimal	Fraction	Decimal
1/64	.015625	11/32	.34375	11/16	.6875
1/32	.03125	23/64	.359375	45/64	.703125
3/64	.046875	3/8	.375	23/32	.71875
1/16	.0625	25/64	.390625	47/64	.734375
5/64	.078125	13/32	.40625	3/4	.750
3/32	.09375	27/64	.421875	49/64	.8125
7/64	.109375	7/16	.4375	25/32	.828125
1/8	.125	29/64	.453125	51/64	.796875
9/64	.140625	15/32	.46875	13/16	.8125
5/32	.15625	31/64	.48438	53/64	.828125
11/64	.171875	1/2	.500	27/32	.84375
3/16	.1875	33/64	.515625	55/64	.859375
13/64	.203125	17/32	.53125	7/8	.875
7/32	.21875	35/64	.546875	57/64	.890625
15/64	.234375	9/16	.5625	29/32	.90625
1/4	.250	37/64	.578125	59/64	.921875
17/64	.265625	19/32	.59375	15/16	.9375
9/32	.28125	39/64	.609375	61/64	.953125
19/64	.296875	5/8	.625	31/32	.96875
5/16	.3125	41/64	.640625	63/64	.984375
21/64	.328125	21/32	.65625	1	1.000

Problem: Find the decimal equivalent of the dimension *5/32 in.*

Solution:

1. In Table 21-1, find the fraction *5/32* in the first column.
2. Read its decimal equivalent opposite the fraction *5/32*. This is .15625
3. Since the fraction is in inches, the decimal also is in inches.
4. Therefore, the *decimal equivalent* is *.15625 in.*

Check: If you desire to check the accuracy of the table, divide the numerator *5* by the denominator *32* to prove that *5/32* is equivalent to the decimal *.15625*

Converting a Decimal Listed in the Table to a Common Fraction

Find the specified decimal in the proper column of the decimal equivalent table (Table 21-1); then read its corresponding fraction.

Problem: Find the fractional equivalent
      of the decimal dimension *.8125 in.*

Solution:

1. In the table, find .8125 in the decimal
   column.
2. Read its fractional equivalent *13/16*
   opposite the decimal.
3. Since the decimal is in inches, the
   fraction also is in inches.
4. Therefore, the *fractional equivalent*
   of .8125 in. is $^{13}/_{16}$ in.

Check: To prove this correct, multiply
   the decimal *.8125* by *16* to obtain the
   numerator *13*.

Converting a Decimal Not Listed in the Table to a Common Fraction

Determine the two decimals that the fraction falls between. The decimal
that is closer is to be used to determine the fractional equivalent.

Problem: Determine the fractional equiva-
      lent of the decimal *.64512* in.

Solution:

1. Examine the table to find the two
   decimals that the decimal .64512 falls
   between.

   .640625
   $\rightarrow$
   .656250

2. Find the difference between the
   larger number and .64512

   .656250
   $-$ .645120
   ‾‾‾‾‾‾‾‾
   .011130

3. Find the difference between the
   smaller number and .64512

   .645120
   $-$ .640625
   ‾‾‾‾‾‾‾‾
   .004495

4. Examine the results of these two
   subtractions.

   .011130
   .004495

5. The smaller difference indicates that
   the smaller decimal *.640625* in the
   table corresponds more closely to the
   decimal *.64512*. Therefore, its fractional equivalent is the correct common fraction.

   .640625 = 41/64

6. The *fractional equivalent* is $^{41}/_{64}$ in.

Dealing With Whole Numbers

The whole numbers are merely retained as whole numbers.

Problem 1:   Determine the decimal equivalent of the fractional dimension *3 3/16 in.*

Solution:

1. Find the common fraction *3/16* in the table (Table 21-1).
2. The decimal equivalent of the fraction *3/16* is *.1875*
3. The *decimal equivalent* of $3\frac{3}{16}$ in. is 3.1875 in.

Problem 2:   Determine the fractional equivalent of the decimal dimension *4.59375 in.*

Solution:

1. Find .59375 in the table.
2. The fractional equivalent of the decimal *.59375* is the common fraction.
3. The *fractional equivalent* of 4.59375 in. is $4\frac{19}{32}$ in.

Unit **22**

Tables and Charts
for Shop Use

In many shop operations, various tables and charts are often required to complete the job exactly as the drawing indicates (Fig. 22-1).

The precision sheet metalworker often must determine the correct table or chart for his specific purpose. Then, he must be careful to read it correctly. In addition to the decimal equivalent table (Table 21-1) and the bend allowance chart in Table 27-1, the precision sheet metalworker uses the following tables, which are in the Appendix:

Table 1. Decimal Equivalents of Number Size Drills.
Table 2. Decimal Equivalents of Letter Size Drills.
Table 3. American National Coarse and Fine Thread Dimensions.
Table 4. Tap Drill Sizes.
Table 5. Tap Drill Sizes for Fractional Size Threads.
Table 6. Approximate Pressures Required for Punching Round Holes in Mild Steel Sheet.
Table 7. Standard Gauges and Equivalents in Decimals of an Inch.
Table 8. Galvanized Carbon Steel Sheets.
Table 9. Sheet Gauges and Weights—Carbon Steel and Brass.
Table 10. Sheet Gauges and Weights—Copper and Zinc.
Table 11. Stainless Steel Sheets.

The following problems can be solved from the tables in the Appendix:

Problem 1:   What twist drill number size would you need for a .1160″ diameter hole?

91

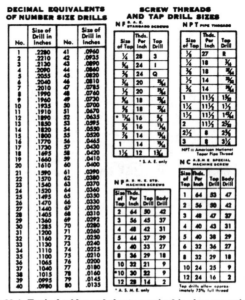

DECIMAL EQUIVALENTS OF NUMBER SIZE DRILLS

No.	Size of Drill in Inches	No.	Size of Drill in Inches
1	.2280	41	.0960
2	.2210	42	.0935
3	.2130	43	.0890
4	.2090	44	.0860
5	.2055	45	.0820
6	.2040	46	.0810
7	.2010	47	.0785
8	.1990	48	.0760
9	.1960	49	.0730
10	.1935	50	.0700
11	.1910	51	.0670
12	.1890	52	.0635
13	.1850	53	.0595
14	.1820	54	.0550
15	.1800	55	.0520
16	.1770	56	.0465
17	.1730	57	.0430
18	.1695	58	.0420
19	.1660	59	.0410
20	.1610	60	.0400
21	.1590	61	.0390
22	.1570	62	.0380
23	.1540	63	.0370
24	.1520	64	.0360
25	.1495	65	.0350
26	.1470	66	.0330
27	.1440	67	.0320
28	.1405	68	.0310
29	.1360	69	.0292
30	.1285	70	.0280
31	.1200	71	.0260
32	.1160	72	.0250
33	.1130	73	.0240
34	.1110	74	.0225
35	.1100	75	.0210
36	.1065	76	.0200
37	.1040	77	.0180
38	.1015	78	.0160
39	.0995	79	.0145
40	.0980	80	.0135

SCREW THREADS AND TAP DRILL SIZES

NF S.A.E. STANDARD SCREWS

Size of Tap	Thds. Per Inch	Tap Drill
1/4	28	3
5/16	24	I
3/8	24	Q
7/16	20	25/64
1/2	20	29/64
9/16	18	33/64
5/8	18	37/64
* 11/16	16	5/8
3/4	16	11/16
7/8	14	13/16
1	14	15/16
1 1/8	12	1 3/64

* S. A. E. only

NPT PIPE THREADS

Size of Tap	Thds. Per Inch	Tap Drill
1/8	27	R
1/4	18	7/16
3/8	18	37/64
1/2	14	23/32
3/4	14	59/64
1	11 1/2	1 5/32
1 1/4	11 1/2	1 1/2
1 1/2	11 1/2	1 47/64
2	11 1/2	2 7/32
2 1/2	8	2 5/8
3	8	3 1/4

NPT = American National Taper Pipe Thread

NF A. S. M. E. STD. MACHINE SCREWS

Size of Tap	Thds. Per Inch	Tap Drill	Body Drill
2	64	50	42
3	56	45	37
4	48	42	31
5	44	37	29
6	40	33	27
8	36	29	18
10	32	21	9
*10	30	22	9
12	28	14	2

* A. S. M. E. only

NC A.S.M.E. SPECIAL MACHINE SCREW

Size of Tap	Thds. Per Inch	Tap Drill	Body Drill
1	64	53	47
2	56	50	42
3	48	47	37
4	40	43	31
5	40	38	29
6	32	36	27
8	32	29	18
10	24	25	9
12	24	16	2

Tap drills allow approximately 75% full thread

Fig. 22-1. Typical tables and charts required in shop operations.

Solution:

1. Find the correct chart. It is "Decimal Equivalents of Number Size Drills" in Table 1 in the Appendix.
2. Find .1160" in the column "Size of Drill in Inches."
3. Find the corresponding number in the column "No."
4. The twist drill *number size* is *32*.

Problem 2: Find the letter size of a twist drill with a .261" diameter.

Solution:

1. Find the correct chart. It is "Decimal Equivalents of Letter Size Drills" in Table 2 in the Appendix.
2. Find .261" in the column "Size of Drill in Inches."
3. Find the corresponding letter in the column "Letter."
4. The *letter size* of the twist drill is *G*.

Problem 3: If a hole is to be tapped with a 7/16" National Fine thread, find the decimal equivalent of the tap drill.

Solution:

1. Find the correct chart. It is "American National Coarse and National Fine Thread Dimensions" in Table 3 in the Appendix.

2. Find $\frac{7}{16}$" in the "Size" column and find the line with a number in the column for National Fine (NF).
3. Read the number in the "Decimal Equivalent of Tap Drill" column.
4. The *decimal equivalent* of the tap drill is *.3906"*.

Problem 4:   Find the approximate pressure required for punching a hole with a .4375" diameter in a piece of 18-gauge mild steel.

Solution:

1. Find the correct chart. It is "Approximate Pressures Required for Punching Round Holes in Mild Steel Sheet" in Table 6 in the Appendix.
2. In the "Hole Diameter" column, find .4375 and find the column marked 18-gauge. Read the corresponding number.
3. The *pressure* required is *1.6 tons*.

Problem 5:   Find the thickness in decimals of 10-gauge brass by the Brown and Sharpe standard.

Solution:

1. Find the correct chart. Brass is listed in the "Sheet Gauges and Weights" in Table 9 in the Appendix.
2. In the "B&S Gauge No." column, find 10 gauge. Read the number in the "Decimal Thickness" column.
3. The *thickness* in decimals is *.1019"*.

Problem 6:   If a sheet of copper is measured with a micrometer and is .049", find its gauge number.

Solution:

1. Find the correct chart. Copper is listed on the "Sheet Gauges and Weights" in Table 10 in the Appendix.
2. In the "Decimal Thickness" column, find .049. Read the corresponding number in the "Stub's Gauge Number" column.
3. The *sheet* of copper is *18-gauge*.

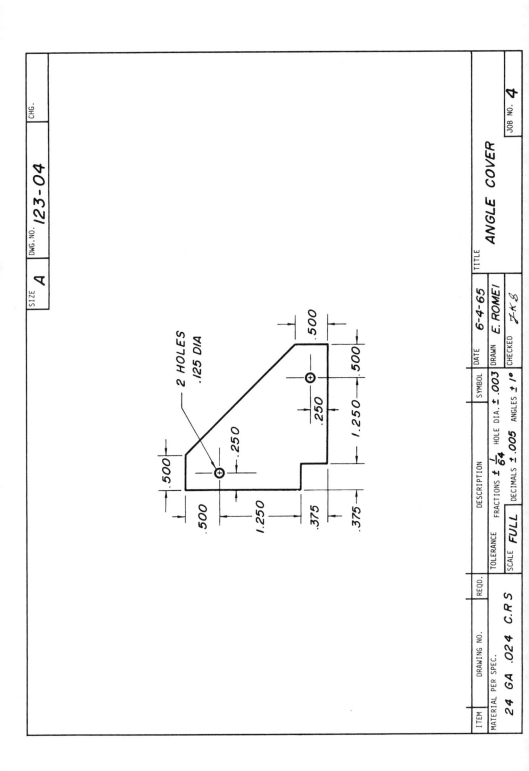

2 HOLES
.125 DIA

.500

.250

.500

.500

.250

.500

1.250

1.250

.375

.500

.375

SIZE **A**   DWG. NO. **123-04**   CHG.

ITEM	DRAWING NO.	REQD.	DESCRIPTION	SYMBOL	DATE **6-4-65**	TITLE

MATERIAL PER SPEC.

24 GA .024 C.R S

TOLERANCE   FRACTIONS $\pm\frac{1}{64}$ HOLE DIA. $\pm$ .003   DRAWN **E. ROMEI**

SCALE **FULL**   DECIMALS $\pm$ .005   ANGLES $\pm$ 1°   CHECKED *J.K.B*

ANGLE COVER

JOB NO. **4**

Reading the Micrometer

The smallest measurement that the precision sheet metalworker can make with a steel rule is $\frac{1}{64}''$ in fractions and $0.01''$ in decimals. To measure more closely, as in 1000ths, a micrometer (Fig. 23-1) is used by the precision sheet metalworker to measure metal thickness and the diameters of punches, taps, and twist drills. A *bar* micrometer is used to measure blank sizes. It is read in the same manner that a micrometer is usually read, but the bar micrometer is more convenient in measuring the longer lengths of metal, due to the interchangeable metal peg that can be inserted on the bar at $1''$ graduations. A fractional dimension must be converted to its decimal equivalent, before the measurement can be performed with a micrometer.

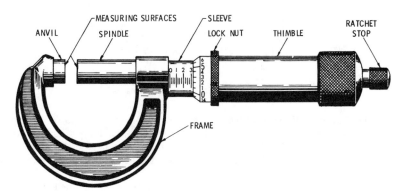

Fig. 23-1. Micrometer with parts.

95

Micrometers can be purchased with the graduations in either 1000ths or 10,000ths, depending on the needs of the user. The visible parts of the micrometer are shown in Fig. 23-1, including the anvil, frame, measuring surfaces, spindle, lock nut, sleeve, thimble, and ratchet stop.

An accurately ground screw, actually a part of the spindle, rotates in a fixed nut. This screw opens and closes the distance between the two measuring surfaces, which are the ends of the spindle and the anvil. When the micrometer is closed, with the spindle touching the anvil, the reading is zero. To measure an object with the micrometer:

1. Turn the thimble, opening the micrometer far enough that the object to be measured fits between the anvil and spindle. The thimble and spindle both move the same distance. As the thimble moves, it uncovers the markings on the sleeve.

2. Insert the part being measured against the anvil.

3. Turn the thimble until the spindle also touches the object.

4. Read the markings on both the sleeve and the thimble to determine the required dimension.

Reading the Micrometer Graduated in 1000ths

Both the thimble and the sleeve have markings that must be read. The sleeve has 40 equal divisions. Each vertical line represents $\frac{1}{40}$" or .025" (Fig. 23-2). Every fourth line is longer, and it designates 10ths; that is, the line marked *1* indicates 0.100"; the line marked *2* indicates 0.200"; etc.

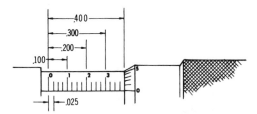

Fig. 23-2. Micrometer sleeve graduations.

The beveled edge of the thimble is divided into 25 equal parts, each representing 0.001" (Fig. 23-3). For convenience, every fifth line is usually numbered, such as 5, 10, etc. Therefore, one complete turn of the thimble (from 0 to 0) is equal to 25 × 0.001" (25 one-thousandths of an inch); or it is written as 0.025".

Now, the relation of the sleeve and thimble can be determined. One complete turn of the thimble (.025") is equal to one division on the sleeve (.025"). To read the measurement, multiply the number of vertical lines visible on the sleeve by .025"; add to this .001" for each mark indicated on the thimble. The thimble mark to read is the one that coincides (lines up) with the longitudinal line on the sleeve.

Trade Problem

Problem: Find the reading on the micrometer in Fig. 23-3.

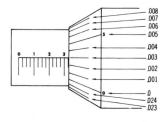

Fig. 23-3. Micrometer thimble graduations.

Solution:

1. On the sleeve, line *3* is visible. This represents .300   .300″

2. On the sleeve, one additional line is visible. This represents: (.025″ × 1), or .025″.   .025″

3. Line *3* on the thimble coincides with the longitudinal line on the thimble, representing (3 × .001″), or .003.   .003″
.328″

4. Adding these values, the *reading* is .328″.

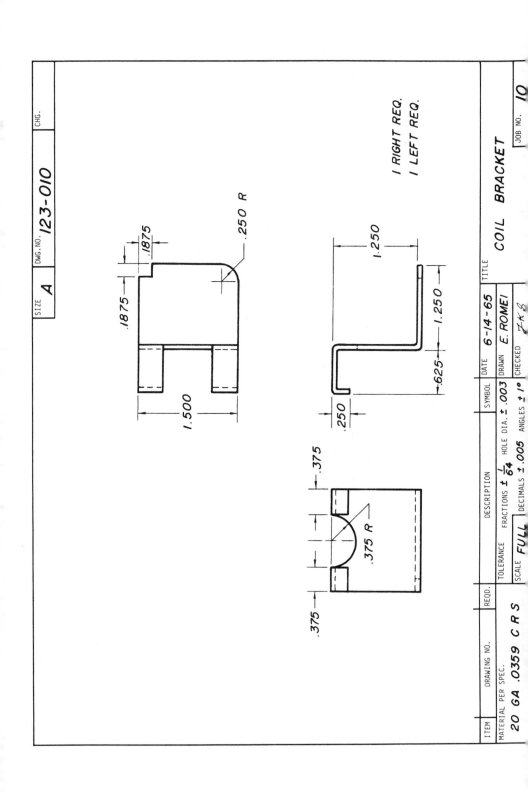

1 RIGHT REQ.
1 LEFT REQ.

.250 R

.1875

.1875

.1875

1.500

1.250

1.250

.625

.250

.375

.375 R

.375

SIZE **A** | DWG. NO. **123-010** | CHG.

TITLE **COIL BRACKET**

JOB NO. **10**

ITEM	DRAWING NO.	REQD.	DESCRIPTION	SYMBOL	DATE **6-14-65**

MATERIAL PER SPEC.
20 GA .0359 C R S

TOLERANCE   FRACTIONS ± $\frac{1}{64}$ HOLE DIA. ± .003

SCALE **FULL**   DECIMALS ± .005   ANGLES ± 1°

DRAWN **E. ROMEI**   CHECKED

Unit **24**

Reading the
Vernier Caliper

The precision sheet metalworker uses a vernier caliper (Fig. 24-1) to check the blank sizes of parts that are to be formed. It is used to measure both the inside and the outside dimensions of the parts that have been formed and to check various features, such as slots, holes, and distances from the edges of

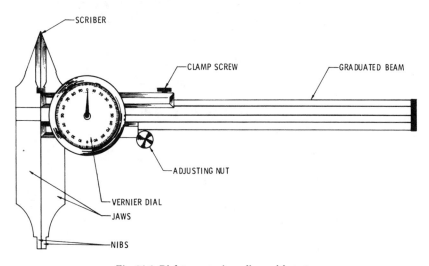

Fig. 24-1. Dial-type vernier caliper with parts.

99

holes. The vernier caliper is also used as an aid in setting up machinery. The precision sheet metalworker uses the vernier caliper much more frequently than he uses the micrometer.

The vernier caliper consists of two basic parts—a *stationary* part and a *movable* part. The stationary part is the graduated steel rule or beam which has a fixed measuring jaw. The movable part moves the jaw and the vernier plate or dial along the graduated beam. A vernier caliper has either a vernier plate or a vernier dial. The caliper in Fig. 24-1 has a vernier dial. Therefore, the movable part contains a jaw, a nib, a clamp screw, an adjusting nut, and a vernier dial. Attached to the graduated beam are the opposite jaw and nib. The *inside* surfaces of both jaws contact the work being measured in measuring an *outside* dimension. The *outside* surfaces of the nibs must contact the work being measured when measuring an *inside* dimension.

Reading the Caliper Dial

The movable jaw uncovers the numbered graduations along the beam to measure 10ths of an inch. The dial is then used to measure 100ths and 1000ths.

Problem: Read the caliper setting shown
on the dial in Fig. 24-2.

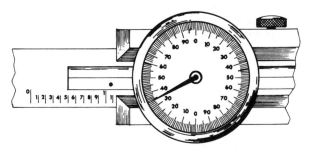

Fig. 24-2. Dial of a vernier caliper.

Solution:

1. Read the highest graduation visible   1.1"
   on the beam.
2. Read the dial, which is marked in
   1000ths.   .034"
3. Combine the two readings by adding.   1.134"
4. The *reading* on the dial is *1.134"*.

Reading the Caliper Plate

The graduated beam is divided into 40ths of an inch, or 0.025". Every fourth division is equal to $\frac{1}{10}$", and it is numbered. The vernier plate is divided into 25 divisions marked at 0, 5, 10, 15, 20 and 25. They occupy the same space that

24 divisions occupy on the beam; thus, they are slightly closer than the divisions on the beam. Each division represents 1/1000″, or 0.001″.

As a measurement increases, the vernier plate moves in the right-hand direction. Therefore, the line to use in reading the beam is the last line that the vernier plate has passed in moving toward the right (last line to the left of the "0" mark on the vernier plate). To determine the small distance from the line, read only to the "0" mark on the vernier plate; find the line on the vernier plate that lines up exactly with a line on the beam (only one line coincides exactly). The line on the vernier plate is the number of 1000ths to add to the reading on the blade.

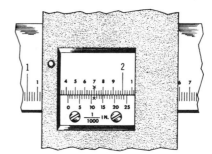

Fig. 24-3. Plate of a vernier caliper.

Problem: Read the vernier caliper setting shown on the plate in Fig. 24-3.

Solution:

1. Read the number on the beam that   1.425″
   the "0" mark on the vernier plate
   has just passed.
2. Find the mark where a line on the
   vernier plate lines up exactly with a
   line on the blade. This occurs at line
   11 on the plate; therefore, the read-
   ing is 11/1000, or .011″.   .011″
3. Add the two numbers.   1.436″
4. The *reading* on the caliper plate is
   1.436″.

Variations in Calipers for Inside Dimensions

Two types of vernier calipers used for measuring inside dimensions are:

1. On the vernier caliper illustrated in Fig. 24-1, the nibs are used on inside dimensions. The usual reading is taken; then .4″ is added for the size of

the nibs. Therefore, if a reading is 3.141″, the inside dimension would be (3.141″ + .4″), or 3.541″.

2. On many vernier calipers, the device for measuring the inside dimension is located above the beam. On these instruments, no adjustment is made. The usual reading is correct.

Tolerances

Since a portion of the cost of a part depends on the required accuracy (due to the time involved), it is important for the precision sheet metalworker to understand tolerances (Fig. 25-1) in order to reduce the time required and to omit unnecessary attention to accuracy. Some features on parts and assemblies do not require extreme accuracy.

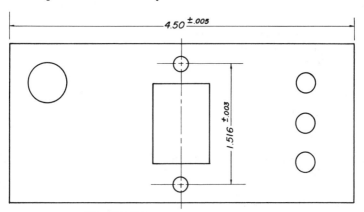

Fig. 25-1. Tolerances for a part dimension.

Accuracy

The following factors determine the accuracy of measurements:
1. Limitations of the measuring instruments.
    a. Steel rule—$\frac{1}{64}''$ to $\frac{1}{100}''$.

103

  b. Micrometer—.001″ to .0001″.

  c. Vernier caliper—.001″.

2. Errors in measurement.

  a. Measuring tools.

   (1). Manufacturer's error (inaccuracy of scale).

   (2). Wear (check the micrometers and the ends of the rules).

   (3). Temperature (affects the fourth decimal place).

  b. Person measuring.

   (1). Eyesight (improper light, not looking directly at the part being measured).

   (2). Touch (develop a sense of feel when using the micrometer).

  c. Good judgment (select the proper measuring instrument and closest division that meets the requirements of the job).

3. Specified limits. These limits are indicated on the drawing as to the degree of accuracy required.

Determining Tolerance Limits

Add the allowable tolerance to the dimension. This is the maximum tolerance to which you can work. Subtract the allowable tolerance from the dimension. This is the minimum tolerance allowable for that dimension.

Problem: A dimension is stated as $3\frac{7}{16}''$ $\pm\frac{1}{64}$. Find the limits of accuracy allowable.

Solution:

1. Add the allowable tolerance to the dimension.

$$\begin{array}{r} 3\frac{28}{64} \\ +\ \frac{1}{64} \\ \hline 3\frac{29}{64} \end{array}$$

2. Subtract the allowable tolerance from the dimension.

$$\begin{array}{r} 3\frac{28}{64} \\ -\ \frac{1}{64} \\ \hline 3\frac{27}{64} \end{array}$$

3. The dimension must be within $3\frac{27}{64}''$ and $3\frac{29}{64}''$.

Trade Problem

Find the lower and upper limits of tolerance or variation allowed on the overall length of the part in Fig. 25-1.

Problem: Add: 4.500″ ± .005

Solution:

1. Add the allowable tolerance (+ .005)
   to the dimension.

	4.500
+	.005
	4.505

2. Subtract the allowable tolerance
   (— .005) from the dimension.

	4.500
—	.005
	4.495

3. The *dimension* must be between
   4.495″ and *4.505″*.

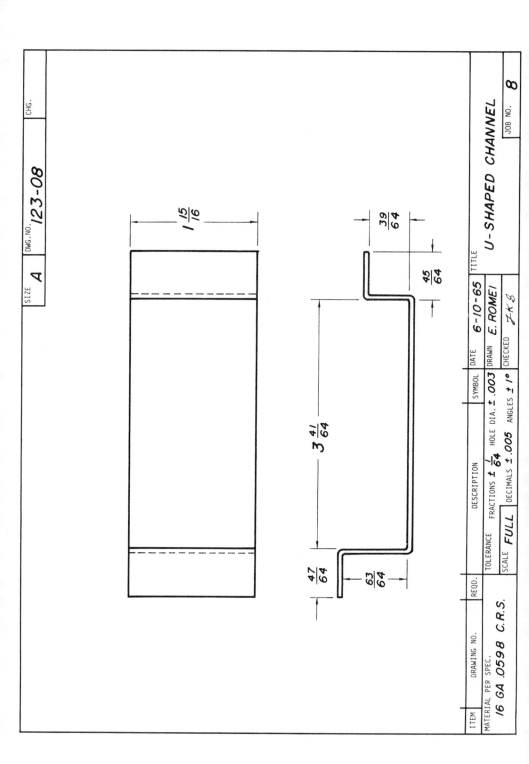

$1\frac{15}{16}$

$3\frac{41}{64}$

$\frac{39}{64}$

$\frac{45}{64}$

$\frac{47}{64}$

$\frac{63}{64}$

ITEM	DRAWING NO.	REQD.		DESCRIPTION	SYMBOL	DATE 6-10-65	TITLE

MATERIAL PER SPEC.
16 GA .0598 C.R.S.

TOLERANCE FRACTIONS $\pm\frac{1}{64}$ HOLE DIA. $\pm$.003
DECIMALS $\pm$.005 ANGLES $\pm$ 1°
SCALE FULL

DRAWN E. ROMEI
CHECKED J.K.B

TITLE U-SHAPED CHANNEL

JOB NO. 8

SIZE A   DWG. NO. 123-08   CHG.

Inside and Outside Dimensions

The precision sheet metalworker must realize the difference between an inside dimension and an outside dimension, and he must use them accurately and correctly. An inside dimension is the dimension inside the item—that is, it does not include the metal thickness of a side. It is referred to as ID (Fig. 26-1).

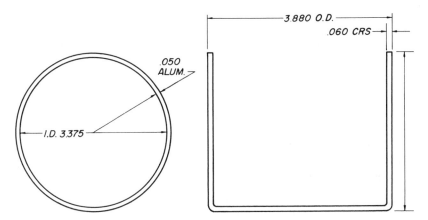

Fig. 26-1. An inside dimension.

An outside dimension is the dimension from end to end of an object, including the metal thickness of a side. It is referred to as OD (Fig. 26-2). The preci-

107

sion sheet metalworker uses inside dimensions, unless stated otherwise, in mathematics problems.

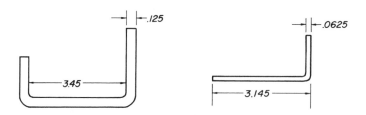

Fig. 26-2. An outside dimension.

Converting an Inside Dimension (ID) to an Outside Dimension (OD)

To convert a dimension from an inside dimension to an outside dimension, the metal thickness of each side that must be included is added to the given inside dimension.

Find the outside dimension.

Problem: ID = 3.45″; metal thickness
= .125″

Solution:

1.	Add the metal thickness of each side to the given inside dimension.	3.450 .125 .125 —— 3.700

2. The *outside* dimension is *3.700 in.*

Converting an Outside Dimension (OD) to an Inside Dimension (ID)

To convert a dimension from an outside dimension to an inside dimension, subtract the metal thickness of each included side from the given outside dimension.

Find the inside dimension.

Problem: OD = 3.145″; metal thickness = .0625″

Solution:

1.	Subtract the metal thickness for each included side from the given outside dimension.	3.1450 − .0625 —— 3.0825

2. The *inside* dimension is *3.760 in.*

Trade Problem

Find the outside dimension in Fig. 26-1.

Problem 1: ID = 3.375"; metal thickness = .050"

Solution:

1. Add the metal thickness of each included side to the given inside dimension.

3.375
.050
.050
3.475

2. The *outside* dimension is *3.475 in.*

Find the inside dimension in Fig. 26-2.

Problem 2: OD = 3.880"; metal thickness = .060"

Solution:

1. Subtract the metal thickness for each included side (.060" + .060" = .120") from the outside dimension.

3.880
− .120
3.760

2. The *inside* dimension is *3.760 in.*

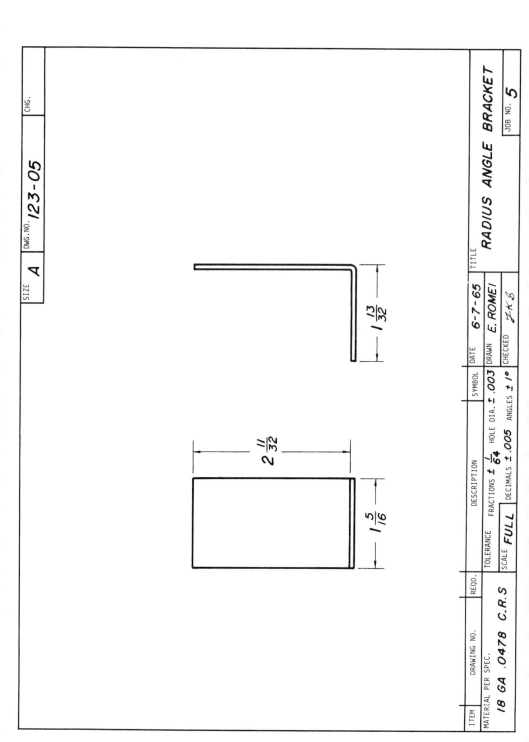

$1\frac{13}{32}$

$2\frac{11}{32}$

$1\frac{5}{16}$

SIZE	DWG. NO.	CHG.
A	123-05	

ITEM	DRAWING NO.		REQD.	DESCRIPTION		SYMBOL	DATE	6-7-65	TITLE	

MATERIAL PER SPEC.

18 GA .0478 C.R.S

TOLERANCE   FRACTIONS $\pm\frac{1}{64}$ HOLE DIA. $\pm$ .003

SCALE   FULL   DECIMALS $\pm$ .005   ANGLES $\pm$ 1°

DRAWN   E. ROMEI

CHECKED   J. K. B.

RADIUS ANGLE BRACKET

JOB NO. 5

Bend Allowances

The bend allowance is the length a of material that must be added to the total length of the flat pattern to allow for forming the part (Fig. 27-1). The bend allowance depends on two factors—the inside radius of the bend and the thickness of the metal. Inside dimensions are used by the precision sheet metalworker to determine the bend allowances.

Fig. 27-1. Bend allowance for a part.

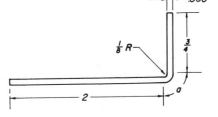

The precision sheet metalworker must know the three methods of determining the bend allowance, depending on the bend, for the following:

1. A sharp 90° angle.

2. A 90° angle with a designated radius.

3. Angles other than 90°

Bend Allowance for a 90° Sharp Bend

Depending on the thickness of the metal, use one of the following rules:

1. If the metal thickness is less than .125″, multiply the metal thickness by 40 percent (0.40).
2. If the metal thickness is .125″ or thicker, multiply the metal thickness by 50 percent (0.50).

Problem 1: Find the bend allowance for a sharp 90° angle with a metal thickness of .115″.

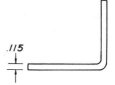

Solution:

1. The metal thickness is less than .125″; therefore, multiply the metal thickness (.115″) by 0.40.
2. The *bend allowance* is *.046″*.

$$\begin{array}{r} .115 \\ \times\ .40 \\ \hline .04600 \end{array}$$

Problem 2: Find the bend allowance for a sharp 90° angle with a metal thickness of .1875″.

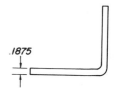

Solution:

1. The metal thickness is more than .125″; therefore, multiply the metal thickness by .50
2. The *bend allowance* is *.093750″*.

$$\begin{array}{r} .1875 \\ \times\ .50 \\ \hline .093750 \end{array}$$

Bend Allowance for a 90° Angle With a Designated Radius

To determine the bend allowance for a 90° angle with a designated radius, use Table 27-1. Each metal thickness has the usual radius sizes given. This table is used in many shops. However, if a shop requires either more or less accuracy, a different table may be used. With this table, no computation is necessary; merely use the bend allowance listed.

Table 27-1. Bend Allowance for 90° Angle With Designated Radius

Stock	Radius	B.A.	Stock	Radius	B.A.
.020	⅟₁₆	.109	.064	⅟₁₆	.138
.032	⅟₁₆	.119		³⁄₃₂	.190
	³⁄₃₂	.168		⅛	.241
				³⁄₁₆	.338
	⅛	.218		¼	.437
	³⁄₁₆	.315			
	¼	.414	.078	⅟₁₆	.152
				³⁄₃₂	.201
.040	⅟₁₆	.125		⅛	.251
	³⁄₃₂	.174		³⁄₁₆	.348
	⅛	.224		¼	.447
	³⁄₁₆	.321			
	¼	.420	.093	⅟₁₆	.162
.050	⅟₁₆	.132		³⁄₃₂	.203
	³⁄₃₂	.181		⅛	.256
	⅛	.231		³⁄₁₆	.359
	³⁄₁₆	.328		¼	.457
	¼	.427			
.060	⅟₁₆	.139	.125	⅟₁₆	.175
	³⁄₃₂	.188		³⁄₃₂	.234
	⅛	.238			
				⅛	.284
	³⁄₁₆	.335		³⁄₁₆	.381
	¼	.434			
				¼	.480

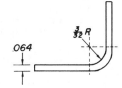

Problem: Find the bend allowance required for a 90° angle with a radius of ³⁄₃₂″ for .064″ metal.

Solution:

1. Find the stock thickness required in the table.

2. Find the required radius; then read the bend allowance opposite this radius.

3. The *bend allowance* is *.190"*.

Determining the Size (Degrees) of the Bends

The size of the angle used to determine the bend allowance is the number of degrees in the angle formed from the flat piece to the formed shape.

Bend Allowance for Angles Other Than 90°

To determine the exact bend allowance for bends other than 90°, use Table 27-2. The table is used in this manner:

Table 27-2. Bend Allowance—Steel Sheet

Gauge	24	22	20	18	16	14	12	11	1/8	10	5/32	3/16	1/4	5/16
Mat'l. Thick.	.0239	.0299	.0359	.0478	.0598	.0747	.1046	.1196	.125	.1345	.1562	.1875	.250	.3125
Inside Radius	BEND ALLOWANCE FOR 1° ANGLE													
1/32	.00073	.00077	.00082	.00091										
1/16	.00128	.00132	.00138	.00146	.00155	.00167								
3/32	.00182	.00187	.00191	.00200	.00210	.00221	.00245							
1/8	.00237	.00241	.00247	.00255	.00265	.00276	.00299	.00311	.00315					
5/32	.00291	.00295	.00300	.00309	.00319	.00330	.00354	.00365	.00370	.00377	.00394			
3/16	.00345	.00350	.00355	.00364	.00373	.00385	.00408	.00420	.00424	.00432	.00449	.00473		
7/32	.00398	.00404	.00409	.00418	.00428	.00439	.00463	.00474	.00479	.00486	.00503	.00527		
1/4	.00454	.00458	.00463	.00472	.00482	.00493	.00516	.00528	.00533	.00540	.00557	.00581	.00630	
9/32	.00508	.00513	.00518	.00527	.00537	.00548	.00572	.00583	.00588	.00595	.00612	.00636	.00685	
5/16	.00563	.00568	.00573	.00582	.00591	.00603	.00626	.00638	.00642	.00649	.00666	.00691	.00740	.00788
11/32	.00618	.00622	.00627	.00636	.00646	.00657	.00681	.00692	.00697	.00704	.00721	.00745	.00794	.00843
3/8	.00672	.00677	.00682	.00691	.00700	.00712	.00735	.00747	.00751	.00758	.00775	.00800	.00849	.00897
13/32	.00727	.00731	.00736	.00745	.00755	.00766	.00790	.00801	.00806	.00813	.00830	.00854	.00903	.00952
7/16	.00781	.00786	.00790	.00800	.00809	.00821	.00844	.00856	.00860	.00867	.00884	.00909	.00958	.01006
15/32	.00835	.00840	.00845	.00854	.00863	.00875	.00898	.00910	.00914	.00922	.00939	.00963	.01012	.01061
1/2	.00890	.00895	.00899	.00909	.00918	.00930	.00953	.00965	.00969	.00976	.00993	.01018	.01067	.01115
17/32	.00944	.00949	.00954	.00963	.00972	.00984	.01007	.01019	.01023	.01031	.01048	.01072	.01121	.01170
9/16	.00999	.01004	.01008	.01018	.01027	.01039	.01062	.01074	.01078	.01085	.01102	.01127	.01175	.01224
19/32	.01053	.01058	.01063	.01072	.01081	.01093	.01116	.01128	.01132	.01140	.01157	.01181	.01230	.01279
5/8	.01108	.01113	.01117	.01127	.01136	.01147	.01171	.01183	.01187	.01194	.01211	.01235	.01284	.01333

Table 27-2. Bend Allowance—Steel Sheet—(cont'd)

Gauge	24	22	20	18	16	14	12	11	1/8	10	5/32	3/16	1/4	5/16
Matl. Thick.	.0239	.0299	.0359	.0478	.0598	.0747	.1046	.1196	.125	.1345	.1562	.1875	.250	.3125
Inside Radius	BEND ALLOWANCE FOR 1° ANGLE													
21/32	.01162	.01167	.01171	.01181	.01190	.01202	.01225	.01237	.01241	.01249	.01266	.01290	.01339	.01387
11/16	.01217	.01222	.01226	.01235	.01245	.01256	.01280	.01292	.01296	.01303	.01320	.01345	.01383	.01442
23/32	.01271	.01276	.01281	.01290	.01299	.01311	.01334	.01346	.01350	.01357	.01374	.01399	.01448	.01496
3/4	.01326	.01331	.01335	.01344	.01354	.01365	.01389	.01400	.01405	.01412	.01429	.01453	.01502	.01551
25/32	.01380	.01385	.01390	.01400	.01408	.01419	.01443	.01455	.01459	.01466	.01483	.01508	.01557	.01605
13/16	.01435	.01439	.01444	.01453	.01463	.01474	.01498	.01509	.01514	.01521	.01538	.01562	.01611	.01660
27/32	.01489	.01494	.01498	.01508	.01517	.01529	.01552	.01564	.01568	.01575	.01592	.01617	.01666	.01714
7/8	.01544	.01548	.01553	.01562	.01571	.01583	.01607	.01618	.01623	.01630	.01647	.01671	.01720	.01769
29/32	.01598	.01603	.01607	.01617	.01626	.01638	.01661	.01673	.01677	.01684	.01701	.01726	.01775	.01823
15/16	.01653	.01657	.01662	.01671	.01681	.01692	.01716	.01727	.01732	.01739	.01756	.01780	.01829	.01878
31/32	.01707	.01712	.01716	.01726	.01735	.01747	.01770	.01782	.01786	.01793	.01810	.01835	.01883	.01932
1	.01762	.01766	.01771	.01780	.01790	.01801	.01825	.01836	.01841	.01848	.01865	.01889	.01938	.01987

1. Find the column with the desired material thickness across the top of the table.
2. In this column, find the line across the table for the desired inside radius; here you will find the allowance *per degree*.
3. Multiply this number by the number of degrees in the bend. The result is the total bend allowance.

Problem: Find the bend allowance for a 35° bend with a metal thickness of .125″ and a radius of 17/32″.

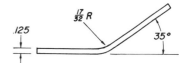

Solution:

1. Find the column across the top of the table for a metal thickness of .125
2. In this column, find the line across the table for the inside radius of 17/32. The number is .01023, which is the allowance per degree.
3. Multiply .01023 by the degrees in the bend *35°*.

```
  .01023
×     35
  ─────
   5115
  3069
  ──────
 .35805
```

4. The total *bend allowance* is *.35805 in.*

Formula for Determining Bend Allowance

To determine the exact bend allowance for bends other than 90° when either the exact radius or the material thickness is not in the table, the following formula must be used. This formula was also used to obtain the two mentioned previously:

1° b.a. = (.01743 × inside radius) + (.0078 × thickness)

The total bend allowance is the number derived from the formula times the degrees in the bend.

Problem: Find the bend allowance for an inside radius of .125″ with a metal thickness of .0478″ and a bend of 56°.

Solution:

1. Multiply .01743 by the inside radius.

$$
\begin{array}{r}
.01743 \\
\times\ \ .125 \\
\hline
8715 \\
3486 \\
1743 \\
\hline
.00217875
\end{array}
$$

2. Multiply .0078 by the thickness of the metal.

$$
\begin{array}{r}
.0478 \\
\times .0078 \\
\hline
3824 \\
3346 \\
\hline
.00037284
\end{array}
$$

3. Add these two numbers.

$$
\begin{array}{r}
.00217875 \\
+\ .00037284 \\
\hline
.00255159
\end{array}
$$

4. Round the sum to five places; then multiply by the number of degrees in the bend (56).

$$
\begin{array}{r}
.00255 \\
\times\ \ \ \ 56 \\
\hline
1530 \\
1275 \\
\hline
.14280
\end{array}
$$

5. The total *bend allowance* is *.1428 in.*

To check the formula, find in the table the bend allowance for ⅛″ inside radius (.125) and a metal thickness of .0478 for a 1° angle. This number should be identical to the sum (.00255) obtained before multiplying by 56°.

Computing Blank Sizes When Using 90-Degree Radius Bends

To compute the blank size for a part, use the inside dimensions (later explained more thoroughly in Units 52, 53, 54, and 57). The radius of the bend also must be considered in the dimension for the straight parts.

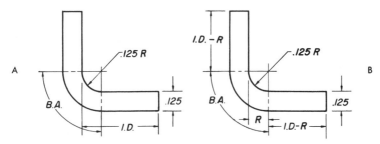

Fig. 27-2. Computing blank sizes for 90° radius bends.

In Fig. 27-2A, the length of the straight portion is used as an inside dimension. However, it can be seen that this overlaps the bend allowance. As shown in Fig. 27-2B, the overlap equals the inside radius. Therefore, the dimension added to the bend allowance is the inside dimension of the straight length minus the inside radius of the bend. The same calculation must be made for the straight length extending upward.

Computing Blank Sizes When Using Radius Bends That are Less Than 90 Degrees

The dimensions specified are either to the middle of the bend (Fig. 27-3A) or to the beginning of the bend (Fig. 27-3B). Use the dimension specified in computing the blank size. This results in sufficient accuracy for the problems in this text.

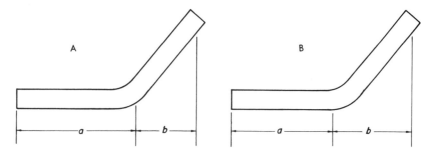

Fig. 27-3. Blank sizes for radius bends that are less than 90°. The dimensions are made: (A) To the middle of the bends, and (B) To the beginning of the bend.

If more accuracy is required, the degrees of the bend, as a fractional part of 90 degrees, multiplied by the inside radius is subtracted from the inside dimension to determine the length of each straight piece. In the shop, it is usually less time consuming to use the method described first—make a sample part to check whether the blank size is sufficiently accurate.

Computing Blank Sizes When Using Radius Bends That Are More Than 90 Degrees

The dimensions specified are usually outside dimensions. When computing the blank size, the metal thickness should be subtracted from the outside dimension of each straight length (Fig. 27-4A).

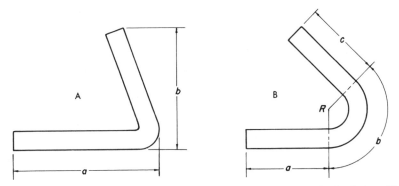

Fig. 27-4. Blank sizes for radius bends that are more than 90°. To compute the blank size: (A) Subtract the metal thickness from the outside dimension, and (B) Use the dimensions of the straight parts.

If more accuracy is required, the degrees of the bend, as a fractional part of 90, multiplied by the inside radius is subtracted from the inside dimension to determine the length of each straight piece. However, in the shop, it is usually less time-consuming to use the method described first—make a sample part to check whether the blank size is sufficiently accurate.

If a relatively large radius is required (Fig. 27-4B), the drawing is usually made as illustrated; then the dimensions of the straight parts to use in the calculations are those given.

Trade Problem

Find the bend allowance a for the part in Fig. 27-1.

Problem: Angle = 90°; inside radius = ⅛"; and metal thickness = .060".

Solution:

1. Since the bend is a 90° bend with a specified inside radius, Table 27-1 can be used.
2. Find a metal thickness of .060 and an inside radius of ⅛; then read the bend allowance.
3. The bend allowance a is *.238 in.*

Linear Measurements

In precision sheet metalwork, inches and feet are the units used in measurements (Fig. 28-1). Therefore, it is necessary for the precision sheet metalworker to understand the linear measurement table, if he is to convert either feet or inches to the other unit and to add, subtract, multiply, and divide feet and inches (Table 28-1).

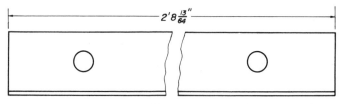

Fig. 28-1

When working with problems that involve both feet and inches, much time can be saved and many errors can be avoided if all units in feet or inches are labeled correctly each time they are used during the computations. In addition to using the abbreviation (in.) for inches, the symbol (″) can be used, as in 3″. The abbreviation for feet (ft) and the symbol (′) can be used, since time is required to write the words.

Converting Inches to Feet and Inches

Since 12 in. = 1 ft, the inches can be changed to feet and inches by dividing the number of inches by 12. The result is in feet and the remainder (if there is one) remains in inches.

119

Problem: Convert 37″ to feet and inches.

Solution:

1. Convert 37″ to feet by dividing by 12.   3 ft
2. The quotient is in feet, and the re-   12 / 37 in.
    mainder is still in inches.   36
3. The result is *3 ft 1 in.*   r. = 1 in.

Converting Feet and Inches to Inches

Since 12 in. = 1 ft, the feet and inches can be converted to inches by multiplying the number of feet by 12 and then adding the number of inches stated previously.

Problem 1:   Convert 2′ 5″ to inches.

Solution:

1. Convert the 2 ft to inches by multi-   12
    plying by 12.   × 2
                                                          24 in.

2. Add the inches (5).   24 in.
                                                          + 5 in.
3. The result is *29 in.*   29 in.

Problem 2:   Convert 7 ft 9¼ in. to inches.

Solution:

1. Convert 7 ft to inches by multiplying   12
    by 12.   × 7   in.
                                                         84   in.
2. Add the inches (9¼).   84   in.
                                                        + 9¼ in.
3. The result is *93 1/4 in.*   93¼ in.

Trade Problem

Find the length 2′ 8$\frac{13}{64}$″, in inches, of the part in Fig. 28-1.

Problem: Convert 2 ft 8 $\frac{13}{64}$ in. to
              inches.

Solution:

1. Convert 2 ft to inches by multiplying   12
    by 12.   × 2
                                                          24 in.

2. Add the inches ($8^{13}\!/_{64}$).

$$\begin{array}{rl} 24 & \text{in.} \\ +\ 8^{13}\!/_{64} & \text{in.} \\ \hline 32^{13}\!/_{64} & \text{in.} \end{array}$$

3. The *length* of the part is $32^{13}\!/_{64}$ *in.*

Table 28-1. Linear Measurements

12 in.	= 1 ft
3 ft	= 1 yd
16½ ft	= 1 rd
5½ yd	= 1 rd
320 rd	= 1 mi
1760 yd	= 1 mi
5280 ft	= 1 mi

in. = inches; ft = feet; yd = yards; rd = rods; mi = miles

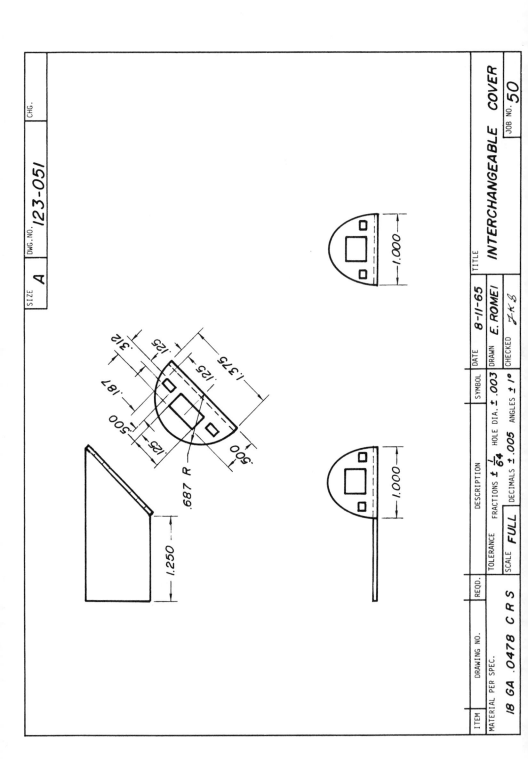

SIZE **A**   DWG. NO. **123-051**   CHG.

ITEM	DRAWING NO.	REQD.	DESCRIPTION		SYMBOL	DATE **8-11-65**	TITLE

MATERIAL PER SPEC.

18 GA .0478 C R S

TOLERANCE FRACTIONS ± 1/64 HOLE DIA. ± .003

DECIMALS ± .005 ANGLES ± 1°

SCALE **FULL**

DRAWN **E. ROMEI**

CHECKED **JKB**

TITLE **INTERCHANGEABLE COVER**

JOB NO. **50**

.312

.125
.125

.187

.500

1.375

.125

.687 R

.500

1.250

1.000

1.000

Addition of Linear Dimensions

Since the dimensions on the drawings that the precision sheet metalworker uses are designated in inches, he must be able to add inches and to add inches and feet, retaining the units of linear measure (Fig. 29-1).

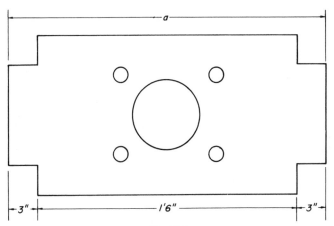

Fig. 29-1

To add the units of linear measure, place the units in like columns; then add each column separately. Express the sum in its lowest terms.

123

Problem 1:   Add: 7 ft 4 in. and 2 ft. 3 in.

Solution:

1. Arrange the numbers in columns of
   like units.
2. Add each column separately.
3. The *sum* is *9 ft 7 in.*

$$\begin{array}{r} 7 \text{ ft } 4 \text{ in.} \\ +2 \text{ ft } 3 \text{ in.} \\ \hline 9 \text{ ft } 7 \text{ in.} \end{array}$$

Problem 2:   Add: 14 ft 9 in. and 5 ft 5 in.

Solution:

1. Arrange the numbers in columns of
   like units.
2. Add each column separately.
3. Convert the total inches to feet and
   inches.
4. Add the 1 ft 2 in. to the 19 ft.

$$\begin{array}{r} 14 \text{ ft } \ \ 9 \text{ in.} \\ + \ 5 \text{ ft } \ \ 5 \text{ in.} \\ \hline 19 \text{ ft } 14 \text{ in.} \end{array}$$

14 in. = 1 ft 2 in.

$$\begin{array}{r} 19 \text{ ft} \\ + \ 1 \text{ ft } 2 \text{ in.} \\ \hline 20 \text{ ft } 2 \text{ in.} \end{array}$$

5. The *sum* is *20 ft 2 in.*

Trade Problem

Find the total length of the part in Fig. 29-1.

Problem: 1 ft 6 in. + 3 in. + 3 in.
Solution:

1. Arrange the numbers in columns of
   like units.

2. Add each column separately.
3. Convert the total inches to feet.
4. Add this total to 1 ft.

5. The *length* of the part is *2 ft.*

$$\begin{array}{r} 1 \text{ ft } \ 6 \text{ in.} \\ 3 \text{ in.} \\ 3 \text{ in.} \\ \hline 1 \text{ ft } 12 \text{ in.} \end{array}$$

12 in. = 1 ft

$$\begin{array}{r} 1 \text{ ft} \\ +1 \text{ ft} \\ \hline 2 \text{ ft} \end{array}$$

Subtraction of Linear Dimensions

Since the dimensions on the drawings that the precision sheet metalworker works with are indicated in inches, he must be able to subtract inches and inches and feet, retaining the correct units of linear measure (Fig. 30-1).

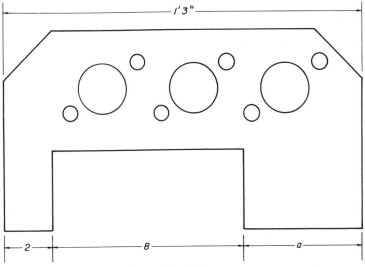

Fig. 30-1

125

To subtract units of linear measure, place the like units in columns; then subtract each column separately. If the number of inches is not large enough to subtract from, borrow 1 ft (12 in.) from the *ft* column.

Problem 1: Subtract 7 ft 7 in. from 12 ft 11 in.

Solution:

1. Arrange the numbers in columns of like units.	12 ft 11 in.
	− 7 ft 7 in.
2. Subtract each column.	5 ft 4 in.
3. The *difference* is *5 ft 4 in.*	

Problem 2: Subtract 5 ft 9 in. from 17 ft 5 in.

Solution:

1. Arrange the numbers in columns.	17 ft 5 in.
2. Since the number of inches is not large enough to subtract from, borrow 1 ft from the 17 ft and add 1 ft or 12 in. to the 5 in. (5 in. + 12 in. = 17 in.).	− 5 ft 9 in.
	16 ft 17 in.
	− 5 ft 9 in.
3. Subtract each column.	11 ft 8 in.
4. The *difference* is *11 ft 8 in.*	

Problem 3: Subtract 3 ft 7½ in. from 5 ft 6 in.

Solution:

1. Arrange the numbers in columns of like units.	5 ft 6 in.
	− 3 ft 7½ in.
2. Borrow 1 ft from 5 ft, and add to 6 in.	4 ft 18 in.
	− 3 ft 7½ in.
3. Subtract each column.	1 ft 10½ in.
4. The *difference* is *1 ft 10½ in.*	

Trade Problem

Find the dimension a in the part in Fig. 30-1.

Problem: Add 8″ + 2″; then subtract
      this sum from 1′ 3″.

Solution:

1. Add the first two numbers.

$$\begin{array}{r} 8'' \\ +2'' \\ \hline 10'' \end{array}$$

2. Subtract this sum (10″) from the
   total length (1′ 3″).

$$\begin{array}{r} 1'\ 3'' \\ -\ 10 \end{array}$$

3. Borrow 1 ft or 12″ from the ft
   column; then add the 1 ft (12″) to
   the 3″. Thus, 12″ + 3″ = 15″.

4. Subtract 10″.

$$\begin{array}{r} 15'' \\ -10'' \\ \hline 5'' \end{array}$$

5. The *difference* or dimension a is 5″.

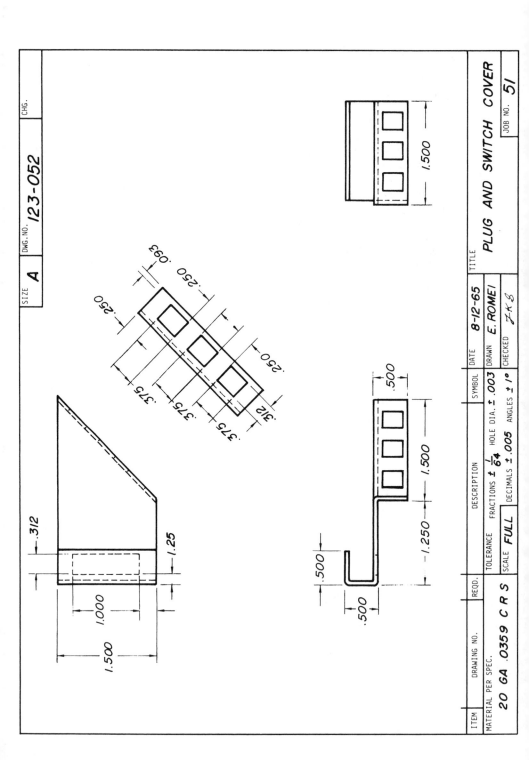

SIZE **A**   DWG. NO. *123-052*   CHG.

.250   .093
.250
.250
.375
.375
.312

.312
1.000
1.25
1.500

.500
.500
.500
1.500
1.250

1.500

ITEM	DRAWING NO.	REQD.	DESCRIPTION	SYMBOL	DATE *8-12-65*	TITLE

MATERIAL PER SPEC.
20 GA .0359 C R S

TOLERANCE   FRACTIONS ± $\frac{1}{64}$ HOLE DIA. ± .003
SCALE *FULL*   DECIMALS ± .005   ANGLES ± 1°

DRAWN   E. ROMEI
CHECKED   *JKB*

TITLE
PLUG AND SWITCH COVER
JOB NO. *51*

Multiplication of
Linear Dimensions

Since the dimensions on the drawings that the precision sheet metalworker works with are indicated in inches, he must be able to multiply by inches and inches and feet, retaining the units of linear measure (Fig. 31-1).

To multiply, place the units of measure in columns; then multiply each column by the number needed. Write the product in its lowest terms. Some-

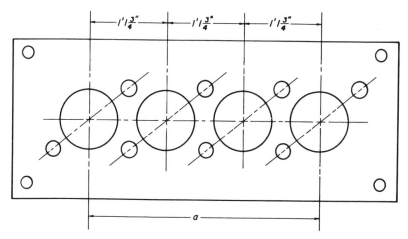

Fig. 31-1

129

times, it is easier to convert the dimensions to inches (if in inches and feet), and then reconvert the product to feet and inches, if necessary.

Problem 1: Find the total length required for a piece of metal to produce five pieces, each 1 ft 3 in. in length.

Solution:

1. Arrange the problem in columns.	1 ft 3 in.
	× 5
2. Multiply each column by 5.	5 ft 15 in.
3. Convert the inches (15) to inches and feet.	15 in. = 1 ft 3 in.
4. Add the 1 ft 3 in. to 5 ft.	5 ft
	+1 ft 3 in.
	6 ft 3 in.
5. The *total length* required is 6 ft 3 in.	

Problem 2: Find the total length required for a piece of metal to produce seven pieces, each $7\frac{3}{4}$ in. in length.

Solution:

1. Arrange the problem in columns.	7 in. $\frac{3}{4}$ in.
	× 7
2. Multiply each column by 7.	49 in. $2\frac{1}{4}$ in.
3. Convert the improper fraction.	$\frac{21}{4}$ in. = $5\frac{1}{4}$ in.
4. Add to this the 49 in.	
	49 in.
	+ $5\frac{1}{4}$ in.
	$54\frac{1}{4}$ in.
5. The *total length* required is $54\frac{1}{4}$ in.; or converted to feet, it *is 4 ft. 6 $\frac{1}{4}$ in.*	

Problem 3: Find the total length required for a piece of metal to produce four pieces, each 1 ft 2.490 in. in length.

Solution:

1. Convert the dimensions to inches; then add.	1 ft = 12 in.
	12 in. + 2.490 in. = 14.490 in.

2. Multiply the inches by the number
of pieces required (4).

$$14.490 \text{ in.}$$
$$\times\ 4$$
$$\overline{57.960 \text{ in.}}$$

3. The *total length* required
is *57.960 in.*, or *4 ft 9.960 in.*

Trade Problem

Find the dimension a of the part in Fig. 31-1.

Problem: 1 ft 1¾ in. × 3

Solution:

1. Convert the dimension to inches

$$1 \text{ ft} = 12 \text{ in.}$$
$$12 \text{ in.} +\ 1¾ \text{ in.} = 13¾ \text{ in.}$$

2. Multiply the inches by the number of
equal dimensions (3).

$$13¾ \text{ in.}$$
$$\times\ 3$$
$$\overline{39\tfrac{9}{4} \text{ in.}}$$

3. Convert the fraction.

$$9/4 \text{ in.} = 2¼ \text{ in.}$$

4. Add the inches.

$$39 \quad \text{ in.}$$
$$+\ 2¼ \text{ in.}$$
$$\overline{41¼ \text{ in.}}$$

5. The dimension a is 41¼ *in.*,
or *3 ft 5¼ in.*

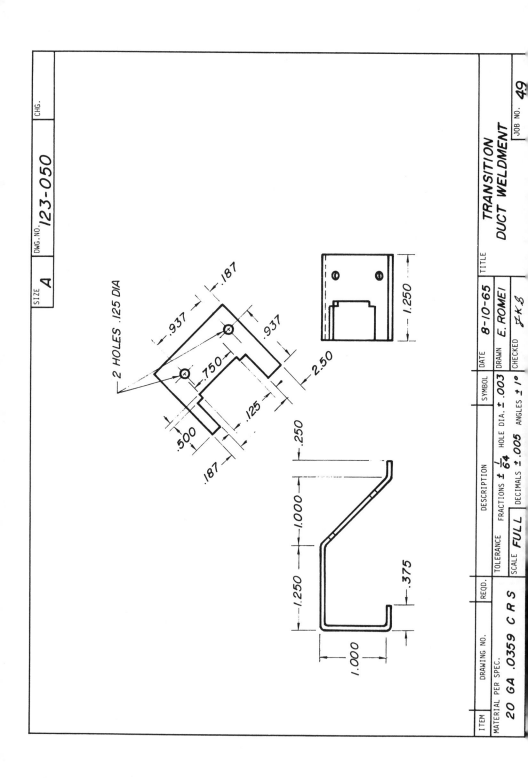

2 HOLES .125 DIA

.187
.937
.937
.750
.500
.125
.187
2.50

.250
1.000
1.250
.375
1.000

1.250

SIZE A   DWG. NO. 123-050   CHG.

ITEM	DRAWING NO.	REQD.	DESCRIPTION	SYMBOL	DATE 8-10-65	TITLE
					DRAWN E. ROMEI	TRANSITION
						DUCT WELDMENT
					CHECKED ℐ•K•B	

MATERIAL PER SPEC.
20 GA .0359 C R S

TOLERANCE
FRACTIONS ± 1/64   HOLE DIA. ±.003
DECIMALS ±.005   ANGLES ±1°
SCALE FULL

JOB NO. 49

Division of
Linear Dimensions

Since the dimensions on the drawings that the precision sheet metal-worker works with are indicated in inches, he must be able to divide inches and inches and feet, retaining the units of linear measure (Fig. 32-1).

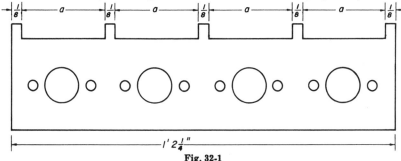

Fig. 32-1

The problem must be arranged in columns, and each column must be divided separately. In some instances, it may be easier to convert fractions to decimals.

Problem 1: Divide 12 ft 4½ in. into two equal parts.

Solution:

1. Arrange the problem in columns.   12 ft 4 in. ½ in.

2. Divide each column separately.

$$2\,\overline{\smash{\big)}\,\begin{array}{l}6\ \text{ft}\ 2\ \text{in.}\ \tfrac{1}{4}\ \text{in.}\\ 12\ \text{ft}\ 4\ \text{in.}\ \tfrac{1}{2}\ \text{in.}\end{array}}$$

3. Each part is *6 ft 2¼ in.*

Problem 2: Divide 2 ft 4½ in. into four equal parts.

Solution:

1. Convert the 2 ft to inches; then ar--range the problem in columns,

$$4\,\overline{\smash{\big)}\,28\ \text{in.}\ \tfrac{1}{2}\ \text{in.}}$$

2. Divide each column separately.
3. *Each* of the four parts is *7⅛ in.*

$$4\,\overline{\smash{\big)}\,\begin{array}{l}7\ \text{in}\ \tfrac{1}{8}\ \text{in.}\\ 28\ \text{in.}\ \tfrac{1}{2}\ \text{in.}\end{array}}$$

Problem 3: If a piece of metal 7′ 3½″ long is divided into two pieces, find the length of each piece.

Solution:

1. Arrange as a division problem.

$$2\,\overline{\smash{\big)}\,7'\,3\tfrac{1}{2}''}$$

2. Divide 7′ by 2. Arrange as a long division problem.

$$\begin{array}{r}3'\\2\,\overline{\smash{\big)}\,7'\,3\tfrac{1}{2}''}\\6\\\hline 1\end{array}$$

3. Convert the remainder of 1 foot to inches; then add the result to the 3 inches.

$$\begin{array}{r}3'\\2\,\overline{\smash{\big)}\,7'\,3\tfrac{1}{2}''}\\6\\\hline 1'=12''\\\hline 15\tfrac{1}{2}''\end{array}$$

4. Divide 15½″ by 2.

$$\begin{array}{r}3'\ 7\tfrac{3}{4}''\\2\,\overline{\smash{\big)}\,7'\,3\tfrac{1}{2}''}\end{array}$$

5. The *length* of each piece is *3′ 7¾″*.

Problem 4: How many pieces, each 3½ in. long, can be obtained from a piece of metal that is 12 in. long? How much metal will remain?

Solution:

1. Convert the fraction to a decimal.

$$3\tfrac{1}{2}=3.5$$

2. Since the total length is in inches, we can divide by inches.
3. The decimal point in the remainder is placed directly below the original

$$\begin{array}{r}3\\3.5\,\overline{\smash{\big)}\,12.0}\\10\ 5\\\hline \text{r.}=1\ 5\end{array}$$

decimal point in the dividend. Therefore, the remainder is 1.5 in.
4. The quotient is 3, with a remainder
   of 1.5 in.
5. Therefore, *three pieces* can be obtained, with 1.5 in. waste.

Problem 5: How many pieces, each 1 ft
1.5 in. long, can be obtained from a
piece of metal that is 96 in. long?

Solution:

1. Convert 1 ft to inches.
2. Divide the total length (96 in.) by
   the length of one piece (13.5 in.).

$$1'\,1.5'' = 13.5''$$

$$13.5\,\overline{\smash{)}\,96.0}\overset{\textstyle 7}{}$$
$$\underline{945}$$
$$\text{r.} = \overline{15}$$

3. The quotient is 7, with a remainder
   of *1.5*.
4. Therefore, *seven pieces* can be obtained, with 1.5 in. waste.

Problem 6: A piece of metal that is 9.5
in. long must be divided into three
equal pieces. Find the length of each
piece corrected to two decimal places.

Solution:

1. Divide, finding the quotient to three
   decimal places (one extra place for
   rounding off to two decimal places).
2. Round off the quotient to two decimal places.
3. The quotient is *3.17″*.
4. Therefore, the *length* of each piece
   is *3.17 in.*

$$3\,\overline{\smash{)}\,9.500}\overset{\textstyle 3.166}{}$$
$$\underline{9}$$
$$\overline{5}$$
$$\underline{3}$$
$$\overline{20}$$
$$\underline{18}$$
$$\overline{20}$$
$$\underline{18}$$

Trade Problem

Find the dimension a in the part in Fig. 32-1.

Problem: From the total length of the
part, subtract the length of each ⅛″
portion. Then, this result must be

divided by 4, the number of pieces marked a.

Solution:

1. Change the overall length to inches.

$$1'\ 2\tfrac{1}{4}'' = 14\tfrac{1}{4}''$$
$$14\tfrac{2}{8}$$
$$-\ \ \tfrac{5}{8}$$

2. From the total length, subtract the length of the five $\tfrac{1}{8}''$ portions. One inch must be borrowed from $14''$, and then added to the fraction.

$$13^{10}\!/_8$$
$$-\ \ \tfrac{5}{8}$$
$$\overline{13\tfrac{5}{8}}$$

3. The total length of the parts marked a is $13\tfrac{5}{8}''$. For greater accuracy, convert $13\tfrac{5}{8}''$ to a decimal.

$$13\tfrac{5}{8} = 13.625$$

4. Divide the total length by the number of parts (4).

$$\begin{array}{r} 3.40625 \\ 4\,\overline{)\,13.62500} \end{array}$$

5. The dimension a of each part is *3.406 in.*

Dividing a Line
Into Equal Parts

The precision sheet metalworker frequently must divide a line into equal parts (Fig. 33-1). A typical example is dividing a given line into equal parts for locating rivet or bolt holes in a given space. A line can be divided either by construction or by computations.

Dividing a Line by Computations

When using computations to divide a line, express the length of the line as a

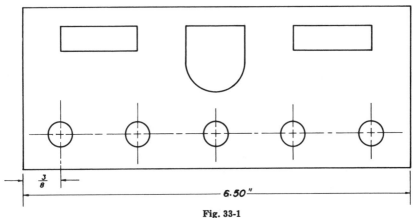

Fig. 33-1

137

decimal. Then, divide by the number of spaces required. Convert the decimal to a fractional equivalent, if necessary.

Problem: Divide a 7½″ line into five
          equal parts.

Solution:

    1. Convert the fraction to a decimal. $½ = 0.5$
    2. Divide the total length by 5.

$$5\,\overline{)\,7.5\,}^{\,1.5}$$

    3. Each equal part is *1.5″*.

Dividing a Line by Bisection

Bisecting a line is dividing a line into two equal parts. The procedure is as follows:

    1. Open your compass until its radius is more than one-half the length of the line. You do not need to measure the length of the line. Place the metal point of the compass at one end of the line. Draw an arc (small portion of a circle) above the line and another arc below the line.

    2. Without changing the compass radius, move the metal point of the compass to the opposite end of the line. Draw arcs both above and below the line, as before. These arcs should intersect the arcs drawn previously, if the first arcs were drawn properly.

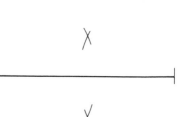

    3. Draw a straight line, connecting the points where the arcs cross. This line is called the *perpendicular bisector* of the original line. The original line has been divided into two equal parts. If the line must be divided into four equal parts, each of the two parts divided previously can be divided further in the same manner.

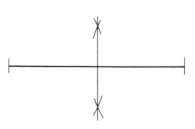

Dividing a Line Into Any Number of Equal Parts

Assuming that we desire to divide the line *OA* into five equal parts, the following procedure to divide a line into any number of equal parts can be used.

1. Draw line *OC*, at any convenient angle with line *OA*.

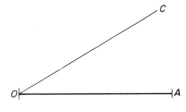

2. On line *OC*, mark off five equal convenient spaces, beginning at *O* (for example, every half inch, quarter inch, etc.) and label these division points *a, b, c, d,* and *e*. Mark five division points, since the line is to be divided into five equal parts.

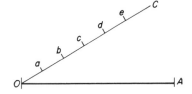

3. Do not be concerned with the measurement of the space from point *e* to point *O*.

4. From point *e*, draw a line to point *A* on the original line.

5. Through points *d, c, b,* and *a* draw lines parallel to line *eA*.

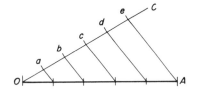

6. The original line has been divided into five equal parts. If it had been divided into nine parts, nine division points would be required on line *OC*.

Dividing a Line Into Equal Parts by Trial and Error

If only three divisions are required, you can use the compass, opening it to a distance that appears to be approximately one-third the length of the line. Try this setting, changing the compass setting until you obtain the correct distance.

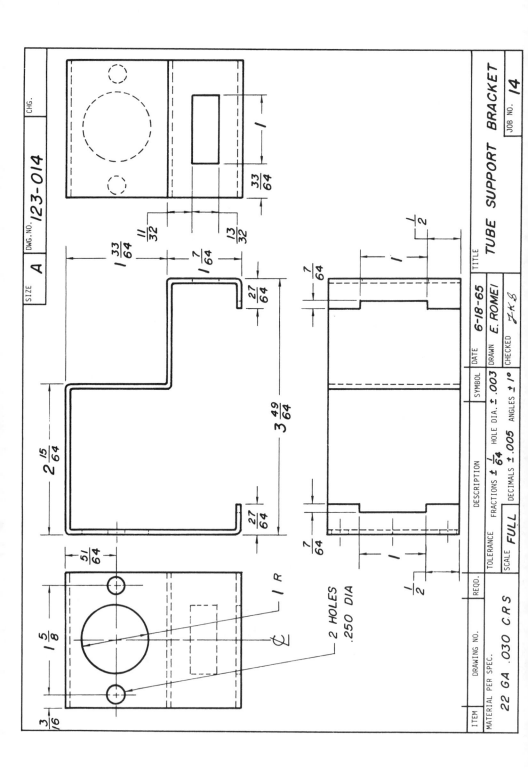

SIZE **A** DWG. NO. **123-014** CHG.

TITLE **TUBE SUPPORT BRACKET**

DATE **6-18-65** JOB NO. **14**

DRAWN **E. ROMEI**

CHECKED **I·K·B**

DESCRIPTION

SYMBOL

REQD.

ITEM DRAWING NO.

MATERIAL PER SPEC.
22 GA .030 C.R.S

TOLERANCE FRACTIONS ± $\frac{1}{64}$ HOLE DIA. ± .003 SCALE **FULL** DECIMALS ± .005 ANGLES ± 1°

$1\frac{33}{64}$

$1\frac{7}{64}$

$2\frac{15}{64}$

$3\frac{49}{64}$

$\frac{27}{64}$

$\frac{27}{64}$

$\frac{11}{32}$

$\frac{13}{32}$

$\frac{33}{64}$

1

$\frac{51}{64}$

$1\frac{5}{8}$

$\frac{3}{16}$

1 R

2 HOLES
.250 DIA

℄

$\frac{7}{64}$

$\frac{1}{2}$

1

$\frac{7}{64}$

$\frac{7}{64}$

1

$\frac{1}{2}$

Unit **34**

Circular Parts

The precision sheet metalworker makes parts that are circular in shape and parts that contain circular holes (Fig. 34-1). Therefore, he must understand the parts of a circle and their relation to each other.

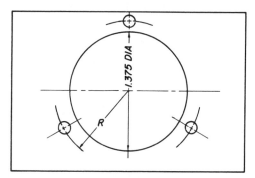

Fig. 34-1

Definition of Terms

1. *Circle.* A plane bounded by a curved line, every point of which is equally distant from the point called the *center.*

2. *Circumference.* The distance around the circle measured in linear units.

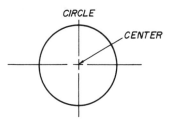

141

3. *Diameter.* A straight line drawn through the center of the circle, terminating at the circumference. It divides the circle into two equal parts called *semicircles.*

4. *Radius.* A straight line drawn from the center of a circle to the circumference.

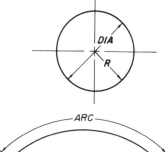

5. *Arc.* Any part of the curved line.

6. *Chord.* A straight line drawn between the ends of an arc.

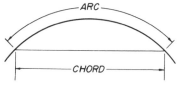

7. *Concentric circles.* Two circles having the same center with different diameters. The diameter of the outer circle is the OD and the inner circle is the ID.

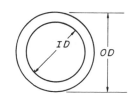

Symbols

The following symbols are commonly used:

1. The symbol for a circle is ⊙.

2. The symbols for the diameter are D and d.

3. The symbols for the radius are R and r.

Relations of the Radius and Diameter of a Circle

The radius of a circle is equal to one-half the diameter; or, the diameter of a circle is twice its radius. The circumference of a circle will be discussed later.

Problem: If the diameter of a circle is $3\frac{1}{4}''$, find its radius.

Solution:

1. Arrange the problem. $\qquad\qquad 3\frac{1}{4} \div 2$

2. Convert the mixed number to an improper fraction. $\qquad 3\frac{1}{4} = \frac{13}{4}$

3. When dividing, invert the divisor and replace the division sign with a multiplication sign. Multiply.

$$\frac{13}{4} \times \frac{1}{2} = \frac{13}{8}$$

4. Convert to a mixed number.
5. The *radius* is 1⅝ in.

$$\frac{13}{8} = 1\frac{5}{8}$$

Problem 2: If the radius of a circle is 2.75″, find the diameter of the circle.

Solution:

1. Arrange the problem and multiply. $2.75 \times 2 = 5.5″$
2. The *diameter* is *5.5 in.*

Trade Problem

Find the radius r of the circle in the part in Fig. 34-1.

Problem: The diameter d is *1.375 in.*

Solution:

1. Arrange the problem. $1.375 \div 2$
2. Divide. $1.375 \div 2 = .6875$
3. The radius r is *.6875 in.*

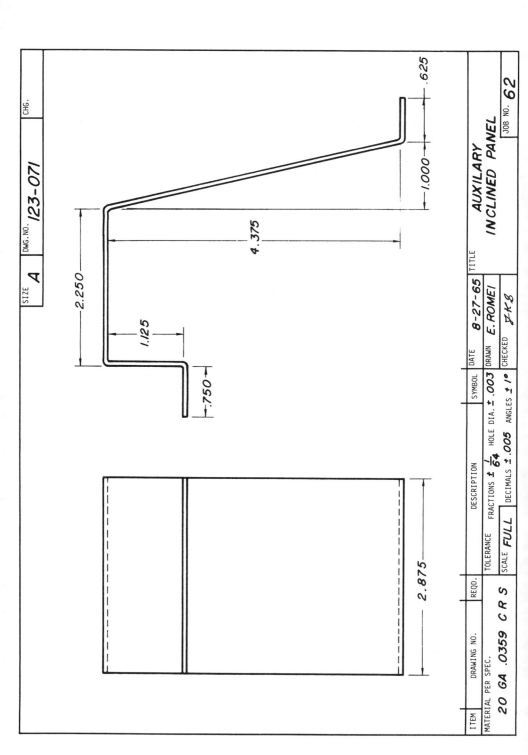

.625

.625

2.250

1.125

4.375

1.000

.750

2.875

SIZE A

DWG. NO. 123-071

CHG.

ITEM	DRAWING NO.	REQD.	DESCRIPTION	SYMBOL	DATE 8-27-65	TITLE
	20 GA .0359 C R S				DRAWN E. ROMEI	AUXILARY

MATERIAL PER SPEC.

TOLERANCE FRACTIONS ± 1/64 HOLE DIA. ± .003

SCALE FULL DECIMALS ± .005 ANGLES ± 1°

CHECKED ℱKℬ

AUXILARY
INCLINED PANEL

JOB NO. 62

Unit **35**

Units of
Angular Measurement

Angles are required in most parts made by the precision sheet metalworker (Fig. 35-1). Therefore, they must be understood thoroughly.

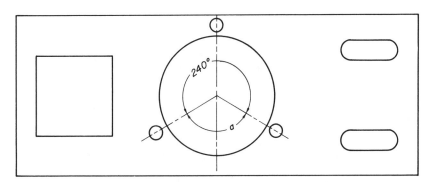

Fig. 35-1

Definition of Terms

1. *Angle.* The opening between two lines which meet at a point.

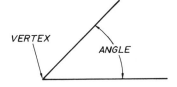

145

2. *Vertex.* The point at which the two
   lines of an angle intersect.

Designating Angular Measure

Angles are measured in degrees, minutes, and seconds. These measurements can be added, subtracted, multiplied, and divided in a manner similar to that used in units of linear measure. The symbols are:

1. A *degree* symbol is a small zero (°): for example, 3°.
2. A *minute* symbol is a single prime ('): for example, 2'.
3. A *second* symbol is a double prime: ("): for example, 4".
4. An *angle* symbol is: ∠

Angular Measurements

1 circle = 360 degrees
1 degree = 60 minutes
1 minute = 60 seconds

Abbreviations

degrees = deg or (°)
minutes = min or (')
seconds = sec or (")

Identifying an Angle

The common method of identifying an angle is a small letter placed inside the angle.

As you will realize when we begin using a protractor to measure an angle, the number of degrees in the angle is not related to the length of the lines or sides of the angle.

Since a circle consists of 360 degrees, the degrees in the following portions of a circle are:

1. *Quarter* circle. 360° × ¼ = 90°.
2. *Half* circle. 360° × ½ = 180°.
3. *Three-quarter* circle. 360° × ¾ = 270°.

Problems Converting Degrees, Minutes, and Seconds

Problem 1:   Convert 120° to a fractional part of a circle.

Solution:

1. Place the number of degrees being considered above the total number of degrees in a circle.

$$\frac{120°}{360°}$$

2. Reduce the fraction to its lowest terms.

$$\frac{120°}{360°} = \frac{1}{3}$$

3. The *fractional part* of a circle is ⅓ circle.

Problem 2:   Convert 45 minutes to degrees.

Solution:

1. Place the number of minutes being considered above the total number of minutes in a degree.

$$\frac{45'}{60'}$$

2. Reduce the fraction to its lowest terms.

$$\frac{45'}{60'} = \frac{3}{4}$$

3. The number of degrees is ¾ or *.75 degree.*

Problem 3:   Convert .25 degrees to minutes.

Solution:

1. Multiply the number of degrees being considered (.25) by the number of minutes in a degree (60).

2. The number of minutes is *15'*.

$$.25 \times 60' = 15'$$

Trade Problem

Find the number of degrees a in the portion of the circle in the part in **Fig.** 35-1.

Problem: Circle = 360°; designated portion = 240°.

Solution:

1. Subtract the number of degrees (240) in the portion of the circle that is labeled from the number of degrees in a complete circle (360).

$$\begin{array}{r} 360° \\ -240° \\ \hline 120° \end{array}$$

2. The number of degrees a is *120°*.

Reading the
Bevel Protractor

A protractor is used by the precision sheet metalworker to measure angles. The various types are the semicircular protractor, vernier protractor, bevel protractor, and swinging-blade protractor. The protractor shown in Fig. 36-1 is the bevel protractor.

A bevel protractor consists of two basic parts—the rule and the protractor head. The rule has a groove on one side, which is used to insert it into the lug of the protractor head. When the rule has been inserted into the lug, the screw can be tightened; then the protractor head can no longer slide along the rule.

The protractor scale is stationary, but the outer portion containing the markings for the reading can be moved to measure the angle. The piece to be measured should be held first against the rule; then the protractor head is moved until the base of the protractor also rests firmly against the piece. The screws on the back of the protractor head can be tightened to hold the protractor head in position; then the reading is made.

Reading The Protractor Scale

The bevel protractor scale (Fig. 36-2) is divided into 180°. The scale begins with a reading of 0° on each side and progresses in 1° graduations to 90° at the top. The index mark on either side is used to read the number of degrees in the angle.

When measuring an angle less than 90° (an acute angle), the size of the angle is the reading indicated on the protractor head (Fig. 36-3). When measuring an angle more than 90° (an obtuse angle), the size of the angle is 180° minus the

149

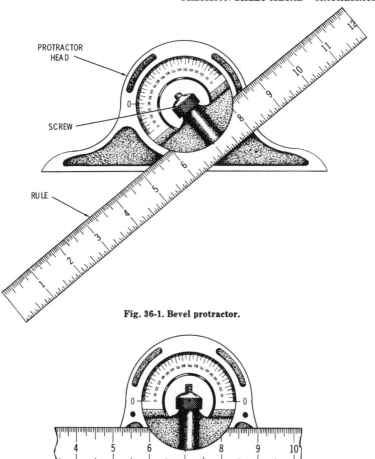

Fig. 36-1. Bevel protractor.

Fig. 36-2. The head of the bevel protractor.

reading. If the angle is more than 90° and the reading is 70°, the angle being measured is $180° - 70° = 110°$.

Trade Problem

Problem: What is the reading on the bevel protractor in Fig. 36-3?

Solution:

1. The piece being measured has been positioned against the rule.

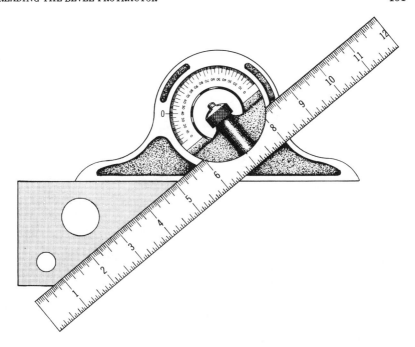

Fig. 36-3. Measuring an acute angle.

2. The protractor head has been moved against the piece.
3. The reading is 40°. Since the angle being measured is less than 90°, this reading *40°* is the exact reading.
4. The measured *angle* is *40°*.

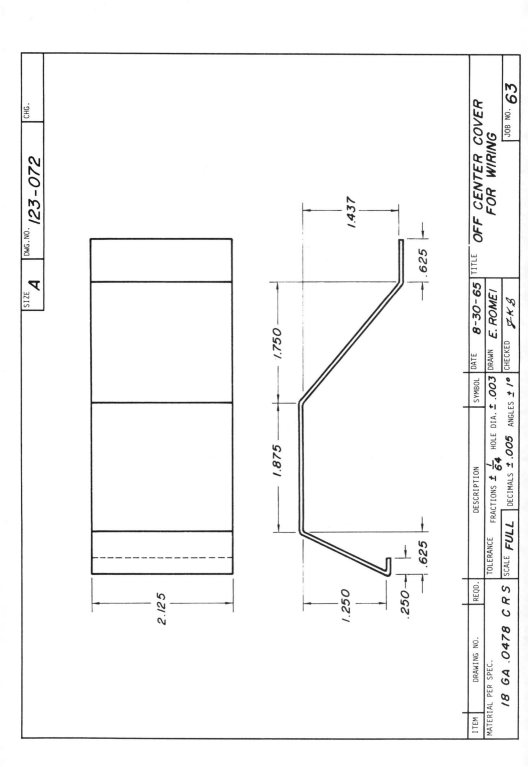

SIZE A | DWG. NO. 123-072 | CHG.

2.125

1.437
1.750
1.875
.625
1.250
.250
.625

| ITEM | DRAWING NO. | REQD. | DESCRIPTION | SYMBOL | DATE 8-30-65 | TITLE OFF CENTER COVER FOR WIRING |

MATERIAL PER SPEC.
18 GA .0478 C R S

TOLERANCE FRACTIONS ± $\frac{1}{64}$ HOLE DIA. ± .003
SCALE FULL DECIMALS ± .005 ANGLES ± 1°

DRAWN E. ROMEI
CHECKED J.K.B

JOB NO. 63

Triangles

A plane figure with three straight sides is a triangle. The principles of the triangle are applied by the precision sheet metalworker in making various parts with inclined surfaces or edges (Fig. 37-1) and in locating a dimension for a series of holes.

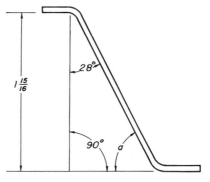

Fig. 37-1. A part with an inclined surface.

Types of Triangles

The sides of a triangle can be either equal or unequal. However, the differences in the lengths of the sides and the sizes of the angles determine the names for the various triangles. Since a triangle has three sides, it also has three angles.

The *lengths of the sides* is one method of dividing triangles into groups and naming them:

153

1. *Equilateral triangle.* A triangle with three sides equal in length.

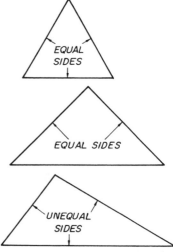

2. *Isosceles triangle.* Two sides are equal in length, with the third side either longer or shorter than the equal sides.

3. *Scalene triangle.* All of the sides are unequal; that is, each of the three sides is a different length.

The *altitude* of a triangle is the distance from the vertex to the base, measured perpendicular to the base. The abbreviation of the word *altitude* is *alt*.

The *size of the angles* is another method of dividing triangles into groups and naming them:

1. *Right triangle.* Includes one right angle (90°).

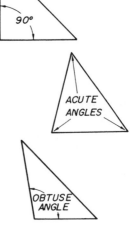

2. *Acute triangle.* All included angles are acute (less than 90°).

3. *Obtuse triangle.* Includes one obtuse angle (more than 90°).

4. *Equiangular* (or equilateral) *triangle*. All the angles are equal. An equiangular triangle is always equilateral. Since the sum of the three angles of a triangle is 180°, each angle in an equiangular or equilateral triangle is (180° ÷ 3), or 60°.

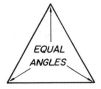

Constructing a Triangle With Three Sides Given

A triangle can be constructed, if the *three sides* are known.

Problem: Draw a triangle with a base 2" in length and sides that are 1⅜" and 1⅞".

Solution:

1. Draw the 2" base line.

2. Using one end of this line for a center, draw an arc with a 1⅜" radius.

3. Using the opposite end of the line for a center, draw an arc with a 1⅞" radius, making sure that the two arcs intersect.

4. Draw a line from the point where the two arcs intersect to each end of the base line to complete the triangle.

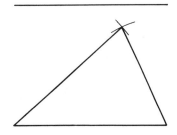

Constructing a Triangle With Two Sides and the Included Angle Given

A triangle can be constructed, if *two sides and the included angle* are known.

Problem: Construct a triangle in which the sides are 1⅜" and 1⅛" and an included angle is 46° (included angle is the angle between the two specified lines).

Solution:

1. Draw a 1⅜" line (the longer of the two specified lines).
2. Construct a 46° angle at one end of the line.

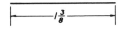

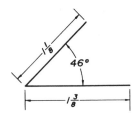

3. Measure 1⅛" (second side) on the constructed line. Mark this point.

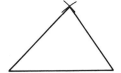

4. Connect this marked point with the opposite end of the first line.

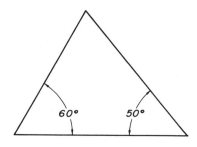

Constructing a Triangle With Two Angles and the Included Side Given

A triangle can be constructed, if *two angles and the included side* are known.

Problem: Construct a triangle in which the base is 2½" and the angles at the ends of the 2½" base are 60° and 50°.

Solution:

1. Draw the 2½" base line.
2. Construct a 60° angle at one end of the base line.
3. Construct a 50° angle at the opposite end of the base line.
4. Extend these two lines until they meet, forming the required triangle.

Basic Principles of Triangles

The basic principles of triangles are:

1. Two triangles are equal if the *three sides* of one triangle are equal to the three sides of the second triangle.
2. Two triangles are equal if *two sides and the included angle* of one triangle are equal to two sides and the included angle of the second triangle.
3. Two triangles are equal if *two angles and the included side* of one triangle are equal to two angles and the included side of the second triangle.
4. If two angles of a triangle are equal, the *sides opposite the two equal angles* are equal. Also, if two sides of a triangle are equal, the *angles opposite the two equal sides* are equal.

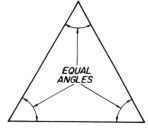

5. The *sum* of the angles in a triangle is 180°.
6. If two triangles are equal, their *corresponding parts* (sides, angles) are equal.

Trade Problem

Note the dimensions on the part in Fig. 37-1. With two angles and the included side given, the slant height and the base length can be determined by constructing the triangle. Find the size of the angle *A*.

Problem: Add: 90° + 28° + angle A =
    180°

Solution:

1. Find the sum of the two angles.   90°
2. The sum of the angles in a triangle   + 28°
   is 180°.   ────
                                                                     118°
3. Subtract the sum of the two angles   180°
   from 180°.   −118°
                                                                    ────
4. The unknown angle *A* is 62°.   62°
5. Constructing the triangle will determine the *base length* and the *slant height*.

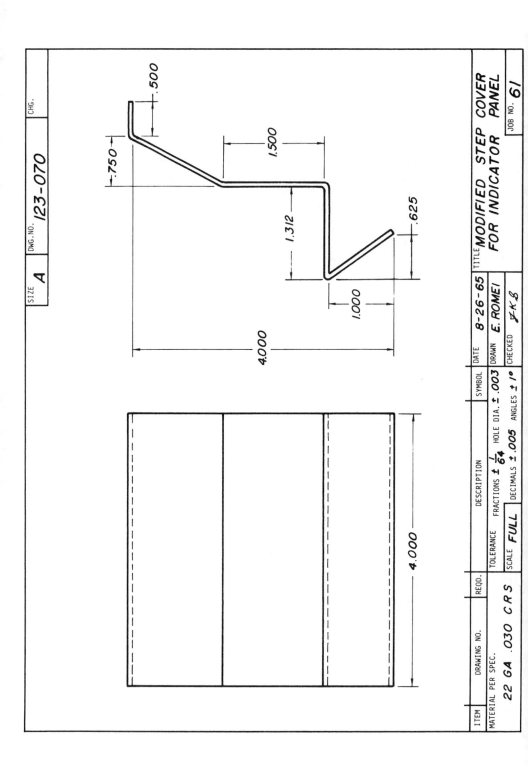

SIZE **A**   DWG. NO. **123-070**   CHG.

.500
.750
.500
1.500
1.312
.625
1.000
4.000

4.000

ITEM	DRAWING NO.	REQD.	DESCRIPTION	SYMBOL	DATE 8-26-65	TITLE MODIFIED STEP COVER

MATERIAL PER SPEC.
22 GA .030 CRS

TOLERANCE   FRACTIONS ± 1/64   HOLE DIA. ± .003
DECIMALS ± .005   ANGLES ± 1°

SCALE **FULL**

DRAWN E. ROMEI
CHECKED ₣K̅B̅

TITLE **MODIFIED STEP COVER**
FOR INDICATOR PANEL
JOB NO. **61**

Intersecting Lines

An understanding of the construction of lines is essential for the precision sheet metalworker, because most parts consist of straight lines. Straight lines are found at various angles to each other (Fig. 38-1). They are *perpendicular* lines if they are at 90° to each other. They are *oblique* lines, if they are at any degree other than either 90° or 180° to each other.

Fig. 38-1. Part with straight lines at various angles.

An angle more than 90°, but less than 180°, is an *obtuse* angle. An angle less than 90° is an *acute* angle. A 90° angle is a *right* angle.

Perpendicular Lines

Perpendicular lines intersect at 90°; or they will intersect at a 90° angle if they are extended until they meet. The symbol that represents the term *perpendicular* is ⊥.

Perpendicular lines can be in any position. They are not necessarily horizontal and vertical.

Constructing a Perpendicular to a Line From a Point On the Line

This procedure results in construction of a right angle from a given point on the line.

Problem: Construct a perpendicular to the given line from a point C on the line.

Solution:

1. With the given point C as the center, draw two arcs with equal radii. Use any convenient radius, and be sure that the arcs intersect the line. The points of intersection are the points A and B.

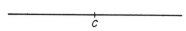

2. With the points A and B as the centers and a convenient radius (longer than AC or BC), draw two arcs that intersect at point D.

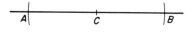

3. Draw a straight line connecting points D and C. This line is perpendicular to the given line. The two angles are each 90°.

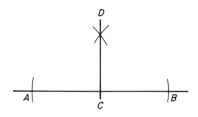

Constructing a Perpendicular to a Line From a Point Above the Line

This procedure results in constructing a right angle from a point above the line.

Problem: Construct a perpendicular to the line from point C above the line.

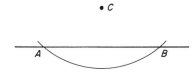

Solution:

1. Using point C as the center and a convenient radius, draw an arc intersecting the line at points A and B.

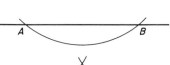

2. Using points A and B as centers and a convenient radius, draw two arcs intersecting at point D on the opposite side of the line from point C.

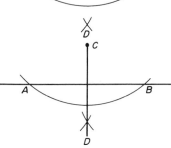

3. Draw a line from point C to point D. This line is perpendicular to the line and passes through the point C. Each angle formed is 90°.

Constructing a Perpendicular to a Line From a Point at the End of the Line

This procedure results in constructing a right angle from the end of a line.

Problem: Construct a perpendicular to the line from point C at the end of the line.

Solution:

1. Using the point C at the end of the line as the center, draw a conveniently large arc.

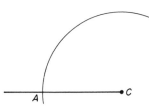

2. Using the same radius, use point A as center and mark point B on the arc with the compass. Then, using point B as center, mark point D on the arc with the compass.

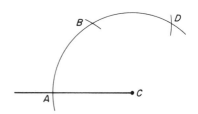

3. Using points B and D as centers, draw intersecting arcs with the same radius. They intersect at point E. Connect points C and E.

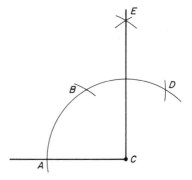

4. The angle formed is 90°.

Dividing an Angle Into Equal Parts

Dividing an angle into two equal parts is called *bisecting* the angle. When this is completed, each angle can be bisected further to form four equal angles.

Problem: Divide the angle ACB into four equal parts.

Solution:

1. First, the angle must be bisected. Using point C as a center and a convenient radius, draw an arc intersecting the sides of the angle at points A and B.

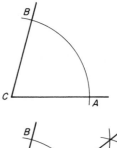

2. With a convenient radius, use points A and B as centers to draw two arcs intersecting at point E.

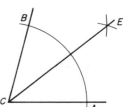

3. Connect points E and C; the angle is bisected. The two angles formed are ACE and ECB.

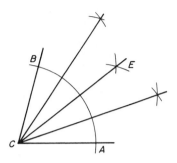

4. Repeat Steps No. 2 and No. 3 with both angles ACE and ECB, bisecting each angle. Therefore, the original angle ACB has been divided into four equal angles.

Transferring an Angle

Problem: Transfer the given angle ACB to the given line ST, using point S as the vertex.

Solution:

1. Using the vertex C of the angle as the center, draw arc AB. Using the same radius and point S on the line as the center, draw an arc intersecting line ST and extending upward.

 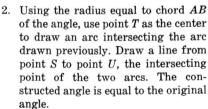

2. Using the radius equal to chord AB of the angle, use point T as the center to draw an arc intersecting the arc drawn previously. Draw a line from point S to point U, the intersecting point of the two arcs. The constructed angle is equal to the original angle.

Relation of the Angles

The angles formed by intersecting lines are related as follows:

1. The total number of degrees extending around a given point is 360°. Therefore, angle A can be determined by subtracting 310° from 360°, which is equal to 50°.

2. If the sum of two angles results in a straight line, or 180°, they are called *supplementary* angles. A 180° angle is, therefore, a *straight* angle.

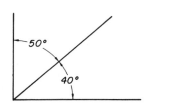

3. If the sum of two angles results in a right angle, or 90°, the angles are *complementary* angles.

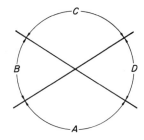

4. If two straight lines intersect, the opposite angles are equal.

   a. *Given:*
      Angle $A = 116°$
      Angle $B = 64°$
   b. *Therefore:*
      Angle $C = 116°$
      Angle $D = 64°$

Unit **39**

Parallel Lines

Parallel lines are used by the precision sheet metalworker in making many parts (Fig. 39-1). Parallel lines are lines that are equally distant (equidistant) at all points. They never meet, regardless of the distance they are extended. The symbol for the term *parallel* is $\parallel$.

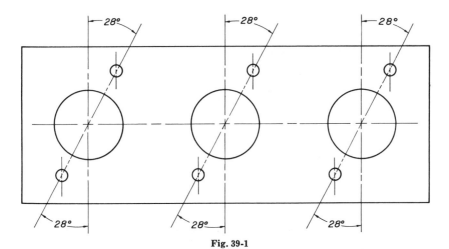

Fig. 39-1

Constructing Parallel Lines by Using Perpendiculars

Problem: Construct two parallel lines 1″ apart.

Solution:

1. Begin with a base line.

2. On this line, mark two points 1 inch apart.

3. Construct perpendiculars to the base line at each of the two points.

4. Since each of the two lines is perpendicular to the same line, they are parallel to each other.

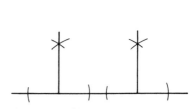

Constructing Parallel Lines by Using Equal Exterior–Interior Angles

Problem: Construct a line through point *P*, parallel to line *AB*.

Solution:

1. Draw a line through point *P* and across line *AB*. Label the point *S* where the lines intersect.

2. Place the compass point on point *S*. Using any radius, draw an arc, intersecting both lines. Label the points *C* and *D* where the arc intersects the lines.

3. Without changing the radius, move the compass point to point *P*. Draw an arc about the same size as the previous arc. Label the point *I* where the arc intersects line *PS*.

4. Move the compass point to point *C*. Adjust the radius to equal the distance *CD*. Place the compass point at point *T*, and draw an arc through the arc that passes through point *T*. Label the point *U* where the arcs intersect.

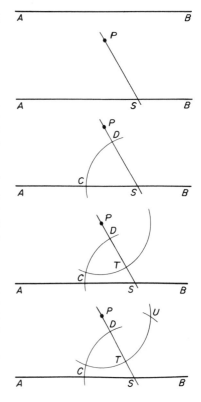

5. Draw a straight line through points *P* and *U*. This line is parallel to line *AB*.

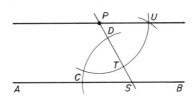

Constructing Parallel Lines by Using Arcs of Circles

Problem: Construct two parallel lines 1″ apart.

Solution:

1. Draw a base line. Construct perpendiculars to this line near the ends. Be sure that each perpendicular is longer than 1″.

2. Using points *A* and *B* as centers, draw arcs with 1″ radius. Label the points *C* and *D* where the arcs intersect the perpendiculars.

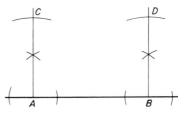

3. Draw a line connecting points *C* and *D*. The line is parallel to the base line.

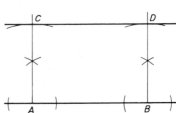

Dividing a Line Into Equal Parts With the Steel Rule

Problem: Divide a line 2″ long into nine
 equal parts.

Solution:

 1. Draw a line perpendicular to the
    given line at one end.

 2. Place a steel rule at an angle to the
    line, so that the number of required
    parts divide evenly into the distance
    on the rule. Nine ¼″ divisions are
    used.

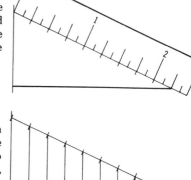

 3. Draw lines from these divisions on
    the steel rule to the given line; the
    lines must be drawn perpendicular to
    the given line. The lines are parallel,
    because they are perpendicular to the
    same line.

Dividing a Line Into Equal Parts by Using Parallel Lines

Problem: Divide the given line, 2½″ long,
 into three equal parts.

Solution:

 1. Draw two lines parallel to each other
    from the ends of line *AB*. These lines
    are *AR* and *BS*, making angle *ABS*
    equal to angle *BAR*.
 2. Beginning with point *A*, mark three
    equal divisions on line *AR* with the
    compass at a convenient radius.
    Using the same radius, mark three
    equal divisions on line *BS*, beginning
    with point *B*.

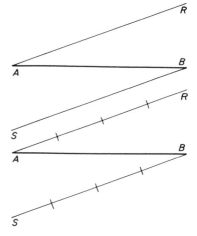

3. Connect the points on the two lines
    with parallel lines which divide line
    AB into *three* equal parts.

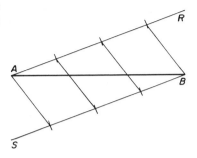

Dividing a Line Into Equal Parts by Transferring Angles

Problem: Divide the given line, 2″ long,
into five equal parts.

Solution:

1. Draw line *AX* at an angle to line *AB*.
    Using a compass, mark five equal
    parts on line *AX*, labeling them *1, 2,
    3, 4,* and *5.*

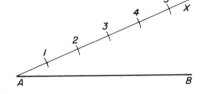

2. Draw a line connecting points *5* and
    B.

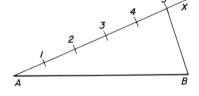

3. Angle *A5B* has been formed. Con-
    struct an equal angle at points *4, 3,
    2,* and *1.* Be sure that the lines which
    complete these angles cross line *AB.*

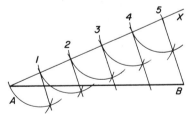

4. The points at which the lines cross line AB divide line AB into five equal parts.

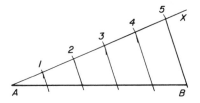

5. Therefore, any given line length can be divided into any number of equal parts.

Alternate Interior and Exterior Angles

When two parallel lines are crossed by a third line, the alternate interior angles and the alternate exterior angles are equal. All angles located between the two parallel lines are interior angles; all angles located above the top line and below the bottom line are exterior angles. Therefore, the *interior* angles are C, D, E, and F; the *exterior* angles are A, B, G, and H.

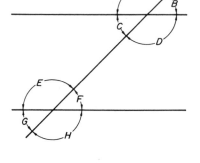

Alternate angles are angles that are equal in size. Therefore, alternate interior angles are angles C and F and angles D and E; the alternate exterior angles are angles A and H and angles B and G. The equal angles are:

$$\text{angle } A = \text{angle } H$$
$$\text{angle } B = \text{angle } G$$
$$\text{angle } C = \text{angle } F$$
$$\text{angle } D = \text{angle } E$$

Squares, Rectangles, Parallelograms, and Trapezoids

Squares, rectangles, parallelograms, and trapezoids are four-sided polygons (plane figures with several angles and sides, usually more than four) which appear in most parts made by the precision sheet metalworker. Sometimes, several of these polygons are involved in making a single part (Fig. 40-1).

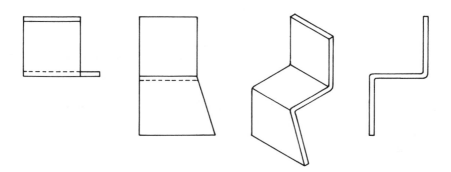

Fig. 40-1. Various shapes used in sheet metal parts.

171

Square

A *square* is a four-sided polygon in which all four sides are equal and all four angles are 90° angles. A small square ☐ is the symbol for the square. The small letter s represents the length of one side of a square. A square is constructed from perpendiculars, as follows:

1. Begin with a line the length desired for each side.

2. Construct perpendiculars to the line at each end of the line.

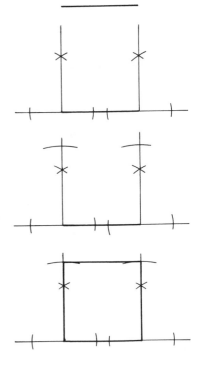

3. With a compass, measure the length of the original line. Use this measurement to mark the length on each perpendicular line.

4. Draw a line connecting these two marks to complete the square.

Rectangle

A *rectangle* is a four-sided polygon with four right angles, but its adjacent sides are not equal. The opposite sides are equal and parallel. The symbol for a rectangle is a small rectangle ☐ . The small letter l represents the length of the longer side, and the small letter w represents the

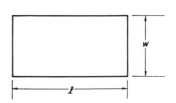

width or length of the shorter side. The rectangle is constructed in the same manner that a square is constructed, except that both the length and width are given and must be measured separately.

Parallelogram

A *parallelogram* is a four-sided polygon in which the opposite sides are parallel. Therefore, squares and rectangles are special types of parallelograms. However, not all parallelograms have the adjacent sides perpendicular (90° angles). The opposite sides are equal, and the sum of the angles is 360°.

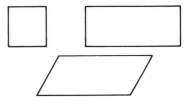

The small letter *b* represents the base, and the small letter *a* represents the height or altitude. The altitude is not equal to the length of a side, as shown in the diagram.

To construct a parallelogram, three dimensions must be given—the length of two sides (not the altitude) and one angle. To construct a parallelogram with sides equal to 2″ and 1½″ and an angle of 75°, the steps are:

1. Draw one line (usually the longer line) to the exact length. The 2″ line is labeled *AB*.
2. Construct the angle with its vertex at point *A*. Draw the line at least 1½″, the length required for the parallelogram. The angle is 75°.
3. Measure this line and mark it at 1½″ from point *A*. Label this point *C*.

4. Construct a line passing through point *C* and parallel to line *AB*.
5. Mark this line 2″ from point *C*. Label this point *D*.

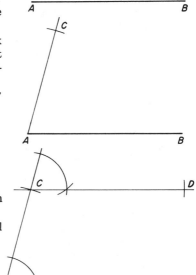

6. Connect points B and D to complete the parallelogram.

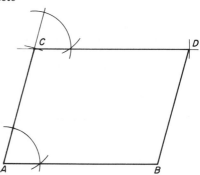

Trapezoid

A *trapezoid* is a four-sided polygon in which only two of its sides are parallel. These two parallel sides are not equal in length. The sum of its four included angles is equal to 360°, as in all parallelograms.

A capital letter B represents the length of the larger base, a small letter b represents the length of the smaller base, and the small letter a represents the altitude.

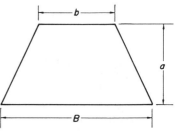

To construct an *isosceles* trapezoid, three dimensions must be given—the lengths of the two bases and the altitude. To construct an isosceles trapezoid with bases 1″ and 2″ and an altitude of 1″, follow these steps:

1. Draw a base line at least 2″ long. Construct perpendiculars 1″ apart.

2. On these perpendiculars, mark off a distance 1″ from the base line. Draw a line between these two points. This line is the smaller base line.

3. Since the larger base line is 1″ longer than the smaller base line, one half (½″) of this additional length must be placed on each side of the 1″ base. Therefore, mark off ½″ on each side of the perpendicular lines on the lower base line.

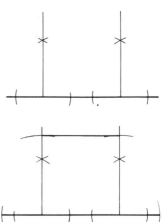

4. Connect each of these two points with the upper base line on each side to form an isosceles trapezoid.

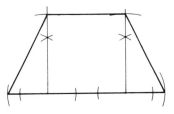

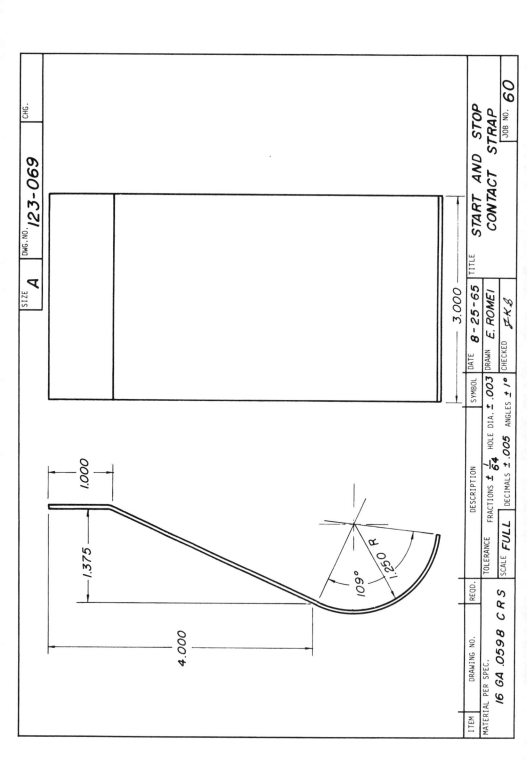

ITEM | DRAWING NO. | REQD. | DESCRIPTION | SYMBOL | DATE 8-25-65 | SIZE A | DWG. NO. 123-069 | CHG.

MATERIAL PER SPEC.
16 GA .0598 CRS

TOLERANCE
FRACTIONS ± 1/64   HOLE DIA. ± .003
DECIMALS ± .005   ANGLES ± 1°
SCALE FULL

DRAWN E. ROMEI
CHECKED

TITLE START AND STOP
CONTACT STRAP
JOB NO. 60

1.000

1.375

4.000

3.000

109°

1.250 R

Arcs and
Tangents of Circles

When constructing precision sheet metal parts that involve circles or arcs of circles, it is sometimes necessary to divide a circle or an arc and to have a tangent to the circle (Fig. 41-1).

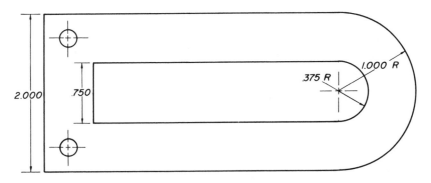

Fig. 41-1

An *arc* of a circle is a portion of its circumference. A *tangent* to a circle is a straight line of any length which touches the circumference at only one point, but does not pass through it. A *chord* is a straight line that connects the two ends of an arc.

177

Bisecting an Arc

An arc is bisected in a manner similar to dividing an angle into two equal parts (or bisecting an angle):

1. Construct an angle with its vertex at the center of the circle and with its sides extending to the ends of the arc.

2. Bisect the angle. Be sure to extend the bisecting line through the arc. This line also *bisects* the arc.

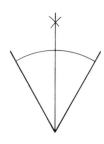

An arc also can be bisected in a manner similar to that for dividing a line into two equal parts:

1. Draw a chord to the arc.

2. With points *A* and *B* of the arc as centers and a radius equal to a convenient distance more than one-half the length of the line, draw arcs that intersect at points *C* and *D* above and below the line.

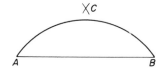

3. Draw a straight line through points *C* and *D*. This line *bisects* both the line and the arc.

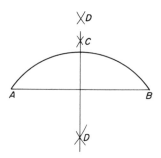

Dividing a Half Circle Into Four and Eight Equal Parts

A half circle can be divided into four or eight equal parts:

1. Construct two lines perpendicular to each other and passing through the center of the half circle.

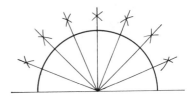

2. This divides the half circle into two equal parts. Bisect each of the angles formed. The half circle is then divided into four equal parts.

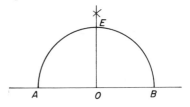

3. Bisect each of the four angles to divide the half circle into *eight* equal parts.

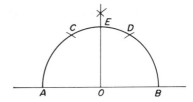

Dividing a Half Circle Into Six Equal Parts

A half circle also can be divided into six equal parts:

1. Construct two lines perpendicular to each other and passing through the center of the half circle.

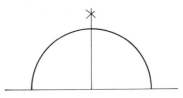

2. Using point A as the center and a radius equal to AO, draw an arc intersecting the half circle at point C. Using point B as a center and the same radius, draw an arc intersecting the half circle at point D.

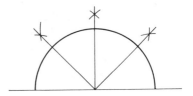

3. Using point *E* as the center and the same radius, draw arcs intersecting the half circle at points *F* and *G*. This divides the half circle into *six* equal parts.

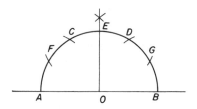

Constructing a Tangent to a Circle

A *tangent* to a circle is perpendicular to the radius or diameter that extends to the point at which the tangent contacts the circle. To construct a tangent to a circle at a given point, follow these steps:

1. Draw a line from the center of the circle through the given point *A* on the circle, extending the line outside the circle.

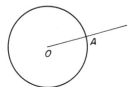

2. Draw a perpendicular to the line *OA*. Point *A* is the point of tangency.

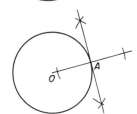

Constructing Tangents to Two Circles

The following steps are required:

1. Draw a line connecting the centers of the two circles.

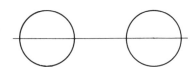

2. Draw a perpendicular to the line from the center point of each circle.

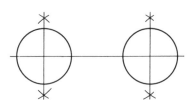

3. Draw the lines connecting the points
   of tangency (the points at which the
   perpendicular lines cross the circles).

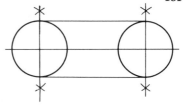

The constructed diagram is semicircular-sided and consists of two semicircles (one at each end) and either a rectangle or a square, depending on the distance between the centers of the circles. The width (height) is equal to twice the radius or to the diameter of the circle. The length of the diagram is twice the radius plus the distance between the centers of the semicircles.

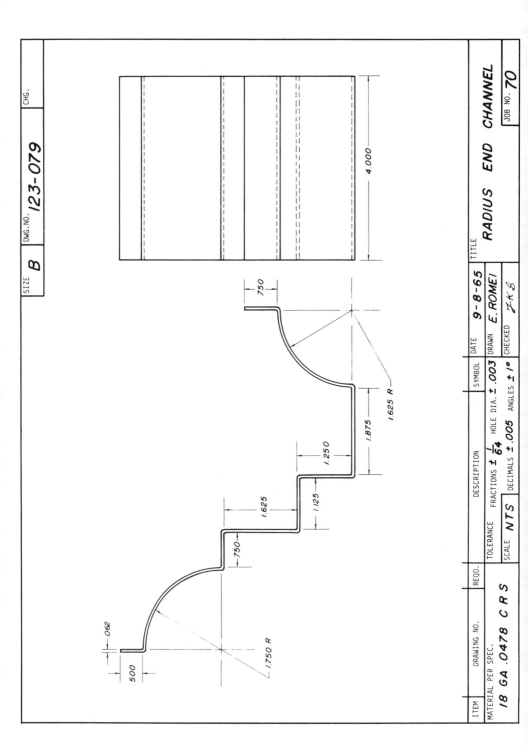

SIZE **B**   DWG. NO. **123-079**   CHG.

.750

1.625 R

1.875

1.250

1.625

1.125

.750

.062

.500

1.750 R

4.000

ITEM	DRAWING NO.	REQD.	DESCRIPTION	SYMBOL	DATE **9-8-65**	TITLE **RADIUS END CHANNEL**

MATERIAL PER SPEC.
18 GA .0478 C R S

TOLERANCE   FRACTIONS $\pm \frac{1}{64}$ HOLE DIA. $\pm$ **.003**
DECIMALS $\pm$ **.005**   ANGLES $\pm 1°$
SCALE **NTS**

DRAWN **E. ROMEI**
CHECKED **J·K·B**

JOB NO. **70**

Mathematical Symbols

The use of the various mathematical symbols must be understood before the precision sheet metalworker can complete many of the required jobs (Fig. 42-1). Therefore, the use of the mathematical signs ($+$), ($-$), ($\times$), and ($/$) or ($\div$) can save much time in the computations. Other symbols include the letters, such as a, b, l, w, and d; parentheses ( ), brackets $\{$ $\}$, braces $[$ $]$, and the bar ‾ are also used.

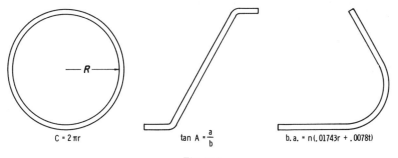

$$C = 2\pi r \qquad \tan A = \frac{a}{b} \qquad \text{b.a.} = n(.01743r + .0078t)$$

Fig. 42-1

Letter Symbols

Letters are used to translate words into mathematical symbols. Some of the common letter symbols are:

d = diameter	p = perimeter
l = length	h = height
w = width	r = radius

183

For example, the length of the first line is *l* and the length of the second line is 2″ longer. The length of the second line can be written: $l + 2″$. If we measure the first line and find it to be 1″, this number can be substituted for the letter *l,* and we find that the length of the second line is: $1″ + 2″ = 3″$.

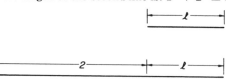

Also, the letters can be used to designate the unknowns, as follows:

1. The *sum* of 5 and *b* is $5 + b$.
2. The *difference* of 3 and *b* is $3 − b$.
3. The product of *a* and *b* is $a × b$ or ab.
4. The quotient of *a* divided by *b* is $a ÷ b$ or a/b.

Adding and Subtracting the Letter Symbols

Like quantities can be added and subtracted, in the same manner that inches, feet, etc. can be dealt with. Therefore, the unlike quantities *3a* and *4b* cannot be added to total *7*. The like quantities *4a* and *5a* can be added:

$$4a + 5a = 9a$$

A line can be divided into five equal parts, each labeled *a*. The total length of the line is: $a + a + a + a + a = 5a$.

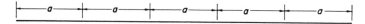

If measured, the dimension *a* is 1″. Therefore, the total length of the line is:

$$1″ + 1″ + 1″ + 1″ + 1″ = 5″$$

or

$$5a = 5 × 1″$$
$$= 5″$$

If two lines are divided into like units (a = 1″ in each line), the two lines can be added to obtain the total length of the two lines. The length of the first line is $a + a + a = 3a$, and the length of the second line is $a + a = 2a$. Adding the two lines, we obtain:

$$3a + 2a = 5a$$

or

$$3'' + 2'' = 5''$$

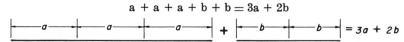

We also can find the difference in the lengths of the two lines. This is done by subtracting:

$$3a - 2a = 1a$$

$$3'' - 2'' = 1''$$

However, if the divisions of the two lines are unequal, they can be neither added nor subtracted in this manner. The length of the first line is $a + a + a$ and the length of the second line is $b + b$. We can add the lengths of the two lines only in this manner:

$$a + a + a + b + b = 3a + 2b$$

The two quantities a and b cannot be added, in the same manner that you cannot add 3″ and 2′ without first converting feet to inches. After measuring the lengths a and b ($a = 1''$; $b = \frac{3}{4}''$), we can add the two lines:

$$1'' + 1'' + 1'' + \tfrac{3}{4}'' + \tfrac{3}{4}'' = 4\tfrac{1}{2}''$$

Or, if we use the sum *3a + 2b:*

$$3a + 2b = (3 \times 1'') + (2 \times \tfrac{3}{4}'')$$

$$= 3'' + 1\tfrac{1}{2}''$$

$$= 4\tfrac{1}{2}''$$

Grouping Symbols

When we must treat a group of numbers or letters as a whole number, we can use special grouping symbols to avoid confusion:

( ) parentheses; { } braces; [ ] brackets; $\overline{}$ bar

The most commonly used grouping symbol is the parentheses. If the parentheses are used previously, the braces are used next, and then the brackets are used:

$$(3 + 2) \times (4 + 7) =$$

then

$$\{(3 + 2) \times (4 + 7)\} + (4 \times 3) =$$

The bar is used above a number, such as $1.\overline{42}$, to indicate where the number begins and ends. This symbol can be convenient when many decimals are used.

When the parentheses are used, the operation required inside them must be completed first, if possible.

Problem 1:   2 (3 + 5)

Solution:

1. Add the numbers inside the parentheses. $3 + 5 = 8$

2. Insert this sum (8) inside the parentheses in the problem. $2 (8) =$

3. Since a number in front of a parenthesis with no sign after it indicates multiplication, the problem can be written: $2 \times 8 =$

4. Multiply. $2 \times 8 = 16$

5. The *product* is *16*.

Problem 2:   3 (a + b)

Solution:

1. If the values of a and b are unknown, the problem cannot be solved.

2. Multiply each unknown inside the parentheses by 3.

$$\begin{array}{r} a + b \\ \times\ 3 \\ \hline 3\,a + 3\,b \end{array}$$

3. The result is *3a + 3b*, which is equal to 3 (a + b).

Problem 3:   3 (a + b) in which: a = 2; b = 5.

Solution:

1. Substitute the known values for a and $b;$ then complete the required operation inside the parentheses.

$$a + b =$$
$$2 + 5 = 7$$

2. Place this sum inside the parentheses. $3 (7) =$

3. Multiply. $3 \times 7 = 21$
4. The result is *21*.

Also, in a division problem, the operation inside the parentheses is completed first. The steps progress from left to right. Let $a = 3$; $b = 1$.

$$\frac{2 (a + b)}{2} = \frac{2 (3 + 1)}{2} = \frac{2 (4)}{2} = \frac{8}{2} = 4$$

The opposite procedure also can be used. This involves removing the common factors:

$$2a + 2b = 2(a + b)$$

$$ad + ac = a(d + c)$$

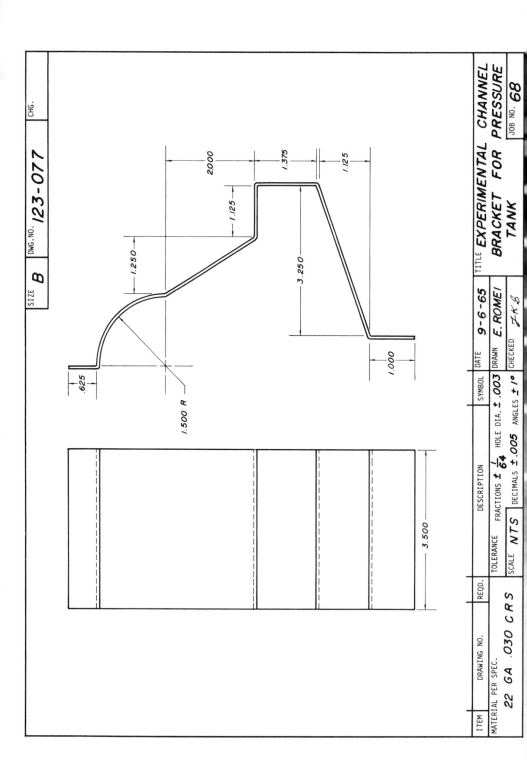

SIZE **B** | DWG. NO. **123-077** | CHG.

2.000

1.375

.125

1.125

1.250

3.250

.625

1.500 R

1.000

3.500

ITEM | DRAWING NO. | REQD. | DESCRIPTION | SYMBOL

MATERIAL PER SPEC.

22 GA .030 CRS

TOLERANCE
FRACTIONS ± $\frac{1}{64}$ HOLE DIA. ±.003
DECIMALS ±.005   ANGLES ±1°

SCALE **NTS**

DATE **9-6-65** | DRAWN **E. ROMEI** | CHECKED *JKB*

TITLE **EXPERIMENTAL CHANNEL BRACKET FOR PRESSURE TANK**

JOB NO. **68**

Introduction to Formulas

A formula is a mathematical rule expressed by means of signs, letters, and symbols. The use of letters and symbols to represent numbers and words permits much quicker and easier solving of formulas for the precision sheet metalworker (Fig. 43-1). Each symbol in a formula represents a number; to use the formula, merely substitute the given or known values for the letters or symbols. Formulas are often used by the precision sheet metalworker. When he becomes familiar with a formula, however, he does not actually write it on paper; he merely retains it in his mind.

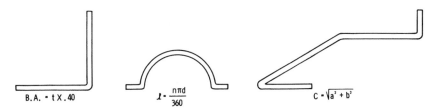

B.A. = t X .40 $l = \dfrac{n\pi d}{360}$ $C = \sqrt{a^2 + b^2}$

Fig. 43-1. Formulas commonly used in making metal parts.

To solve a problem, the steps include:
1. Determining the formula to be used.
2. Substituting the numbers for the letters or symbols.
3. Performing the computations required to find the correct answer.

Problem: How many 2½" pieces can be
cut from a piece of metal that is 10"
long?

189

Solution:

1. The formula is:

$$\text{number of pieces} = \frac{\text{total length of metal}}{\text{length of one piece}}$$

2. Simplify the formula by substituting letters: number of pieces $= N$; total length of metal $= L$; and length of one piece $= l$.

$$N = \frac{L}{l}$$

3. Substitute in the formula.

$$N = \frac{10''}{2\frac{1}{2}''}$$

4. Solve the problem.

$$2.5\overline{\smash{\big)}\,10.0}^{\;4.}$$

5. The *number of pieces* is *4*.

Perimeter of a Square

The perimeter of a polygon is the distance around it expressed in units of linear measure—inches, feet, etc. (Fig. 44-1). A square is a four-sided polygon with all its sides equal in length and its four angles equal to 90°. The perimeter of a square is required by the precision sheet metalworker to determine the blank size of a part.

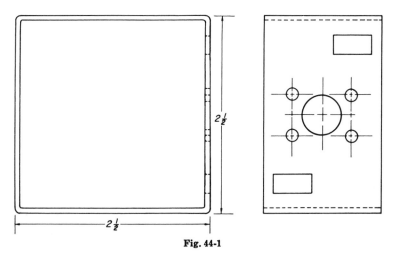

Fig. 44-1

The perimeter P of a square is equal to four times the length of one side, or $4s$, since all four sides are equal. The formula can be written:

191

$$P = 4s$$

in which

    P is perimeter.

    s is length of one side.

Trade Problem

Problem: Find the perimeter of the part in Fig. 44-1.

Solution:

1. Use the formula.
2. Substitute.
3. Solve.
4. The *perimeter* is *10″*.

$$P = 4s$$
$$= 4 \times 2\tfrac{1}{2}''$$
$$= 10''$$

Perimeter
of a Rectangle

It is necessary for the precision sheet metalworker to determine the perimeter of a rectangle when calculating the total blank size for a part (Fig. 45-1). A rectangle is a four-sided polygon with two pairs of equal opposite sides and four 90° angles. The longer dimension is usually the length l, and the shorter dimension is the width w.

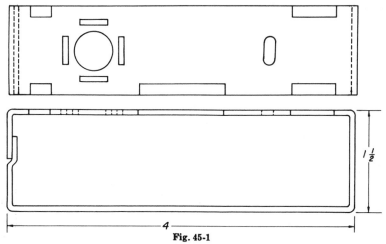

Fig. 45-1

The *perimeter of a rectangle* is equal to twice the length plus twice the width. The formula is:

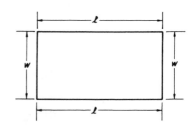

$$P = 2\,l + 2\,\text{w}$$

Trade Problem

Problem: Find the perimeter of the part in Fig. 45-1.

Solution:

1. Determine the formula.
2. Substitute.
3. Solve.

4. The *perimeter* is *11"*.

$P = 2\,l + 2\,\text{w}$
$= (2 \times 4") + (2 \times 1\frac{1}{2}")$
$= 8" + 3"$
$= 11"$

Circumference
of a Circle

The precision sheet metalworker must be able to determine the circumference of a circle when calculating the blank size for a part that is circular in shape (Fig. 46-1).

Fig. 46-1

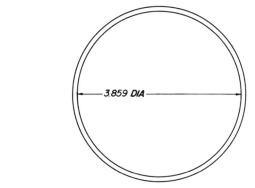

3.859 DIA

The *circumference* is the length or distance around the circle. The formula for determining the circumference of a circle assumes that the diameter d (twice the radius r) is known. The circumference is then found by multiplying the diameter by 3.1416 (*pi* with its symbol π). For less accurate work, 3.14 is sufficient. However, we will use 3.1416 in precision sheet metalwork for more accuracy. The formula is:

195

$$C = \pi d$$

or

$$C = 2 \pi r$$

in which

d is the diameter.

r is the radius.

Trade Problem

Problem: Find the circumference of the
circular part in Fig. 46-1.

Solution:

1. Determine the formula.
2. Substitute.
3. Multiply.

$$C = \pi d$$
$$= 3.1416 \times 3.859''$$

```
        3.1416
      × 3.859
      282744
      157080
      251328
       94248
    12.1234344
```

4. The *perimeter* or circumference *C,*
to the nearest 1000th, is *12.123 in.*

Perimeter of a Semicircular-Sided Part

A semicircular-sided part is composed of two half circles and either a rectangle or a square (Fig. 47-1). The precision sheet metalworker may be required to make a part of this shape. Therefore, he must be able to determine its circumference.

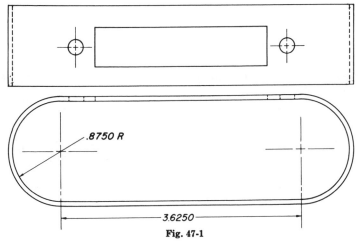

.8750 R

3.6250

Fig. 47-1

197

The height of the part is equal to the diameter of one of the half circles or twice its radius. The length is equal to twice the radius plus the distance between the centers of the two circles.

The perimeter is equal to the arcs of the two half circles plus twice the distance between the half circles. The arcs of the two half circles are equal to the circumference of one circle, since both half circles are the same radius. Therefore, the formula is:

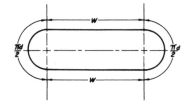

$$P = \pi d + 2w$$

in which

    P is the perimeter.
    d is the diameter of a half circle.
    w is the distance between the half circles.

Trade Problem

Problem: Find the perimeter or circumference of the part in Fig. 47-1.

Solution:

1. Determine the formula.
2. Substitute.
3. Multiply the separate quantities; then substitute.

$$P = \pi d + 2w$$
$$= \pi \times 1.750 + (2 \times 3.625)$$

```
        3.1416
      ×  1.75
      ─────────
      157080
      219912
       31416
      ─────────
      5.497800
```

$$= 5.4978 + 7.25$$
$$= 12.7478$$

4. The perimeter P or circumference is *12.7478 in.;* rounded to 1000ths, it is *12.748 in.*

Ratio of Dimensions

If two objects of like units of measure must be compared and if they differ in size, number, etc., they can be compared by expression of a ratio (Fig. 48-1).

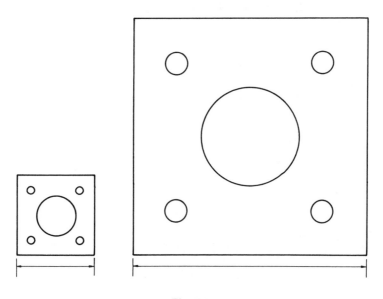

Fig. 48-1

Ratio is the indicated division between two quantities of the same type. A ratio can be written as a fraction if both the numerator and the denominator are in the same units (both inches or both feet). The fraction $\frac{1}{2}$ is a ratio if the units are the same for both numbers. That is, both the numerator and denominator must be in inches or both must be in feet; one number cannot be in inches and the other in feet. A ratio of unlike numbers, such as inches to pounds, is meaningless.

A ratio also can be written with a colon—for example, 2:3. It is read "two to three," but for computation purposes, it is written as a fraction $\frac{2}{3}$.

Ratios are usually reduced to their lowest terms. For example, the ratio between 3 inches and 9 inches is 1 to 3. A ratio between feet and inches, for example, can be determined; however, the feet must first be changed to inches.

Problem: Find the ratio of the two parts
        in Fig. 48-1.

Solution:

1. Measure their lengths. They are $\frac{3}{4}$"
    and 3".

2. Write the lengths in decimals as a   .75/3.0
    ratio.

3. Reducing to the least terms, the *ratio*
    is $\frac{1}{4}$ or *1 to 4*.

Unit **49**

Ratios of Scale Drawings

Ratios are used frequently on precision sheet metal drawings. Sometimes it is neither practical nor necessary to make a full-size drawing of a large part. In precision sheet metalwork, however, some details are necessary, and the drawing is easier to read if it is larger than the actual part to be made (Fig. 49-1). Therefore, drawings are made half-size, double-size, etc. Double-size drawings are used commonly to illustrate small details of the part.

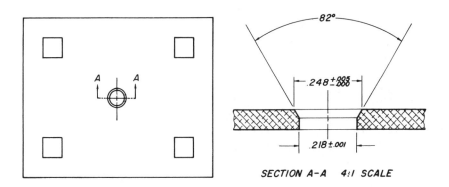

Fig. 49-1

The terms *half-size* and *double-size* refer to the ratio of the lengths of the lines on the drawing to those of the part to be made. Some of the scales commonly used include:

Drawing	*Scales*	*Ratios*
double-size	$2'' = 1''$	2:1 or $\frac{2}{1}$
full-size	$1'' = 1''$	1:1 or $\frac{1}{1}$
half-size	$\frac{1}{2}'' = 1''$	1:2 or $\frac{1}{2}$
quarter-size	$\frac{1}{4}'' = 1''$	1:4 or $\frac{1}{4}$

To determine a dimension for a part to be made, *divide* the length of the line on the drawing by the scale ratio. The first number in a ratio refers to the drawing. The second number in the ratio refers to the part.

Problem 1:   A line on a drawing is $\frac{1}{2}$ inch. The scale is 2:1. Find the actual length of the $\frac{1}{2}''$ dimension on the finished part.

Solution:

1. Arrange the problem. $\frac{1}{2} \div \frac{2}{1} =$

2. Change the sign to multiply and invert the fraction. $\frac{1}{2} \times \frac{1}{2} =$

3. Multiply. $\frac{1}{2} \times \frac{1}{2} = \frac{1}{4}$

4. The *actual length* is $\frac{1}{4}$ *in.*

Problem 2:   A line on a drawing is $\frac{1}{4}''$. The scale is 1:2. Find the actual dimension of the finished part.

Solution:

1. Arrange the problem. $\frac{1}{4} \div \frac{1}{2} =$

2. Change the sign to multiply, and invert the fraction. Then multiply. $\frac{1}{4} \times \frac{2}{1} = \frac{2}{4}$

3. Reducing to lowest terms, the *actual dimension* is $\frac{1}{2}$ *in.*

Trade Problem

Examine the drawing in Fig. 49-1. The scale is 4:1, but each part is labeled the actual size of the finished part. This method is used by sheet metal draftsmen. Therefore, conversion is not actually necessary. However, the specified scale helps to visualize the part to be made.

Allowance for
an Edge or Hem

The precision sheet metalworker might be required to put a special hem or edge on some parts to eliminate a raw edge, to reinforce the edge, or for the sake of appearance. A hem is a fold at the edge of the material (Fig. 50-1). It is necessary to increase the total length of the material to allow for a hem or fold on a metal part.

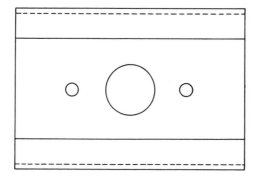 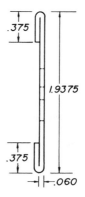

Fig. 50-1

203

Single-Hem Edge

The single-hem edge is commonly called the Dutch hem. The total length of the piece of metal required is: the outside measurement of the piece l plus the outside measurement of the hem h minus one-half the metal thickness t. The formula is:

$$total\ length = l + h - \tfrac{1}{2}\,t$$

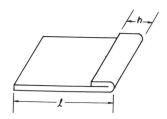

in which

  l is length of piece (OD).
  h is length of hem (OD).
  t is metal thickness.

Problem: Find the total length of the metal required for the part diagram.

Solution:

1. Determine the formula.
2. Substitute dimensions.
3. Solve.

4. The *total length* of the metal required is $1^{15}\!/_{32}''$.

$$
\begin{aligned}
\text{length} &= l + h - \tfrac{1}{2}\,t \\
&= 1\tfrac{1}{4}'' + \tfrac{1}{4}'' - (\tfrac{1}{2} \times \tfrac{1}{16}) \\
&= 1\tfrac{1}{2} - \tfrac{1}{32} \\
&= 1^{15}\!/_{32}
\end{aligned}
$$

Wired Edge

The allowance for a wired edge is two and one-half times the diameter D of the wire. The formula is:

$$allowance = 2\tfrac{1}{2}D$$

Problem. Find the allowance required for the wired edge using wire with a diameter of $\tfrac{7}{32}''$, correct to the nearest 1000th.

DIA. OF WIRE

Solution:

1. Select the formula.   allowance $= 2\frac{1}{2}D$
2. Substitute the dimensions. $= 2\frac{1}{2} \times \frac{7}{32}$
3. Multiply. $\frac{7}{32} = .21875$

$$2\frac{1}{2} = \times\ \ 2.5$$
$$\overline{109375}$$
$$43750$$
$$\overline{.546875}$$

4. Rounded to the nearest 1000th, the *edge allowance* is *.547"*.

Curling, or False Wiring

Curling, or false wiring, is identical to a wired edge; however, the wire is not left inside the edge. Therefore, the allowance is the same as for a wired edge.

Trade Problem

Problem: Find the total length of metal required for the part in Fig. 50-1.

Solution:

1. Determine the formula.   total length
$$= l + h + h - \frac{1}{2}t - \frac{1}{2}t$$
or
$$= l + 2h - t$$
2. Substitute the dimensions. $= 1.9375 + (2 \times .375) - .060$
3. Solve. 1.9375
$$+\ .7500$$
$$\overline{2.6875}$$
$$-\ .0600$$
$$\overline{2.6275}$$

4. The *total length* of metal required is *2.6275 in.*

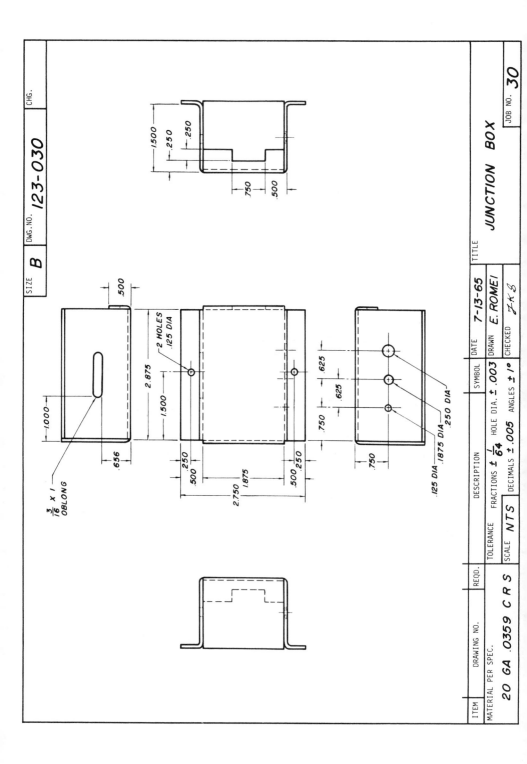

SIZE **B**   DWG. NO. *123-030*   CHG.

$\frac{3}{16} \times 1$ OBLONG

1.000

.656

.500

2 HOLES
.125 DIA

2.875

1.500

.250
.500

2.750

1.875

.500 .250

1.500

.250

.625

.625

.750

.750

.125 DIA
.1875 DIA
.250 DIA

1.500

.250

.750

.500

ITEM	DRAWING NO.	REQD.	DESCRIPTION	TOLERANCE	SYMBOL	DATE 7-13-65	TITLE *JUNCTION BOX*

MATERIAL PER SPEC.
20 GA .0359 C R S

TOLERANCE
FRACTIONS ± $\frac{1}{64}$ HOLE DIA. ± .003
DECIMALS ± .005   ANGLES ± 1°

SCALE *NTS*

DRAWN **E. ROMEI**
CHECKED ∓K8

JOB NO. **30**

Unit **51**

Allowance for a Seam

Many types of seams are used by the precision sheet metalworker to join pieces of metal. An allowance is required for additional metal for a seam (Fig. 51-1).

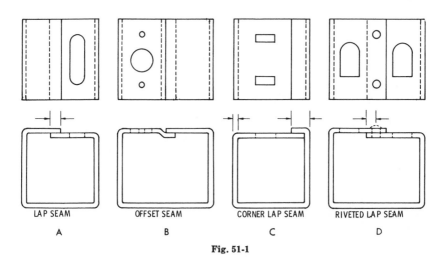

| LAP SEAM | OFFSET SEAM | CORNER LAP SEAM | RIVETED LAP SEAM |
| A | B | C | D |

Fig. 51-1

Lap Seam

The allowance for a lap seam (Fig. 51-1A) is equal to the width of the seam. For example, if the seam is ⅜", the allowance is also ⅜".

207

Offset Seam

The allowance for an offset seam (Fig. 51-1B) requires the addition of the two bend allowances. The total length of the metal required is computed by adding the straight lengths and then adding the two bend allowances. Frequently, the precision sheet metalworker determines the blank size for an offset seam by making a sample piece.

Corner Lap Seam

The allowance for a corner lap seam (Fig. 51-1C) is the width of the seam plus the bend allowance.

Riveted Lap Seam

The allowance for a riveted lap seam (Fig. 51-1D) is twice the specified dimension, because the dimension is from the center of the rivet hole to the edge of the lap.

Unit **52**

Blank Size for a
Box-Shaped Part

Before making a metal part, the precision sheet metalworker must determine the blank size to know exactly how much metal he must use. Box-shaped parts are the most common shape in precision sheet metalwork (Fig. 52-1). To compute the blank size for this type of part, the bend allowance must be added to the total length or width of the part.

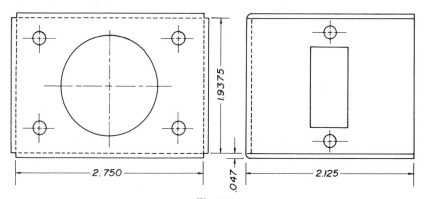

Fig. 52-1

209

Bend Allowance

The bend allowances must be added to the length and to the width of the part, along with the height of each side. Use inside dimensions. Refer to Fig. 27-1, concerning bends with a given radius.

1. Length of blank = l + 2h + each bend allowance.
2. Width of blank = w + 2h + each bend allowance.

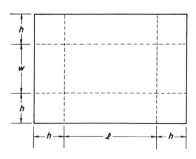

Problem: If the length of a box is 1.5", the width is 1", and the height of each of the four sides is .5", find the blank size required. The bends are 90° sharp, and the metal thickness is .125".

Solution:

1. Formula for the length.

   length of blank = l + 2h + b.a.

2. Substitute the dimensions.

   = 1.5 + (2 × .5) + 2 (.125 × .50)

3. Solve.

   = 1.5 + 1.0 + .125

4. Complete the computations.

   1.500
   1.000
   .125
   ‾‾‾‾‾
   2.625

5. The *length* of the blank required is *2.625".*

6. Formula for the width.

   width of blank = w + 2h + b.a.

7. Substitute the dimensions

   = 1.0 + (2 × .5) + 2 (.125 × .50)

8. Solve.

   = 1.0 + 1.0 + .125

9. Complete the computation.

   1.000
   1.000
   .125
   ‾‾‾‾‾
   2.125

10. The *width* of the blank size is *2.125".*

Trade Problem

Problem: Find the blank size (90° sharp bends) for the part in Fig. 52-1.

Solution:

1. Formula for the length.

   length of
   blank $= l + 2h +$ b.a.

2. Substitute the numbers.

   $= 2.750 + (2 \times 2.125) + 2$
   $\qquad (.047 \times .40)$
   $= 2.750 + 4.250 + .3760$
   $= 7.376$

3. The *length* of the blank required is *7.376 in.*

4. Formula for the width.

   width of
   blank $= w + 2h +$ b.a.

5. Substitute the numbers.

   $= 1.9375 + (2 \times 2.125) + 2$
   $\qquad (.047 \times .40)$
   $= 1.9375 + 4.250 + .3760$
   $= 6.5635$

6. The *width* of the blank required is *6.5635 in.*

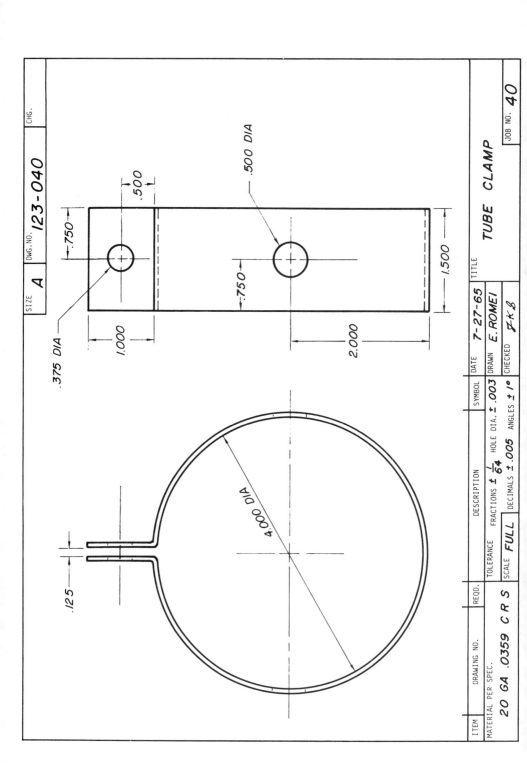

.375 DIA

.750
.500

1.000

.500 DIA

.750

1.500

2.000

.125

4.000 DIA

SIZE **A** DWG. NO. **123-040** CHG.

MATERIAL PER SPEC.

20 GA .0359 C R S

TOLERANCE FRACTIONS $\pm \frac{1}{64}$ HOLE DIA. $\pm .003$

SCALE **FULL** DECIMALS $\pm .005$ ANGLES $\pm 1°$

DRAWN E. ROMEI

CHECKED ᖶ K B

TUBE CLAMP

JOB NO. **40**

Blank Size
for a Circular Part

Before making a metal part, the precision sheet metalworker must determine the blank size to know exactly how much metal to use. The length of the blank for a circular part is found by adding the circumference of the end and the allowance for a seam, if there is a seam, edge, or flange (Fig. 53-1). Also, an allowance must be made for the metal lost in shrinkage due to rolling. In effect,

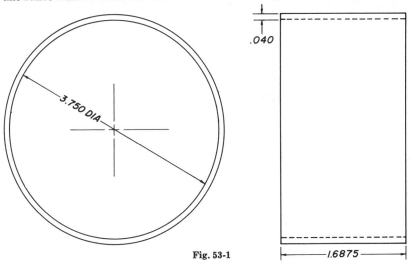

.040

3.750 DIA

1.6875

Fig. 53-1

213

the inside dimension is reduced by the metal thickness; the outside dimension is increased by the metal thickness. Therefore, if no allowance were made, neither the inside dimension nor the outside dimension of the formed part would be the correct dimension.

The inside diameter is reduced in a part $1\frac{1}{2}''$ in diameter with $\frac{1}{16}''$ metal thickness, if no allowance is made for the metal thickness. The inside dimension is then ($1\frac{1}{2}'' - \frac{1}{16}''$), or $1\frac{7}{16}''$, and the outside dimension is ($1\frac{1}{2} + \frac{1}{16}''$), or $1\frac{9}{16}''$ (Fig. 53-2). Refer to Fig. 27-1, in regard to bends with a given radius.

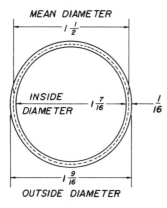

Fig. 53-2. A reduced inside diameter results when no allowance is made for metal thickness.

Inside Dimension Required

If the inside dimension is required, add the thickness of the metal to the given diameter.

1. Length of blank $= \pi\,d +$ metal thickness.
2. Width of blank $=$ width of part.

Problem: Determine the blank size for a part that is to be $2''$ wide with a $2\frac{1}{4}''$ inside diameter; the metal thickness is $\frac{1}{16}''$.

Solution:

1. Formula for the length.

   length of
   blank $= \pi d +$ thickness of metal.

2. Substitute.

   $= (3.1416 \times 2.25) + .0625$

3. Solve.

   $= 7.0686 + .0625$

   $$\begin{array}{r} 7.0686 \\ + \ .0625 \\ \hline 7.1311 \end{array}$$

4. The *length* of the blank, in 1000ths, is *7.131 in.*
5. The width of the blank is merely the width of the part (2 in.).
6. The *width* of the blank is *2 in.*

Outside Dimension Required

If the outside dimension is required, subtract the thickness of the metal from the given diameter.

1. Length of blank $= \pi d$ − metal thickness.
2. Width = width of part.

Problem: Find the blank size required for a part that is to be 2″ wide with 2¼″ outside diameter and with ¹⁄₁₆″ metal thickness.

Solution:

1. Formula for length.

length of
blank $= \pi d$ − m.t.

2. Substitute.

$= (3.1416 \times 2.25)$ − .0625

3. Solve.

$= 7.0686$ − .0625

$$\begin{array}{r} 7.0686 \\ -\ .0625 \\ \hline 7.0061 \end{array}$$

4. The *length* of the blank, in 1000ths, is *7.006 in.*
5. The width of the blank is merely the width of the part (2 in.)
6. The *width* of the blank is *2 in.*

Trade Problem

Problem: Determine the blank size required for the part in Fig. 53-1.

Solution:

1. Select the correct formula.

length of
blank $= \pi d$ + m.t.

2. Substitute.

$= (3.1416 \times 3.750)$ + .040

3. Solve.

$= 11.7810$ + .040
$= 11.821$

4. The *length* of the blank, in 1000ths, is *11.821 in.*
5. The *width* of the blank is the width of the part, or *1.6875 in.*

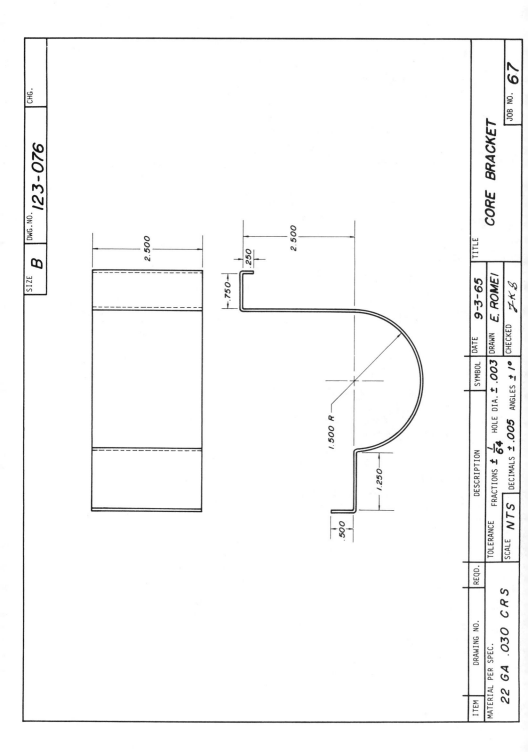

SIZE **B** DWG. NO. **123-076** CHG.

2.500

2.500

.250

.750

1.500 R

1.250

.500

| ITEM | DRAWING NO. | REQD. | DESCRIPTION | SYMBOL | DATE 9-3-65 | TITLE |

Blank Size for a Semicircular-Sided Part

Before making a metal part, the precision sheet metalworker must determine the blank size if he is to know precisely how much metal he needs. Determining the blank size of a semicircular part is similar to the procedure for a circular part, except that the straight lengths must be added to the circular length (Fig. 54-1).

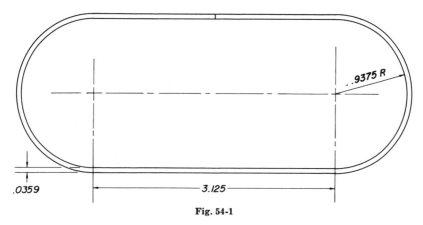

Fig. 54-1

There is a semicircle (half circle) at each end of the part. Therefore, the blank size of a whole circle can be included in the formula. The length of each straight

217

part plus each bend allowance is added to the blank size of the circular part. Refer to Fig. 27-1, in regard to bends with a given radius.

Problem: Find the blank size for the part
    in the diagram.

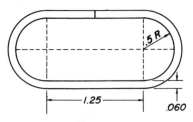

Solution:

1. Determine the formula. Angles are not involved in this part.

   length of
   blank $= \pi d$ + m.t. + 2 l

2. Substitute.

   $= (3.1416 \times 1.0)$ + .060
   $+ (2 \times 1.25)$

3. Solve.

   3.1416
   .0600
   2.5000
   ——————
   5.7016

4. The *length* of the blank, to the nearest 1000th, is *5.702 in.*

Trade Problem

Problem: Determine the blank size for the part in Fig. 54-1.

Solution:

1. Determine the formula.

   length of
   blank $= \pi d$ + m.t. + 2 l

2. Substituting.

   $= (3.1416 \times 1.875)$ + .0359
   $+ (2 \times 3.125)$

3. Solve.

   $= 5.8905$ + .0359 + 6.250
   $= 12.1764$

4. The *length* of the blank, to the nearest 1000th, is *12.176 in.*

Length of Wire
for a Wired Edge

The wire in the wired edge of a part provides additional strength to the part made by the precision sheet metalworker. The length of wire required for a part is equal to the perimeter of the part plus an allowance for the bends (Figs. 55-1 and 55-2). Use the inside dimensions.

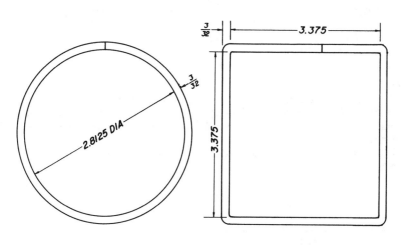

Fig. 55-1   Fig. 55-2

219

Circle

The length of wire required for a circular part (see Fig. 55-1) depends on whether the wiring is done *before* or *after* the part is formed. If it is done before the part is formed, merely use π times the diameter D of the circle (circumference).

If the wiring is done after the part is formed, use the length or the circumference of the circle (πD) plus π times the diameter of the wire (πd). The formula is:

$$length\ of\ wire = \pi\,D + \pi d$$

$$= \pi\,(D + d)$$

Problem: A circular part has a diameter D of $3\frac{1}{4}$" with a wired edge requiring a wire $\frac{1}{8}$" in diameter d. Determine the length of wire required to complete this part if the wiring is done *after* the part is formed.

Solution:

1. Select the formula.

    $length$
    $of\ wire = \pi\,(D + d)$

2. Substitute.

    $= 3.1416\,(3.25 + .125)$

3. Solve.

    $= 3.1416 \times 3.375$
    $= 10.6029$

4. The *length* of wire required is *10.603 in.*, correct to the nearest 1000th.

Square

For square and rectangular parts, the allowance for the bend is one-half the diameter d of the wire for each bend (see Fig. 55-2). Since squares and rectangles have four sides, the allowance for the bends is twice the diameter of the wire.

The length of the wire required for a square part is determined by the formula:

$$length\ of\ wire = 4s + 2d$$

Problem: If the side s of a square is 2.5" and the diameter d of the wire is .125", determine the length of the wire required.

Solution:

1. Select the formula.	length of wire $= 4s + 2d$
2. Substitute.	$= (4 \times 2.5) + (2 \times$
3. Solve.	$.125)$
4. The *length* of the wire required is *10.25 in.*	$= 10 + .250$ $= 10.25$

Rectangle

The length of the wire required for a rectangular part is determined by the formula:

$$length\ of\ wire = 2\,l + 2\,W + 2\,d$$

Problem: If the length *l* of a rectangular part is 2.5″ and the width *w* is 1.5″, determine the length of wire required if the diameter *d* of the wire is .125″.

Solution:

1. Select the formula.	length
2. Substitute.	of wire $= 2\,l + 2\,w + 2d$ $= (2 \times 2.5) + (2 \times 1.5)$
3. Solve.	$+ (2 \times .125)$ $= 5.0 + 3.0 + .250$
4. The *length* of wire required is *8.25 in.*	$= 8.25$

Trade Problem

Problem 1: Determine the length of wire required for the circular part in Fig. 55-1, if the wiring is done after the part is formed.

Solution:

1. Select the formula.	length of wire $= \pi (D + d)$
2. Substitute.	$= 3.1416 (2.8125$ $+ .0937)$
3. Solve.	$= 3.1416 \times 2.9062$ $= 9.13011792$

4. The *length* of wire required
   is *9.13 in.*

Problem 2:   Determine the length of wire
   required for the square part in Fig.
   55-2.

Solution:

1. Select the formula.

2. Substitute.

3. Solve.

length
of wire $= 4s + 2d$
$= (4 \times 3.375) + (2 \times .0937)$
$= 13.500 + .1874$
$= 13.6874$

4. The *length* of wire
   required is *13.69 in.*

Blanks From
a Single Sheet

By positioning the parts on a sheet of metal in various ways, the precision sheet metalworker will find the most economical manner (Fig. 56-1). After several problems have been solved on paper, it will be easier to estimate the most economical method. Considerable savings in materials and maximum profits can result from properly determining the maximum number of blanks that can be obtained from a single sheet of metal. This can be one of the most important economic factors in the manufacture or production of metal parts.

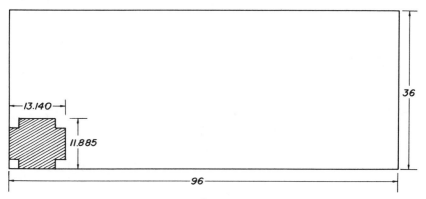

Fig. 56-1

223

The procedure for determining the number of blanks is as follows:

1. Sketch the sheet of metal with the blank size of the metal part in one corner.

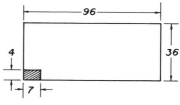

2. Divide the length of the sheet L by the length of the blank size l. Discard the remainder, since this is waste.

$$\frac{L}{l} = \frac{96}{7} = 13 \text{ rows}$$

3. Divide the width of the sheet W by the width of the blank size w. Again, discard the remainder as waste.

$$\frac{W}{w} = \frac{36}{4} = 9 \text{ pieces}$$

4. Multiply the rows (13) by the pieces (9). Therefore, (13x9), or *117* pieces can be obtained from the sheet of metal.

5. Turn the pattern in the opposite direction.

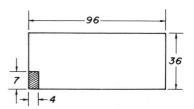

6. Repeat Steps 1 through 4.

$$\frac{L}{l} = \frac{96}{4} = 24 \text{ rows}$$

$$\frac{W}{w} = \frac{36}{7} = 5 \text{ pieces}$$

7. In this manner (24x5), or *120* pieces are obtained.

8. Compare the number of pieces. In this instance, the second method produces more pieces (120).

Trade Problem

Problem: Find the maximum number of pieces that can be obtained from the sheet of metal in Fig. 56-1.

Solution:

1. Divide the length of the sheet of metal by the length of the blank size. Disregard the remainder, since this is waste.

$$\frac{96}{13.14} = 7 \text{ rows}$$

2. Divide the width of the sheet of metal by the width of the blank size. Again, disregard the remainder.

$$\frac{36}{11.885} = 3 \text{ pieces}$$

3. In this manner, 7 rows × 3 pieces, or *21* pieces are obtained.

4. Turning the blank size, repeat Steps 1 through 3.

$$\frac{96}{11.885} = 8 \text{ rows}$$

5. In this manner, 8 rows × 2 pieces, or *16* pieces are obtained.

$$\frac{36}{13.14} = 2 \text{ pieces}$$

6. Comparing the two methods, the first method produces more pieces (21).

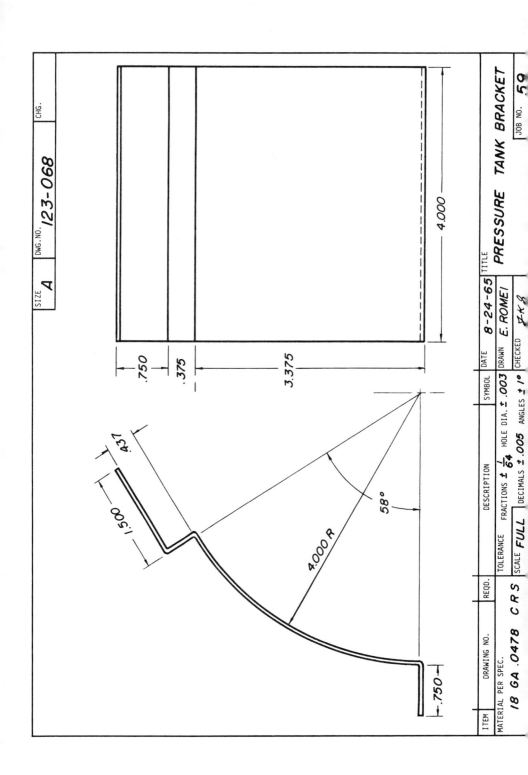

.750

.375

3.375

4.000

.431

1.500

4.000 R

58°

.750

SIZE **A** | DWG. NO. **123-068** | CHG.

ITEM | DRAWING NO. | REQD. | DESCRIPTION | SYMBOL | DATE **8-24-65** | TITLE **PRESSURE TANK BRACKET**
MATERIAL PER SPEC. | | | TOLERANCE FRACTIONS $\pm \frac{1}{64}$ HOLE DIA. $\pm$ .003 | | DRAWN **E. ROMEI** |
18 GA .0478 CRS | | | SCALE **FULL** DECIMALS $\pm$ .005 ANGLES $\pm$ 1° | | CHECKED **EKB** | JOB NO. **59**

Blank Size for
an Arc of a Circle

The precision sheet metalworker needs to be able to calculate the length of an arc of a circle in determining the blank size for making a part that includes a portion of a circle (Fig. 57-1). Refer to Fig. 27-1 in regard to bends with a given radius.

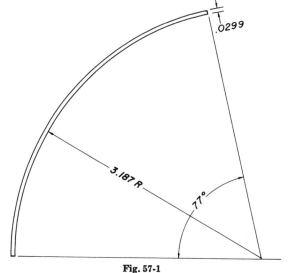

Fig. 57-1

227

Length of an Arc of a Circle

The length of an arc of a circle is equal to the circumference of the circle times the ratio of its central angle to 360°. The formula is:

$$l = \pi d \times \frac{n}{360} = \frac{\pi dn}{360}$$

in which

  l is length of the arc.
  n is number of degrees in the central angle.
  d is diameter of circle or twice the radius.

Problem: Find the length of the arc when the central angle is 51° and the radius is $2\frac{3}{4}$".

Solution:

1. Select the formula. $l = \dfrac{\pi dn}{360}$

2. Substitute. $= \dfrac{51 \times 3.1416 \times 5.5}{360}$

3. Solve $= \dfrac{881.21880}{360}$

4. The *length* of the arc is *2.448 in.* $= 2.44783$ in.

Blank Size for an Arc of a Circle

The blank size for an arc of a circle is equal to the blank size of the entire circle times the ratio of the central angle to 360°. The formulas can be written as follows:

1. Inside dimension $ID = \pi d + \text{m.t.} \times \dfrac{n}{360}$

2. Outside dimension $OD = \pi d - \text{m.t.} \times \dfrac{n}{360}$

Problem: Find the blank size of the arc when its central angle is 51° and the radius of the circle is $2\frac{3}{4}$ in., with a metal thickness of .060". The given radius is an inside dimension.

Solution:

1. Select the correct formula.

$$ID = \pi d + m.t. \times \frac{n}{360}$$

2. Substitute.

$$= (3.1416 \times 5.5) + (.060$$

3. Solve.

$$\times \frac{51}{360})$$

$$= 2.45633$$

4. The *blank size* for the arc is *2.456 in.*

Trade Problem

Problem: Determine the blank size required for the metal part in Fig. 57-1.

Solution:

1. Select the correct formula.

$$\text{blank size} = \pi d + m.t. \times \frac{n}{360}$$

2. Substitute.

$$= (3.1416 \times 6.374) + (.0299$$

3. Solve.

$$\times \frac{77}{360})$$

$$= 4.3108$$

4. The *blank size* required for the arc is *4.311 in.*

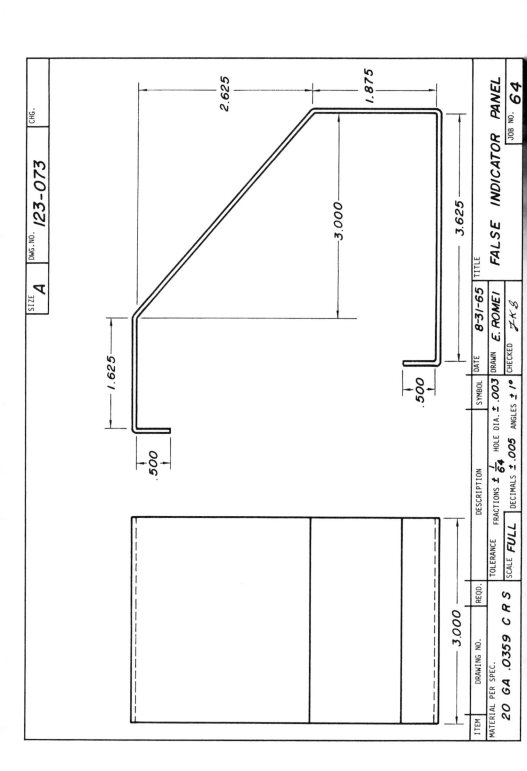

SIZE **A**   DWG. NO. **123-073**   CHG.

2.625

1.875

3.000

3.625

1.625

.500

.500

3.000

ITEM	DRAWING NO.	REQD.	DESCRIPTION	SYMBOL	DATE	TITLE

MATERIAL PER SPEC.
20 GA .0359 C R S

TOLERANCE
FRACTIONS $\pm \frac{1}{64}$ HOLE DIA. $\pm$ .003

SCALE **FULL**   DECIMALS $\pm$ .005   ANGLES $\pm 1°$

8-31-65   DRAWN **E. ROMEI**

CHECKED **J.K.B**

FALSE INDICATOR PANEL

JOB NO. **64**

Square Root

Square root calculations are required in the next unit involving the right triangles. This is extremely important, since the precision sheet metalworker is often required to determine the slant height of a metal part and to locate the position of a series of holes (Fig. 58-1).

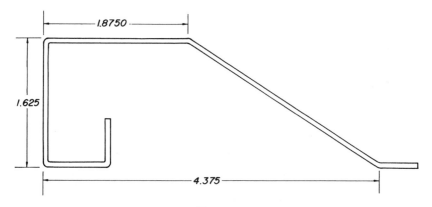

Fig. 58-1

The *square root* of a number is a number which, when multiplied by itself, equals the given number. The operation of extracting the square root is indicated by the symbol $\sqrt{}$. The square root can be found either by inspection or by computation. Inspection can be used for many of the numbers that are perfect squares, as follows:

231

1. The square root of 4 is *2*, because 2 × 2 = 4.
2. The square root of 9 is *3*, because 3 × 3 = 9.
3. The square root of 16 is *4*, because 4 × 4 = 16.
4. The square root of 25 is *5*, because 5 × 5 = 25.

Extracting the Square Root

Abbreviations are used for the complete divisor (c.d.) and the trial divisor (t.d.).

Problem: Find the square root of 137,641.

Solution:

1. Separate the number into periods of two digits each, beginning from the right-hand side. This results in three periods.

$$13'\ \ 76'\ \ 41$$

2. Find the largest perfect square that is either less than or the same as the left-hand period *13*. In period *13*, the largest perfect square is 9, and its square root is *3*, indicated by 3 × 3. Place the root *3* in the answer, above the 13 and place the 9 below the 13.

$$\begin{array}{l} 3 \\ \sqrt{13\ \ 76\ \ 41} \\ 9 \end{array}$$

3. Subtract 9 from 13, obtaining 4. Bring down the second complete period *76*, to obtain 476.

$$\begin{array}{l} 3 \\ \sqrt{13\ \ 76\ \ 41} \\ \underline{9} \\ 4\ \ 76 \end{array}$$

4. Double the first root *3*, which is 6 or the trial divisor. Divide the trial divisor *6* into the first two digits of 476; that is, divide 6 into 47 and the quotient is 7 with a remainder. The 7 is the next digit in the answer.

t. d. = 6

$$\begin{array}{l} 3\ \ \ 7 \\ \sqrt{13\ \ 76\ \ 41} \\ \underline{9} \\ 4\ \ \dot{7}6 \end{array}$$

5. Also, place this 7 after the 6 in the trial divisor, obtaining 67 as the complete divisor. Multiply the complete divisor *67* by 7, obtaining 469, which is placed below 476.

c. d. = 67

$$\begin{array}{l} 3\ \ \ 7 \\ \sqrt{13\ \ 76\ \ 41} \\ 9 \\ 4\ \ 76 \\ 4\ \ 69 \end{array}$$

6. Subtract 469 from 476, obtaining 7. Bring down the third complete period *41*, obtaining 741.

c. d. = 67

$$\begin{array}{l} 3\ \ \ 7 \\ \sqrt{13\ \ 76\ \ 41} \\ 9 \\ 4\ \ 76 \\ 4\ \ 69 \\ \overline{\ \ \ \ 7\ \ 41} \end{array}$$

7. Double the root *37* found previously, with 74 as the new trial divisor. Divide the trial divisor *74* into the first two digits of 741, or 74. The quotient is 1, which is the third digit in the answer. Place the 1 after the 74, the trial divisor, and obtain 741, the complete divisor. Multiply the complete divisor by 1, obtaining 741, which is placed below 741. There is no remainder.

$$\begin{array}{r} 3\quad 7\quad 1 \\ \sqrt{13\ \ 76\ \ 41} \\ 9 \\ \hline \end{array}$$

c. d. = 67   4 76
           4 69

t. d. = 74   7 41
c. d. = 741   7 41

8. Therefore the *square root* of the number *137,641* is *371*.

Returning to Step 4 above in extracting the square root of a number, if the new complete divisor *67* is too large, merely erase the 7 and use the next smaller number (6) to form the complete divisor *66*. The root would be too large, if the number placed below 476 in the problem had been larger than 476, making it impossible to subtract.

The result or square root can be checked by multiplying 371 by 371 to obtain the square 137,641.

If the number for which you are required to find the square root involves a decimal, mark off the periods (groups of two numbers) in each direction from the decimal point, as follows:

$$4531.1489 = \quad 45\ 31\ .\ 14\ 89$$

$$37123.374\ = 3\ 71\ 23\ .\ 37\ 40$$

If you are required to find the square root of a number correct to three decimal places (assuming the square root is not even), you must solve to four decimal places; then round off the square root to three decimal places. For each decimal place required in the square root, a period of numbers is required. If there are not enough numbers, add zeros at the right-hand side of the decimal point.

For example, prepare the number *341.573* for finding its square root, correct to three decimal places.

Solution:

1. Mark off the periods in each direction from the decimal point.

    3 41 . 57 3

2. Since the square root must be correct to three decimal places, it must be first carried to four decimal places. Therefore, zeros must be added to

    3 41 . 57 30 00 00

PRECISION SHEET METAL—MATHEMATICS

Table 58-1. Square Root Table (for numbers 1.0 to 9.99)

No.	0	1	2	3	4	5	6	7	8	9
1.0	1.000	1.005	1.010	1.015	1.020	1.025	1.030	1.034	1.039	1.044
1.1	1.049	1.054	1.058	1.063	1.068	1.072	1.077	1.082	1.086	1.091
1.2	1.095	1.100	1.105	1.109	1.114	1.118	1.122	1.127	1.131	1.136
1.3	1.140	1.145	1.149	1.153	1.158	1.162	1.166	1.170	1.175	1.179
1.4	1.183	1.187	1.192	1.196	1.200	1.204	1.208	1.212	1.217	1.221
1.5	1.225	1.229	1.233	1.237	1.241	1.245	1.249	1.253	1.257	1.261
1.6	1.265	1.269	1.273	1.277	1.281	1.285	1.288	1.292	1.296	1.300
1.7	1.304	1.308	1.311	1.315	1.319	1.323	1.327	1.330	1.334	1.338
1.8	1.342	1.345	1.349	1.353	1.356	1.360	1.364	1.367	1.371	1.375
1.9	1.378	1.382	1.386	1.389	1.393	1.396	1.400	1.404	1.407	1.411
2.0	1.414	1.418	1.421	1.425	1.428	1.432	1.435	1.439	1.442	1.446
2.1	1.449	1.453	1.456	1.459	1.463	1.466	1.470	1.473	1.476	1.480
2.2	1.483	1.487	1.490	1.493	1.497	1.500	1.503	1.507	1.510	1.513
2.3	1.517	1.520	1.523	1.526	1.530	1.533	1.536	1.539	1.543	1.546
2.4	1.549	1.552	1.556	1.559	1.562	1.565	1.568	1.572	1.575	1.578
2.5	1.581	1.584	1.587	1.591	1.594	1.597	1.600	1.603	1.606	1.609
2.6	1.612	1.616	1.619	1.622	1.625	1.628	1.631	1.634	1.637	1.640
2.7	1.643	1.646	1.649	1.652	1.655	1.658	1.661	1.664	1.667	1.670
2.8	1.673	1.676	1.679	1.682	1.685	1.688	1.691	1.694	1.697	1.700
2.9	1.703	1.706	1.709	1.712	1.715	1.718	1.720	1.723	1.726	1.729
3.0	1.732	1.735	1.738	1.741	1.744	1.746	1.749	1.752	1.755	1.758
3.1	1.761	1.764	1.766	1.769	1.772	1.775	1.778	1.780	1.783	1.786
3.2	1.789	1.792	1.794	1.797	1.800	1.803	1.806	1.808	1.811	1.814
3.3	1.817	1.819	1.822	1.825	1.828	1.830	1.833	1.836	1.838	1.841
3.4	1.844	1.847	1.849	1.852	1.855	1.857	1.860	1.863	1.865	1.868
3.5	1.871	1.873	1.876	1.879	1.881	1.884	1.887	1.889	1.892	1.895
3.6	1.897	1.900	1.903	1.905	1.908	1.910	1.913	1.916	1.918	1.921
3.7	1.924	1.926	1.929	1.931	1.934	1.936	1.939	1.942	1.944	1.947
3.8	1.949	1.952	1.954	1.957	1.960	1.962	1.965	1.967	1.970	1.972
3.9	1.975	1.977	1.980	1.982	1.985	1.987	1.990	1.992	1.996	1.997
4.0	2.000	2.002	2.005	2.007	2.010	2.012	2.015	2.107	2.020	2.022
4.1	2.025	2.027	2.030	2,032	2.035	2.037	2.040	2.042	2.045	2.047
4.2	2.049	2.052	2.054	2.057	2.059	2.062	2.064	2.066	2.069	2.071
4.3	2.074	2.076	2.078	2.081	2.083	2.086	2.088	2.090	2.093	2.095
4.4	2.098	2.100	2.102	2.105	2.107	2.110	2.112	2.114	2.117	2.119
4.5	2.121	2.124	2.126	2.128	2.131	2.133	2.135	2.138	2.140	2.142
4.6	2.145	2.147	2.149	2.152	2.154	2.156	2.159	2.161	2.163	2.166
4.7	2.168	2.170	2.173	2.175	2.177	2.179	2.182	2.184	2.186	2.189
4.8	2.191	2.193	2.195	2.198	2.200	2.202	2.205	2.207	2.209	2.211
4.9	2.214	2.216	2.218	2.220	2.223	2.225	2.227	2.229	2.232	2.334
5.0	2.236	2.238	2.241	2.243	2.245	2.247	2.249	2.252	2.254	2.256
5.1	2.258	2.261	2.263	2.265	2.267	2.269	2.272	2.274	2.276	2.278
5.2	2.280	2.283	2.285	2.287	2.289	2.291	2.293	2.296	2.298	2.300
5.3	2.302	2.304	2.307	2.309	2.311	2.313	2.315	2.317	2.319	2.322
5.4	2.324	2.326	2.328	2.330	2.332	2.335	2.337	2.339	2.341	2.343
No.	0	1	2	3	4	5	6	7	8	9

Table 58-1 (Cont'd) Square Root Table (for numbers 1.0 to 9.99)

No.	0	1	2	3	4	5	6	7	8	9
5.5	2.345	2.347	2.349	2.352	2.354	2.356	2.358	2.360	2.363	2.364
5.6	2.366	2.369	2.371	2.373	2.375	2.377	2.379	2.381	2.383	2.385
5.7	2.387	2.390	2.392	2.394	2.396	2.398	2.400	2.402	2.404	2.406
5.8	2.408	2.410	2.412	2.415	2.417	2.419	2.421	2.423	2.425	2.427
5.9	2.429	2.431	2.433	2.435	2.437	2.439	2.441	2.443	2.445	2.447
6.0	2.449	2.452	2.454	2.456	2.458	2.460	2.462	2.464	2.466	2.468
6.1	2.470	2.472	2.474	2.476	2.478	2.480	2.482	2.484	2.486	2.488
6.2	2.490	2.492	2.494	2.496	2.498	2.500	2.502	2.504	2.506	2.508
6.3	2.510	2.512	2.514	2.516	2.518	2.520	2.522	2.524	2.526	2.528
6.4	2.530	2.532	2.534	2.536	2.538	2.540	2.542	2.544	2.546	2.548
6.5	2.550	2.551	2.553	2.555	2.557	2.559	2.561	2.563	2.565	2.567
6.6	2.569	2.571	2.573	2.575	2.577	2.579	2.581	2.583	2.585	2.587
6.7	2.588	2.590	2.592	2.594	2.596	2.598	2.600	2.602	2.604	2.606
6.8	2.608	2.610	2.612	2.613	2.615	2.617	2.619	2.621	2.623	2.626
6.9	2.627	2.629	2.631	2.632	2.634	2.636	2.638	2.640	2.642	2.644
7.0	2.646	2.648	2.650	2.651	2.653	2.655	2.657	2.659	2.661	2.663
7.1	2.665	2.666	2.668	2.670	2.672	2.674	2.676	2.678	2.680	2.681
7.2	2.683	2.685	2.687	2.689	2.691	2.693	2.694	2.696	2.698	2.700
7.3	2.702	2.704	2.706	2.707	2.709	2.711	2.713	2.715	2.717	2.718
7.4	2.720	2.722	2.724	2.726	2.728	2.729	2.731	2.733	2.735	2.737
7.5	2.793	2.740	2.742	2.744	2.746	2.748	2.750	2.751	2.753	2.755
7.6	2.757	2.759	2.760	2.762	2.764	2.766	2.768	2.769	2.771	2.773
7.7	2.775	2.777	2.778	2.780	2.782	2.784	2.786	2.787	2.789	2.791
7.8	2.793	2.795	2.796	2.798	2.800	2.802	2.804	2.805	2.807	2.809
7.9	2.811	2.812	2.814	2.816	2.818	2.820	2.821	2.823	2.825	2.827
8.0	2.828	2.830	2.832	2.834	2.835	2.837	2.839	2.841	2.843	2.844
8.1	2.846	2.848	2.850	2.851	2.853	2.855	2.857	2.858	2.860	2.862
8.2	2.864	2.865	2.867	2.869	2.871	2.872	2.874	2.876	2.877	2.879
8.3	2.881	2.883	2.884	2.886	2.888	2.890	2.891	2.893	2.895	2.897
8.4	2.898	2.900	2.902	2.903	2.905	2.907	2.909	2.910	2.912	2.914
8.5	2.915	2.917	2.919	2.921	2.922	2.924	2.926	2.927	2.929	2.931
8.6	2.933	2.934	2.936	2.938	2.939	2.941	2.943	2.944	2.946	2.948
8.7	2.950	2.951	2.953	2.955	2.956	2.958	2.960	2.961	2.963	2.965
8.8	2.966	2.968	2.970	2.972	2.973	2.975	2.977	2.978	2.980	2.982
8.9	2.983	2.985	2.987	2.988	2.990	2.992	2.993	2.995	2.997	2.998
9.0	3.000	3.002	3.003	3.005	3.007	3.008	3.010	3.012	3.013	3.015
9.1	3.017	3.018	3.020	3.022	3.023	3.025	3.027	3.028	3.030	3.032
9.2	3.033	3.035	3.036	3.038	3.040	3.041	3.043	3.045	3.046	3.048
9.3	3.050	3.051	3.053	3.055	3.056	3.058	3.059	3.061	3.063	3.064
9.4	3.066	3.068	3.069	3.071	3.072	3.074	3.076	3.077	3.079	3.081
9.5	3.082	3.084	3.085	3.087	3.089	3.090	3.092	3.094	3.095	3.097
9.6	3.098	3.100	3.102	3.103	3.105	3.106	3.108	3.110	3.111	3.113
9.7	3.114	3.116	3.118	3.119	3.121	3.122	3.124	3.126	3.127	3.129
9.8	3.130	3.132	3.134	3.135	3.137	3.138	3.140	3.142	3.143	3.145
9.9	3.146	3.148	3.150	3.151	3.153	3.154	3.156	3.158	3.159	3.161
No.	0	1	2	3	4	5	6	7	8	9

Table 58-2. Square Root Table (for numbers 10 to 54.9)

No.	0	1	2	3	4	5	6	7	8	9
10	3.162	3.178	3.194	3.209	3.225	3.240	3.256	3.271	3.286	3.302
11	3.317	3.332	3.347	3.362	3.376	3.391	3.406	3.421	3.435	3.450
12	3.464	3.479	3.493	3.507	3.521	3.536	3.550	3.564	3.578	3.592
13	3.606	3.619	3.633	3.647	3.661	3.674	3.688	3.701	3.715	3.728
14	3.742	3.755	3.768	3.782	3.795	3.808	3.821	3.834	3.847	3.860
15	3.873	3.886	3.899	3.912	3.924	3.937	3.950	3.962	3.975	3.987
16	4.000	4.012	4.025	4.037	4.050	4.062	4.074	4.087	4.099	4.111
17	4.123	4.135	4.147	4.159	4.171	4.183	3.195	4.207	4.219	4.231
18	4.243	4.254	4.266	4.278	4.290	4.301	4.313	4.324	4.336	4.347
19	4.359	4.370	4.383	4.393	4.405	4.416	4.427	4.438	4.450	4.461
20	4.472	4.483	4.494	4.506	4.517	4.528	4.539	4.550	4.561	4.572
21	4.583	4.593	4.604	4.615	4.626	4.637	4.648	4.658	4.669	4.680
22	4.690	4.701	4.712	4.722	4.733	4.743	4.754	4.764	4.775	4.785
23	4.796	4.806	4.817	4.827	4.837	4.848	4.858	4.868	4.879	4.889
24	4.899	4.909	4.919	4.930	4.940	4.950	4.960	4.970	4.980	4.990
25	5.000	5.010	5.020	5.030	5.040	5.050	5.060	5.070	5.079	5.089
26	5.099	5.109	5.119	5.128	5.138	5.148	5.158	5.167	5.177	5.187
27	5.196	5.206	5.215	5.225	5.235	5.244	5.254	5.263	5.273	5.282
28	5.292	5.301	5.310	5.320	5.329	5.339	5.348	5.357	5.367	5.376
29	5.385	5.394	5.404	5.413	5.422	5.431	5.441	5.450	5.459	5.468
30	5.477	5.486	5.495	5.505	5.514	5.523	5.532	5.541	5.550	5.559
31	5.568	5.577	5.586	5.595	5.604	5.612	5.621	5.630	5.639	5.648
32	5.657	5.666	5.675	5.683	5.692	5.701	5.710	5.718	5.727	5.736
33	5.745	5.573	5.762	5.771	5.779	5.788	5.797	5.805	5.814	5.822
34	5.831	5.840	5.848	5.857	5.865	5.875	5.882	5.891	5.899	5.908
35	5.916	5.925	5.933	5.941	5.950	5.958	5.967	5.975	5.983	5.992
36	6.000	6.008	6.017	6.025	6.033	6.042	6.050	6.058	6.066	6.075
37	6.083	6.091	6.099	6.107	6.116	6.124	6.132	6.140	6.148	6.156
38	6.164	6.173	6.181	6.189	6.197	6.205	6.213	6.221	6.229	6.237
39	6.245	6.253	6.261	6.269	6.277	6.285	6.293	6.301	6.309	6.317
40	6.325	6.332	6.340	6.348	6.356	6.364	6.372	6.380	6.387	6.395
41	6.403	6.411	6.419	6.427	6.434	6.442	6.450	6.458	6.465	6.473
42	6.481	6.488	6.496	6.504	6.512	6.519	6.527	6.535	6.542	6.550
43	6.557	6.565	6.573	6.580	6.588	6.595	6.603	6.611	6.618	6.626
44	6.633	6.641	6.648	6.656	6.663	6.671	6.678	6.686	6.693	6.701
45	6.708	6.716	6.723	6.731	6.738	6.745	6.753	6.760	6.768	6.775
46	6.782	6.790	6.797	6.804	6.812	6.819	6.826	6.834	6.841	6.848
47	6.856	6.863	6.870	6.877	6.885	6.892	6.899	6.907	6.914	6.921
48	6.928	6.935	6.943	6.950	6.957	6.964	6.971	6.979	6.986	6.993
49	7.000	7.007	7.014	7.021	7.029	7.036	7.043	7.050	7.057	7.064
50	7.071	7.078	7.085	7.092	7.099	7.106	7.113	7.120	7.127	7.134
51	7.141	7.148	7.155	7.162	7.169	7.176	7.183	7.190	7.197	7.204
52	7.211	7.218	7.225	7.232	7.239	7.246	7.253	7.259	7.266	7.273
53	7.280	7.287	7.294	7.301	7.308	7.314	7.321	7.328	7.335	7.342
54	7.348	7.355	7.362	7.369	7.376	7.382	7.389	7.396	7.403	7.409
No.	0	1	2	3	4	5	6	7	8	9

provide four periods on the right-
hand side of the decimal point.

Finding the Square Root From a Table

The square root table (Table 58-1) can be used to find the square roots of numbers from 1.0 to 9.99, graduated in 100ths. The square root table (Table 58-2) can be used to find square roots of numbers from 10 to 55, graduated in 10ths. Tables are also available for the larger numbers. In these tables, the number is listed in the left-hand column; then either 100ths or 10ths are indicated across the top and bottom.

Problem: In Table 58-1, find the square root of 3.39

Solution:
1. Find the number *3.3* in the left-hand column in Table 58-1.
2. Move across this row to the column marked 9 for .09 at the top of the table.
3. Therefore, the *square root* of 3.39 is *1.841*

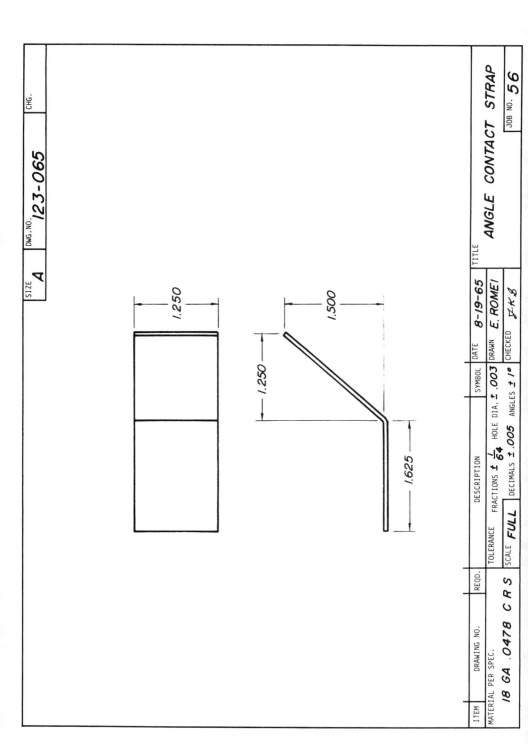

1.250

1.250

1.625

1.500

ITEM	DRAWING NO.	REQD.			DESCRIPTION	SYMBOL	DATE 8-19-65	TITLE

MATERIAL PER SPEC.

18 GA .0478 CRS

TOLERANCE   FRACTIONS ± $\frac{1}{64}$ HOLE DIA. ± .003

SCALE **FULL**   DECIMALS ±.005   ANGLES ± 1°

DRAWN E. ROMEI

CHECKED J·K·B

TITLE ANGLE CONTACT STRAP

JOB NO. 56

SIZE **A**   DWG. NO. **123-065**   CHG.

Law of the
Right Triangle

The precision sheet metalworker must understand the law of the right triangle in determining the length of the slant height and in locating the positions for a series of holes in a part (Fig. 59-1).

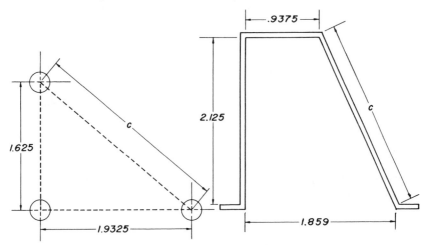

Fig. 59-1

239

A *right triangle* is a triangle with one included 90° angle. The side opposite the 90° angle is the *hypotenuse c*, the *altitude* is the height *a*, and the third side is the base *b*.

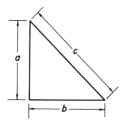

To find the length of the hypotenuse *c* of a right triangle, add the square of the altitude *a* and the square of the base *b;* then find the square root of this sum. The formula is:

$$c = \sqrt{a^2 + b^2}$$

in which

    c is the length of the hypotenuse.
    a is length of the altitude.
    b is the length of the base.

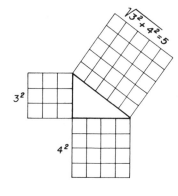

Problem: In a right triangle, the base is 4″ and the altitude is 3″. Find the length of the hypotenuse.

Solution:

   1. Determine the formula.
   2. Substitute.
   3. Solve.

$$c = \sqrt{a^2 + b^2}$$
$$= \sqrt{3^2 + 4^2}$$
$$= \sqrt{9 + 16}$$
$$= \sqrt{25}$$
$$= 5$$

   4. The hypotenuse *c* is *5″*.

With the altitude *a*, base *b*, and hypotenuse *c*, any one of the three lengths can be found when the other two lengths are known:

$$a = \sqrt{c^2 - b^2} \qquad b = \sqrt{c^2 - a^2} \qquad c = \sqrt{a^2 + b^2}$$

Problem: If the base *b* is 3″ and the hypotenuse *c* is 4″, find the altitude *a* of a right triangle, correct to two decimal places.

Solution:

1. Determine the formula.

2. Substitute.

3. Solve.

$$a = \sqrt{c^2 - b^2}$$
$$= \sqrt{4^2 - 3^2}$$
$$= \sqrt{16 - 9}$$
$$= \sqrt{7}$$
$$= 2.645$$

4. The altitude a is *2.65"*.

Trade Problem

Problem 1: Find the slant height c in the right triangle (left) in Fig. 59-1.

Solution:

1. Determine the formula.

2. Substitute.

3. Solve.

$$c = \sqrt{a^2 + b^2}$$
$$= \sqrt{1.625^2 + 1.9325^2}$$
$$= \sqrt{2.63063 + 3.73456}$$
$$= \sqrt{6.36519}$$
$$= 2.523$$

4. The slant height c is *2.523"*.

Problem 2: Find the slant height c in the metal part (right) in Fig. 59-1.

Solution:

1. Determine the formula.

2. To find the length of the base for the slant height c, subtract .9375 from 1.859; then substitute.

3. Solve.

4. Finding the square root of 5.37 in Table 58-1, the slant height c is *2.317"*.

$$c = \sqrt{a^2 + b^2}$$

$$\begin{array}{r} 1.8590 \\ -\ .9375 \\ \hline .9215 \end{array}$$

$$= \sqrt{2.125^2 + .9215^2}$$
$$= \sqrt{4.5156 + .8502}$$
$$= \sqrt{5.3658}$$

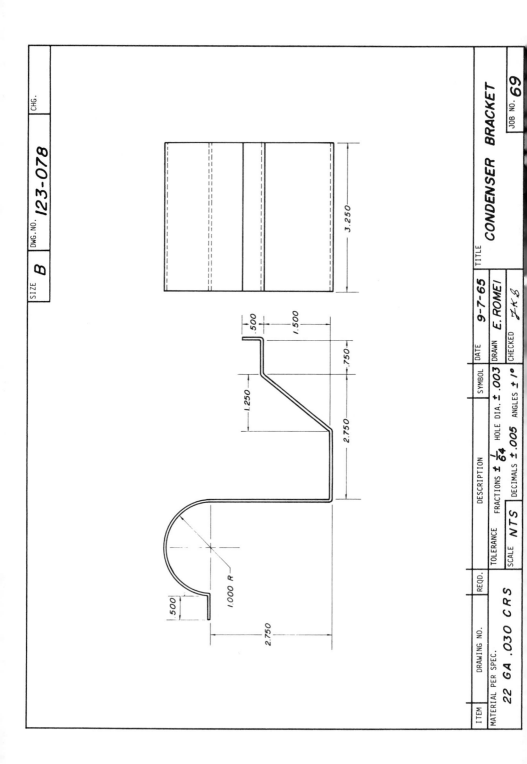

SIZE **B** | DWG.NO. **123-078** | CHG.

3.250

.500
1.500
.750
1.250
2.750
1.000 R
.500
2.750

ITEM	DRAWING NO.	REQD.	DESCRIPTION	SYMBOL	DATE **9-7-65**	TITLE

CONDENSER BRACKET

MATERIAL PER SPEC.
22 GA .030 CRS

TOLERANCE FRACTIONS ± $\frac{1}{64}$ HOLE DIA. ±.003
DECIMALS ±.005 ANGLES ±1°
SCALE **NTS**

DRAWN **E. ROMEI**
CHECKED **J.K.B**

JOB NO. **69**

The Equation

The ability to solve equations is essential in completing the next five units. These equations are used by the precision sheet metalworker in determining the true length of a slant edge, line, or surface (Fig. 60-1).

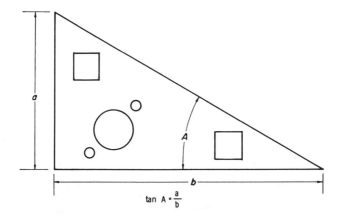

$$\tan A = \frac{a}{b}$$

Fig. 60-1

An *equation* is an expression of equality between two quantities. All the formulas we have used are equations, because they express equalities, such as:

$$c = \sqrt{a^2 + b^2}$$

243

The members of an equation are the expressions, numbers, or letters on each side of the equal sign:

$$3 + 2 = 2 + 3$$

The first member of an equation is the expression on the left-hand side of the equal sign $(3 + 2)$; the second member is the expression on the right-hand side of the equal sign $(2 + 3)$.

A letter in an equation is referred to as an *unknown*. In the following equation, the unknown is the letter x:

$$2x = 7$$

In every equation, both members are equal. When one member of an equation is increased, decreased, multiplied, or divided by any number, the opposite member also must be increased, decreased, multiplied, or divided by the same number to maintain this equality.

When equal members of an equation are increased, decreased, multiplied, or divided by the same number, the results are equal. This equality is shown in the following examples:

1. Addition.
   add 2 to each member;
   equality remains

   $$4 = 4$$
   $$+2 = +2$$
   $$\overline{6 = 6}$$

2. Subtraction.
   subtract 1 from each member;
   equality remains

   $$4 = 4$$
   $$-1 = -1$$
   $$\overline{3 = 3}$$

3. Multiplication.
   multiply each member by 5;
   equality remains

   $$4 = 4$$
   $$\times 5 = \times 5$$
   $$\overline{20 = 20}$$

4. Division.
   divide each member by 2;
   equality remains

   $$4 = 4$$
   $$\div 2 = \div 2$$
   $$\overline{2 = 2}$$

General Rules of Equations

To solve an equation that includes one unknown quantity (letter or symbol), place the unknown quantity alone on one side of the equals sign. This is accomplished through addition, subtraction, multiplication, or division, as shown in the following equations:

1. The following equation requires none of these processes, since the unknown quantity a is alone:

$$a = 3 - 1$$

2. In the following equation, the -3 must be removed from the left-hand member of the equation. This can be accomplished by *adding* $+3$ to both sides of the equation.

$$a - 3 = 6$$
$$a - 3 + 3 = 6 + 3$$
$$a = 9$$

3. In the following equation, the $+7$ must be removed from the left-hand member of the equation. This can be accomplished by *subtracting* 7 from both sides of the equation:

$$a + 7 = 13$$
$$a + 7 - 7 = 13 - 7$$
$$a = 6$$

4. In the following equation, the denominator *2* must be eliminated from the left-hand member of the equation. This can be accomplished by *multiplying* both sides of the equation by 2:

$$\frac{a}{2} = 5$$

$$\frac{a}{2} \times 2 = 5 \times 2$$

$$a = 10$$

5. In the following equation, the 7 must be eliminated from the left-hand member of the equation. This can be accomplished by *dividing* both sides of the equation by 7:

$$7a = 23$$
$$\frac{7a}{7} = \frac{23}{7}$$
$$a = 23 \div 7$$
$$= 3\tfrac{2}{7}$$

6. If it is more convenient to move or transpose the left-hand member to the right-hand side and the right-hand member to the left-hand side, this can be accomplished by merely *transposing* each complete member to the opposite side of the equal sign.

$$23 = 7a$$
$$7a = 23$$
$$a = 23 \div 7$$
$$= 3\tfrac{2}{7}$$

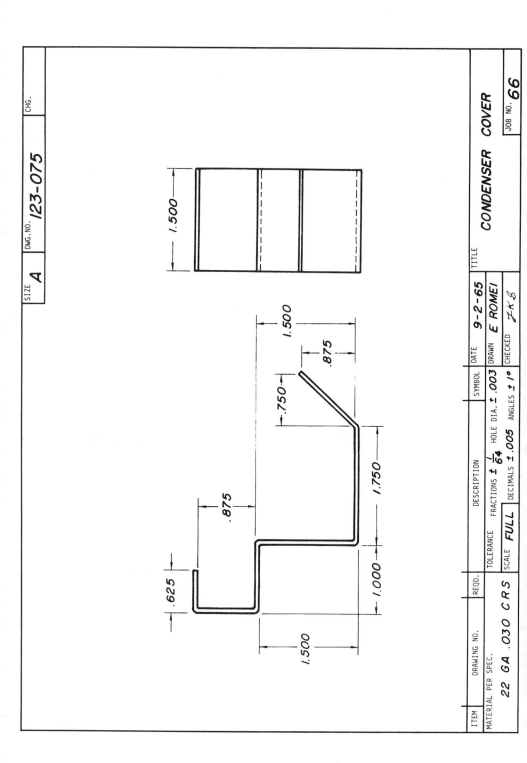

SIZE **A** | DWG. NO. **123-075** | CHG.

ITEM	DRAWING NO.	REQD.	DESCRIPTION	SYMBOL	DATE **9-2-65**	TITLE

MATERIAL PER SPEC.
22 GA .030 CRS

TOLERANCE
FRACTIONS ± $\frac{1}{64}$ HOLE DIA. ± **.003**
SCALE **FULL** DECIMALS ± **.005** ANGLES ± **1°**

DRAWN **E ROMEI**
CHECKED **JKB**

CONDENSER COVER

JOB NO. **66**

Dimensions shown: 1.500, .875, .750, 1.500, .875, 1.750, 1.000, .625, 1.500

Basic
Trigonometric Functions

Trigonometry is used by the precision sheet metalworker to determine a missing dimension for a right triangle (Fig. 61-1). This can be required on parts with slanting surfaces or in locating the positions for a series of holes on some parts.

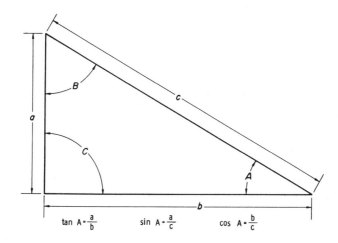

$$\tan A = \frac{a}{b} \qquad \sin A = \frac{a}{c} \qquad \cos A = \frac{b}{c}$$

Fig. 61-1

247

Trigonometry involves both ratio and equation solving. The equations we will use include the terms *sine* (sin) *tangent* (tan) and *cosine* (cos). It must be remembered that only right triangles are used in these computations.

All right triangles include two acute angles (less than 90°) and one 90° angle. The right angle or 90° angle is designated by the capital letter *C,* and the opposite side or hypotenuse is indicated by the small letter *c* (see diagrams).

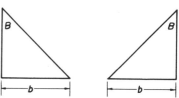

The angle *B* is the angle opposite the base *b* of the triangle.

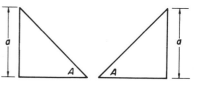

The angle *A* is opposite the remaining side or altitude *a.*

Using angle *A,* the formulas include:

$$\tan A = \frac{a}{b} = \frac{\text{opposite}}{\text{adjacent}} \ ; \sin A = \frac{a}{c} = \frac{\text{opposite}}{\text{hypotenuse}}; \cos A = \frac{b}{c} = \frac{\text{adjacent}}{\text{hypotenuse}}$$

The applications of these equations will be explained later in Units 62 through 65. The letters in the equations correspond to the letters in the diagrams.

In solving these equations, the table of natural trigonometric functions (Table 61-1) must be used. Each of the three ratios is referred to as a trigonometric function. By substituting the following numbers in the ratios, we can learn to use the table:

$$a = 3''; b = 4''; \text{ and } c = 5''$$

Using the tangent column of Table 61-1, the angle nearest .75000 is *37°*.

$$\tan A = \frac{a}{b} = \frac{3}{4} = .75000$$

Using the sine column, the angle nearest .60000 is *37°*.

$$\sin A = \frac{a}{c} = \frac{3}{5} = .60000$$

Using the cosine column, the angle nearest .80000 is *37°*.

$$\cos A = \frac{b}{c} = \frac{4}{5} = .80000$$

Therefore, if you construct a triangle with these dimensions, label it in the proper manner, and measure angle *A,* you will find it to be *37°*.

The table (Table 61-1) will be used to solve the problems; however, in the tables used in most shops, the degrees are divided into minutes to permit more accuracy.

Table 61-1. Table of Natural Trigonometric Functions

Angle°	Sine	Cosine	Tan.	Cotan.	Secant	Cosec.	Angle°	Sine	Cosine	Tan.	Cotan.	Secant	Cosec.
1	.0175	.9998	.0175	57.29	1.000	57.30	46	.7193	.6947	1.0355	.9657	1.439	1.390
2	.0349	.9994	.0349	28.64	1.001	28.65	47	.7314	.6820	1.0724	.9325	1.466	1.367
3	.0523	.9986	.0524	19.08	1.001	19.11	48	.7431	.6691	1.1106	.9004	1.494	1.346
4	.0698	.9976	.0699	14.30	1.002	14.33	49	.7547	.6561	1.1504	.8693	1.524	1.325
5	.0872	.9962	.0875	11.43	1.004	11.47	50	.7660	.6428	1.1918	.8391	1.556	1.305
6	.1045	.9945	.1051	9.514	1.005	9.567	51	.7771	.6293	1.2349	.8098	1.589	1.287
7	.1219	.9925	.1228	8.144	1.007	8.205	52	.7880	.6157	1.2799	.7812	1.624	1.269
8	.1392	.9903	.1405	7.115	1.010	7.185	53	.7986	.6018	1.3270	.7535	1.662	1.252
9	.1564	.9877	.1584	6.314	1.012	6.392	54	.8090	.5878	1.3764	.7265	1.701	1.236
10	.1736	.9848	.1763	5.671	1.015	5.759	55	.8192	.5736	1.4281	.7002	1.743	1.221
11	.1908	.9816	.1944	5.144	1.019	5.241	56	.8290	.5592	1.4826	.6745	1.788	1.206
12	.2079	.9781	.2126	4.705	1.022	4.810	57	.8387	.5446	1.5399	.6494	1.836	1.192
13	.2250	.9744	.2309	4.331	1.026	4.445	58	.8480	.5299	1.6003	.6249	1.887	1.179
14	.2419	.9703	.2493	4.011	1.031	4.134	59	.8572	.5150	1.6643	.6009	1.942	1.167
15	.2588	.9659	.2679	3.732	1.035	3.864	60	.8660	.5000	1.7321	.5773	2.000	1.155
16	.2756	.9613	.2867	3.487	1.040	3.628	61	.8746	.4848	1.8040	.5543	2.063	1.143
17	.2924	.9563	.3057	3.271	1.046	3.420	62	.8829	.4695	1.8807	.5317	2.130	1.133
18	.3090	.9511	.3249	3.078	1.051	3.236	63	.8910	.4540	1.9626	.5095	2.203	1.122
19	.3256	.9455	.3443	2.904	1.058	3.071	64	.8988	.4384	2.0503	.4877	2.281	1.113
20	.3420	.9397	.3640	2.748	1.064	2.924	65	.9063	.4226	2.1445	.4663	2.366	1.103
21	.3584	.9336	.3839	2.605	1.071	2.790	66	.9135	.4067	2.2460	.4452	2.459	1.095
22	.3746	.9272	.4040	2.475	1.078	2.669	67	.9205	.3907	2.3559	.4245	2.559	1.086
23	.3907	.9205	.4245	2.356	1.086	2.559	68	.9272	.3746	2.4751	.4040	2.669	1.078
24	.4067	.9135	.4452	2.246	1.095	2.459	69	.9336	.3584	2.6051	.3839	2.790	1.071
25	.4226	.9063	.4663	2.144	1.103	2.366	70	.9397	.3420	2.7475	.3640	2.924	1.064
26	.4384	.8988	.4877	2.050	1.113	2.281	71	.9455	.3256	2.9042	.3443	3.071	1.058
27	.4540	.8910	'5095	1.963	1.122	2.203	72	.9511	.3090	3.0777	.3249	3.236	1.051
28	.4695	.8829	.5317	1.881	1.133	2.130	73	.9563	.2924	3.2709	.3057	3.420	1.046
29	.4848	.8746	.5543	1.804	1.143	2.063	74	.9613	.2756	3.4874	.2867	3.628	1.040
30	.5000	.8660	.5774	1.732	1.155	2.000	75	.9659	.2588	3.7321	.2679	3.864	1.035
31	.5150	.8572	.6009	1.664	1.167	1.942	76	.9703	.2419	4.0108	.2493	4.134	1.031
32	.5299	.8480	.6249	1.600	1.179	1.887	77	.9744	.2250	4.3315	.2309	4.445	1.026
33	.5446	.8387	.6494	1.540	1.192	1.836	78	.9781	.2079	4.7046	.2126	4.810	1.022
34	.5592	.8290	.6745	1.483	1.206	1.788	79	.9816	.1908	5.1446	.1944	5.241	1.019
35	.5736	.8192	.7002	1.428	1.221	1.743	80	.9848	.1736	5.6713	.1763	5.759	1.015
36	.5878	.8090	.7265	1.376	1.236	1.701	81	.9877	.1564	6.3138	.1584	6.392	1.012
37	.6018	.7986	.7536	1.327	1.252	1.662	82	.9903	.1392	7.1154	.1405	7.185	1.010
38	.6157	.7880	.7813	1.280	1.269	1.624	83	.9925	.1219	8.1443	.1228	8.205	1.007
39	.6293	.7771	.8098	1.235	1.287	1.589	84	.9945	.1045	9.5144	.1051	9.567	1.005
40	.6428	.7660	.8391	1.192	1.305	1.556	85	.9962	.0872	11.4301	.0875	11.47	1.004
41	.6561	.7547	.8693	1.150	1.325	1.524	86	.9976	.0698	14.3007	.0699	14.33	1.002
42	.6691	.7431	.9004	1.111	1.346	1.494	87	.9986	.0523	19.0811	.0524	19.11	1.001
43	.6820	.7314	.9325	1.072	1.367	1.466	88	.9994	.0349	28.6363	.0349	28.65	1.001
44	.6947	.7193	.9657	1.035	1.390	1.439	89	.9998	.0175	57.2900	.0174	57.30	1.000
45	.7071	.7071	1.0000	1.000	1.414	1.414	90	1.0000	.0000				

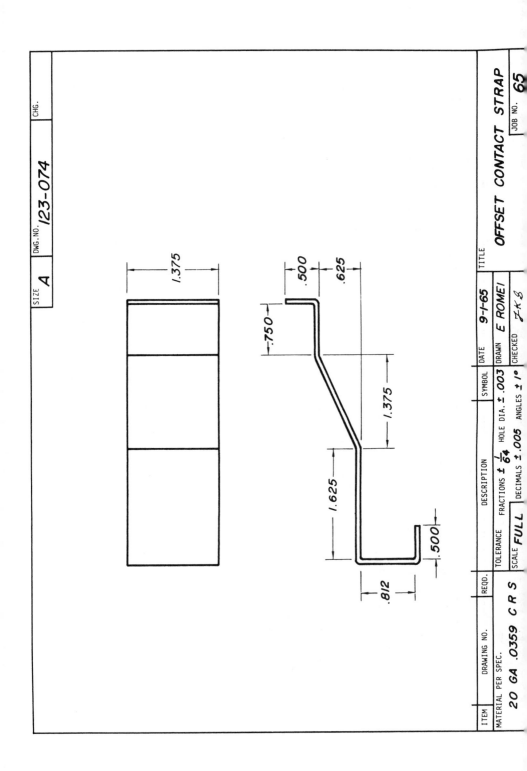

SIZE **A** DWG. NO. **123-074** CHG.

1.375

.750

.500

.625

1.625

1.375

.500

.812

ITEM	DRAWING NO.	REQD.				SYMBOL	DATE **9-1-65**	TITLE

MATERIAL PER SPEC.

20 GA .0359 C R S

TOLERANCE   FRACTIONS **± 1/64**   HOLE DIA. **± .003**

DESCRIPTION

SCALE **FULL** DECIMALS **± .005** ANGLES **± 1°**

DRAWN **E ROMEI**

CHECKED **I·K·B**

OFFSET CONTACT STRAP

JOB NO. **65**

The Tangent Formula

The *tangent formula* is used by the precision sheet metalworker to solve either of the following measurements for a right triangle (Fig. 62-1):

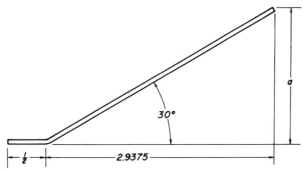

Fig. 62-1

1. An acute angle *A*—if the opposite side *a* and adjacent side *b* are known.

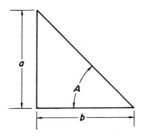

2. The side *b*—if the acute angle *B* and
the adjacent side *a* are known.

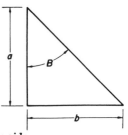

Substituting in the tangent formula: $tan = \dfrac{opposite\ side}{adjacent\ side}$

Angle *A:* $tan\ A = \dfrac{a}{b}$ Angle *B:* $tan\ B = \dfrac{b}{a}$

Solving for an Acute Angle

Problem: Given: A right triangle with
$a = 2''$ and b $= 1.5''$. Solve for angle
A.

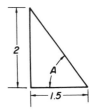

Solution:

1. Determine the correct formula.

$$tan\ A = \frac{a}{b}$$

2. Substitute.

$$= \frac{2}{1.5}$$

3. Solve.

$$= 1.33333$$

4. Find tan 1.33333 in the table (Table
61-1).

$$= 53°$$

5. The acute angle *A* is *53°*.

Solving for a Side

Problem: *Given:* A right triangle with
angle $A = 50°$ and side $b = 3''$.
Solve for side *a.*

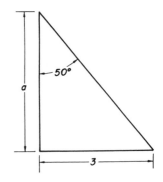

Solution:

1. Determine the correct formula.

$$\tan A = \frac{a}{b}$$

2. Substitute.

$$\tan 50° = \frac{a}{3}$$

3. Solve. Find 50° (tan) in the table (Table 61-1) and substitute.

$$.8391 = \frac{a}{3}$$

$$3 \times .8391 = \frac{a}{3} \times 3$$

$$2.5173 = a$$

4. The side *a* is 2.5173" or $2^{33}\!/_{64}$"

Trade Problem

Problem: Find the length of side *a* of the part in Fig. 62-1.

Solution:

1. Determine the formula.

$$\tan A = \frac{a}{b}$$

2. Substitute.

$$\tan 30° = \frac{a}{2.9375}$$

3. Solve for side *a*. Find 30° (tan) in the table, and substitute.

$$.5774 = \frac{a}{2.9375}$$

$$2.9375 \times .5774 = \frac{a}{2.9375} \times 2.9375$$

$$1.6961 = a$$

4. The side *a* is *1.6961"*.

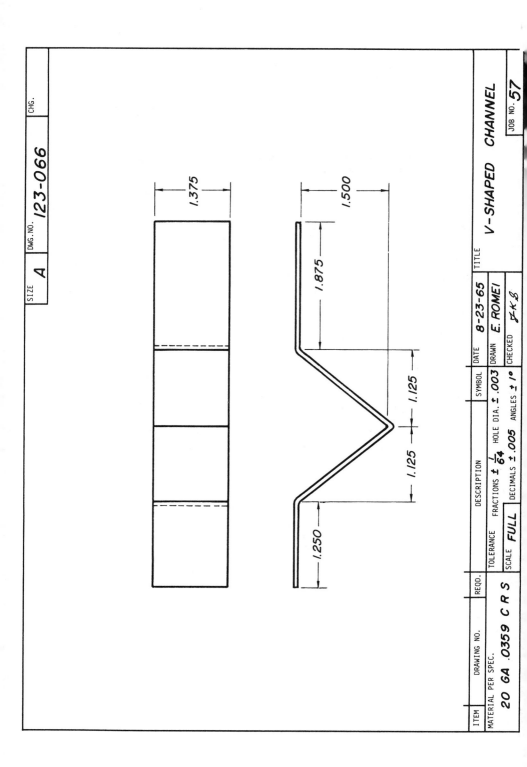

SIZE	DWG. NO.	CHG.
A	123-066	

1.375

1.500

1.875

1.125

1.125

1.250

ITEM	DRAWING NO.	REQD.	DESCRIPTION	SYMBOL	DATE 8-23-65	TITLE
			TOLERANCE FRACTIONS ± 1/64 HOLE DIA. ± .003		DRAWN E. ROMEI	V-SHAPED CHANNEL
MATERIAL PER SPEC. 20 GA .0359 C R S			SCALE FULL DECIMALS ± .005 ANGLES ± 1°		CHECKED FKB	JOB NO. 57

The Sine Formula

The *sine formula* is used by the precision sheet metalworker to determine one of the two components (Fig. 63-1) for a right triangle:

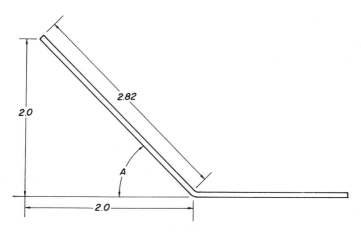

Fig. 63-1

1. An acute angle *A*—if the opposite side *a* and the hypotenuse *c* are known (Fig. 63-1).

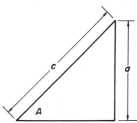

2. A side *b*—if the acute angle *B* opposite side *b* and the hypotenuse *c* are known.

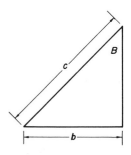

Substituting in the sine formula: $sin = \dfrac{opposite\ side}{hypotenuse}$

Angle *A*: $sin\ A = \dfrac{a}{c}$ Angle *B*: $sin\ B = \dfrac{b}{c}$

Solving for an Angle

Problem: *Given:* A right triangle with side $a = 3''$ and $c = 5''$. Solve for angle *A*.

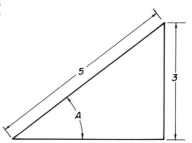

Solution:

1. Determine the correct formula.

$$sin\ A = \dfrac{a}{c}$$

2. Substitute.

$$= \dfrac{3}{5}$$

3. Solve.

$$= .60000$$

4. Find .6000 in the sin column of the table.

$$= 37°$$

5. The acute angle *A* is *37°*.

Solving for a Side

Problem: Given: A right triangle with angle $A = 40°$ and the hypotenuse $c = 2"$. Solve for the side a.

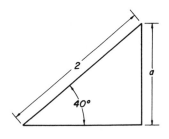

Solution:

1. Determine the correct formula.

$$\sin A = \frac{a}{c}$$

2. Substitute.

$$\sin 40° = \frac{a}{2}$$

3. Complete the computations. First, find sin 40° in the table; substitute the number (.6428).

$$.6428 = \frac{a}{2}$$

$$.6428 \times 2 = \frac{a}{2} \times 2$$

$$1.2856 = a$$

4. The side a is 1.2856", or $1\frac{9}{32}"$.

Trade Problem

Problem: Find the size of the angle A of the part in Fig. 63-1.

Solution:

1. Determine the formula.

$$\sin A = \frac{a}{c}$$

2. Substitute.

$$= \frac{2.0}{2.82}$$

3. Solve for sin A. Find sin .7092 in the table, and substitute.

$$= .7092$$

$$= 45°$$

4. The angle A is *45°*.

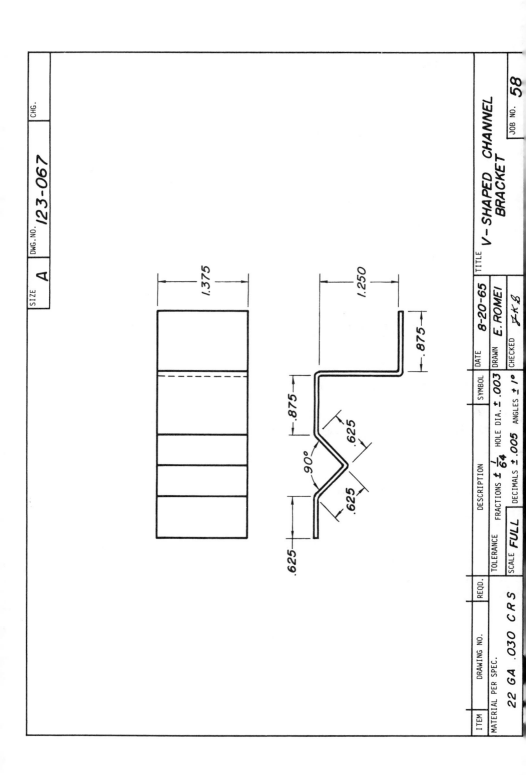

1.375

1.250

.875

.875

.625

90°

.625

.625

.625

SIZE A | DWG. NO. 123-067 | CHG.

| ITEM | DRAWING NO. | REQD. | DESCRIPTION | SYMBOL | DATE 8-20-65 | TITLE V-SHAPED CHANNEL BRACKET |

MATERIAL PER SPEC.

22 GA .030 C R S

TOLERANCE FRACTIONS ± 1/64 HOLE DIA. ± .003

SCALE FULL DECIMALS ± .005 ANGLES ± 1°

DRAWN E. ROMEI

CHECKED F.K.B

JOB NO. 58

Unit **64**

The Cosine Formula

The *cosine formula* is used by the precision sheet metalworker to determine one of the two components (Fig. 64-1) for a right triangle:

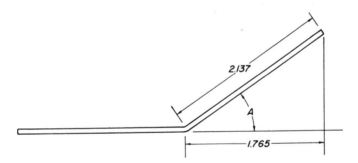

Fig. 64-1

1. An acute angle *A*—if the adjacent side *b* and the hypotenuse *c* are known.

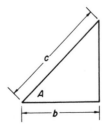

259

2. The side *b*—if the acute angle *A* adjacent to side *b* and the hypotenuse *c* are known.

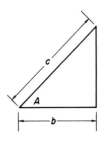

Substituting in the cosine formula: $cos = \dfrac{adjacent\ side}{hypotenuse}$

Angle *A:* $cos\ A = \dfrac{b}{c}$ Angle *B:* $cos\ B = \dfrac{a}{c}$

Solving for an Angle

Problem: *Given:* A right triangle with side $b = 1.5''$ and the hypotenuse $c = 2.5''$ Solve for angle *A*.

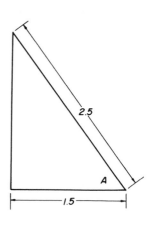

Solution:

1. Determine the correct formula.

$$\cos A = \dfrac{b}{c}$$

2. Substitute.

$$= \dfrac{1.5}{2.5}$$

3. Find 6.0000 in the cos column of the table.

$$= .60000$$
$$= 53°$$

4. Angle *A* is *53°*.

Solving for a Side

Problem: Given: A right triangle with
   angle $A = 44°$ and the hypotenuse
   $c = 3''$. Solve for the base b.

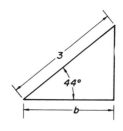

Solution:

1. Determine the correct formula.

$$\cos A = \frac{b}{c}$$

2. Substitute.

$$\cos 44° = \frac{b}{3}$$

3. Find cos 44° in the table, and
   substitute.

$$.7193 = \frac{b}{3}$$

$$.7193 \times 3 = \frac{b}{3} \times 3$$

$$2.1579 = b$$

4. The base b is 2.1579″, or 2$\frac{5}{32}$″.

Trade Problem

Problem: Find the size of the angle A of
   the part in Fig. 64-1.

Solution:

1. Determine the correct formula.

$$\cos A = \frac{b}{c}$$

2. Substitute.

$$= \frac{1.765}{2.137}$$

3. Solve. Find cos .8259 in the table,
   and substitute.

$$= .8259$$
$$\text{angle A} = 34°$$

4. The angle A is *34°*.

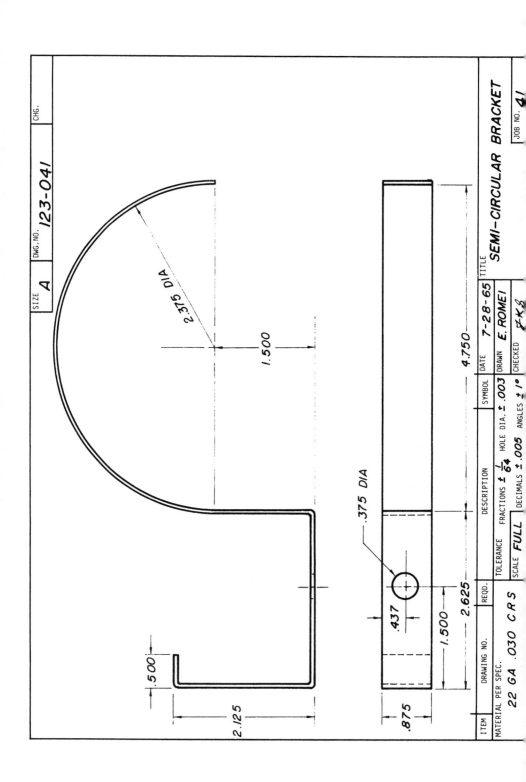

SIZE **A** | DWG. NO. **123-041** | CHG.

2.375 DIA

1.500

.375 DIA

.437

1.500

2.625

.875

.500

2.125

4.750

ITEM	DRAWING NO.	REQD.	DESCRIPTION	SYMBOL

MATERIAL PER SPEC.
22 GA .030 CRS

TOLERANCE
FRACTIONS ± $\frac{1}{64}$ HOLE DIA. ± .003
DECIMALS ±.005   ANGLES ± 1°

SCALE **FULL**

DATE **7-28-65**
DRAWN **E. ROMEI**
CHECKED

TITLE
SEMI-CIRCULAR BRACKET

JOB NO. **41**

Selection of
Correct Formula

To select the correct formula for determining an unknown dimension on a right triangle, the precision sheet metalworker must label the imaginary right triangle correctly (Fig. 65-1).

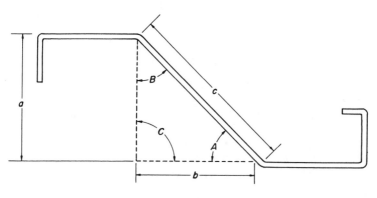

Fig. 65-1

The right angle (90°) is always designated with a capital letter C, and the hypotenuse is labeled with the small letter c. In previous examples, we designated the base b and the altitude a, with the angles opposite these sides angles B and A, respectively. However, if a right triangle is positioned in a manner similar to the right triangle shown, the base is the hypotenuse c, the altitude is the side a, and the angle opposite the side a is angle A. The third side is side b and the angle opposite this side is angle B. As explained previously, the formulas are:

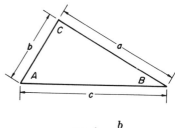

$$tan\ A = \frac{a}{b} \qquad sin\ A = \frac{a}{c} \qquad cos\ A = \frac{b}{c}$$

Solving for an Angle

If the size of an angle is needed, the known information must include one of the following dimensions:

1. Two sides a and b of the right triangle.

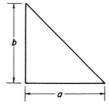

2. One side a or b and the hypotenuse c of the right triangle.

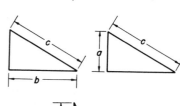

The procedure in solving a problem is:

1. Construct a right triangle; label with the known information. The two sides are $b = 1''$ and $a = 2''$.

2. After each known number, place the letter in parentheses that the number represents.

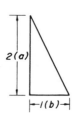

3. Select the formula that includes the two letters a and b.

4. Substitute the numbers into the formula; then solve the problem.

$$\tan A = \frac{a}{b}$$
$$= \frac{2}{1}$$
$$= 2.0000$$
$$= 63°$$

5. The angle A is 63°.

6. To find the size of the acute angle B, subtract the size of angle A from 90°; thus the angle B is $(90° - 63°)$, or 27°. Since the three angles of a triangle equal 180° and the right angle is 90°, the two acute angles in a right triangle total 90°.

Solving for a Side

If the length of a side is required, the known information must include one of the following combinations:

1. One side and one acute angle of a right triangle.

2. The hypotenuse c and one acute angle of a right triangle.

The procedure in solving this type of problem is:

1. Construct a right triangle, and label it with the given information. The hypotenuse c is 2″, and an acute angle A is 57°.

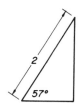

2. After each known number, place the letter that the known number represents in parentheses.

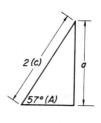

3. Label the side a to be solved for.

4. To determine the formula to use, place the known side c for use as the denominator of a fraction; then place the side a to be solved for as the numerator.

$$= \frac{a}{c}$$

5. Select the formula that includes the designations a and c.

$$\sin A = \frac{a}{c}$$

6. Substitute and solve the problem.

$$\sin 57° = \frac{a}{2}$$

$$.8387 \times 2 = \frac{a}{2} \times 2$$

7. The side a is 1.6774″, or $1\frac{43}{64}$″.

$$1.6774 = a$$

Other Trigonometric Tables

Some trigonometric tables contain columns for the cotangent, secant, and cosecant, in addition to the sine, cosine, and tangent. The formulas for these trigonometric functions are:

$$cotangent = \frac{adjacent\ side}{opposite\ side} \qquad secant = \frac{hypotenuse}{adjacent\ side}$$

$$cosecant = \frac{hypotenuse}{opposite\ side}$$

The formulas eliminate the need for two formulas in finding some of the unknowns.

Trade Problem

Problem: In the part in Fig. 65-1, assume that the hypotenuse c is 3.15 in. and that the base b is 2.61 in. Find the size of angle B.

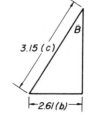

Solution:

1. Label the triangle with the known dimensions and the letters they represent.

2. Since the three formulas that can be used with the table (Table 61-1) are for angle A, we must first find angle A and subtract from 90° to obtain angle B.

3. Select the formula that contains both the known values, c and b.

$$\cos A = \frac{b}{c}$$

4. Substitute for c and b in the equation; then solve the equation.

$$= \frac{2.61}{3.15}$$

$$= .8286$$

$$\text{angle } A = 34°$$

5. The angle A is 34°.

6. The angle B is $(90° - 34°)$, or 56°.

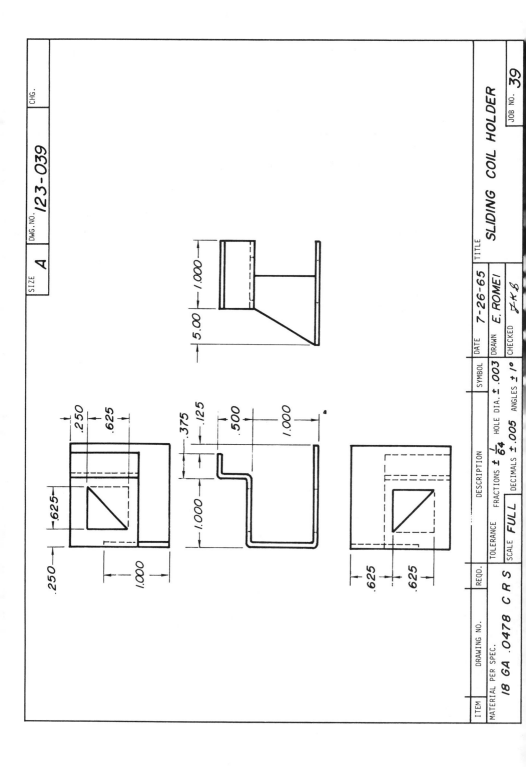

SIZE A | DWG. NO. 123-039 | CHG.

ITEM | DRAWING NO. | REQD. | DESCRIPTION
MATERIAL PER SPEC.
18 GA .0478 C R S

TOLERANCE FRACTIONS ± 1/64 HOLE DIA. ± .003
SCALE FULL DECIMALS ± .005 ANGLES ± 1°

SYMBOL | DATE 7-26-65 | TITLE
DRAWN E. ROME!
CHECKED FKB

SLIDING COIL HOLDER

JOB NO. 39

.250
.625
.625
.250
1.000

.375
.125
1.000
1.000
.500
1.000

.625
.625

5.00
1.000

Trigonometric Formulas
for Oblique Triangles

The precision sheet metalworker may be required to determine the missing dimension of an oblique triangle or the area of an oblique triangle (Fig. 66-1). This can be done by constructing a right triangle, but it is easier and quicker to use the formulas which will be explained later.

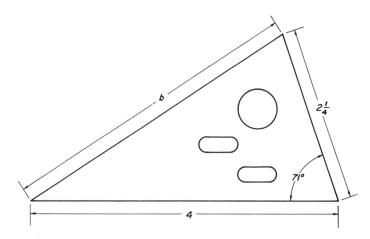

Fig. 66-1

269

An *oblique* triangle is a triangle that *does not have a right angle*. It includes both acute and obtuse angles. If any three dimensions of a triangle are known, with at least one being a side, the other parts can be computed. If only three angles are known, no actual triangle is determined, because three given angles can form many triangles. The angles of the three triangles are the same size, but the sides are of different lengths.

The formula to select depends on the known parts of the triangle. The possible situations include:

1. *Situation 1.* One side and two angles are known.
2. *Situation 2.* Two sides and an angle opposite one of the given sides are known.
3. *Situation 3.* Two sides and the included angle are known.
4. *Situation 4.* Three sides are known.

As mentioned previously, an oblique triangle can be solved by drawing a perpendicular from one of the vertices to the opposite side, forming two right triangles; then solve as for two right triangles. However, after establishing familiarity with the following equations, the following method will be much quicker.

The exact location of the sides a, b, and c in labeling is not important. Merely be sure that the angle opposite each side is labeled to correspond with the side. That is, the angle opposite side a is angle A, the angle opposite side b is angle B, etc.

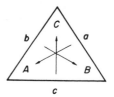

Remember the following formulas, which must be used in this unit. The table of natural trigonometric functions (Table 61-1) also must be used. The formulas are:

$$sine = \frac{opposite\ side}{hypotenuse}$$

$$cosine = \frac{adjacent\ side}{hypotenuse}$$

$$tangent = \frac{opposite\ side}{adjacent\ side}$$

Solving Situations 1 and 2

The following formulas are used in Situations *1* and *2:*

1. One side and two angles are known.

2. Two sides and an angle opposite one of the known sides are given.

Select the following equations for which three of the four values are known. Substitute these values and find the value desired. When two angles are given, the third angle can be found by subtracting the sum of the two angles from 180°.

$$\frac{a}{b} = \frac{sin\ A}{sin\ B} \qquad \frac{a}{c} = \frac{sin\ A}{sin\ C} \qquad \frac{b}{c} = \frac{sin\ B}{sin\ C}$$

Problem: If two angles A and B of a triangle are 110° and 36°, respectively, and the common adjacent side c is 1.750″, find the side b opposite the 36° angle B.

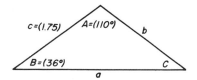

Solution:

1. Label a triangle with the letters, placing the known dimensions in parentheses.

2. Determine the third angle C.

$$\text{angle } C = 180° - 110° - 36°$$
$$= 34°$$

3. Select the formula with three of the four known values.

$$\frac{b}{c} = \frac{\sin B}{\sin C}$$

4. Substitute.

$$\frac{b}{1.75} = \frac{\sin 36°}{\sin 34°}$$
$$= \frac{.5878}{.5592}$$

5. Solve for the side b.

$$b = 1.75 \times \frac{.5878}{.5592}$$
$$= 1.75 \times 1.051$$
$$= 1.83925$$

6. The side b is *1.839 in.*

Solving Situation 3

The following formulas are used in Situation *3* in which two sides and the included angle are known. Select the equation with the letter representing the unknown value on the left-hand of the equal sign. These equations are used to find the third or unknown side.

$$a^2 = b^2 + c^2 - 2bc\ cos\ A$$
$$b^2 = a^2 + c^2 - 2ac\ cos\ B$$
$$c^2 = a^2 + b^2 - 2ab\ cos\ C$$

Problem: If two sides b and c of a triangle are 1.5″ and 1.4375″, respectively, and the included angle A is
  54°, find the third side c.

Solution:

1. Label a triangle with the letters;
   place the known dimensions in parentheses.

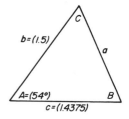

2. Determine the formula. $a^2 = b^2 + c^2 - 2bc \cos A$
3. Substitute the known values. $= 1.5^2 + 1.4375^2 -$
                                          $(2 \times 1.5 \times 1.4375 \times$
                                          $\cos 54°)$
4. Solve. $= 2.25 + 2.066 - 2.534$
                                        $a = \sqrt{1.782}$
                                          $= 1.334$

5. The third side a is *1.334 in.*

Solving Situation 4

The following formulas are used in Situation *4*, in which three sides are given.
Select the formula for the cosine of the angle to be computed. Then use the
table to find the size of the angle.

$$\cos\ A = \frac{b^2 + c^2 - a^2}{2bc}$$

$$\cos\ B = \frac{a^2 + c^2 - b^2}{2ac}$$

$$\cos\ C = \frac{a^2 + b^2 - c^2}{2ab}$$

Problem: If the three sides a, b, and c are
  1.5″, 1.875″, and 2″, respectively,
  find the size of the included angle B
  between sides a and c, which are 1.5″
  and 2″.

Solution:

1. Label a triangle with the letters; then place the known values in parentheses.

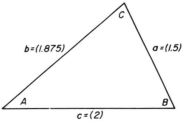

2. Determine the formula.

$$\cos B = \frac{a^2 + c^2 - b^2}{2ac}$$

3. Substitute the known values.

$$= \frac{1.5^2 + 2^2 - 1.875^2}{2 \times 1.5 \times 2}$$

4. Solve.

$$= \frac{2.25 + 4 - 3.516}{6}$$

$$= \frac{2.734}{6}$$

$$= .4557$$

$$\text{angle } B = 63°$$

5. Angle *B* is 63°.

Area of a Triangle

The area of a triangle also can be found by using trigonometry. To use the following formulas, two sides and the included angle must be known. If this is not given, it can be determined by using one or more of the formula mentioned previously. The formulas used to determine the area include:

$$area = \tfrac{1}{2} bc \sin A$$

$$= \tfrac{1}{2} ab \sin C$$

$$= \tfrac{1}{2} ac \sin B$$

Problems: If two sides *a* and *c* are 1.5″ and 2″ and the included angle *B* is 75°, find the area of the triangle.

Solution:

1. Label a triangle with the letters; place the known dimensions in parentheses.

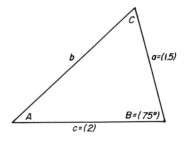

2. Determine the formula.

3. Substitute the known values.

4. Solve.

$$\text{area} = \tfrac{1}{2} \, ac \sin B$$
$$= \tfrac{1}{2} \times 1.5 \times 2 \times \sin 75°$$
$$= \tfrac{1}{2} \times 1.5 \times 2 \times .9659$$
$$= 1.5 \times .9659$$
$$= 1.44885$$

5. The area of the triangle is *1.449 sq in.*

Trade Problem

Problem: Find the length of the third side *b* of the part in Fig. 66-1.

Solution:

1. Label a triangle with the letters and place the known dimensions in parentheses.

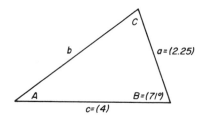

2. Determine the formula.

3. Substitute the known values.

4. Solve.

$$b^2 = a^2 + c^2 - 2ac \cos B$$
$$= 2.25^2 + 4^2 - (2 \times 2.25 \times 4 \times \cos 71°)$$
$$= 5.0625 + 16 - (18 \times .3256)$$
$$= 21.0625 - 5.8608$$
$$b = \sqrt{15.2017}$$
$$= 3.889$$

5. The third side *b* is *3.889 in.*

Constructing a Regular Polygon

The precision sheet metalworker may find it necessary to construct an object with all sides and all angles equal and with any given number of sides (Fig. 67-1).

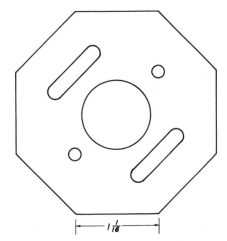

Fig. 67-1

In a regular polygon, all the sides are equal, and all the angles are equal. These polygons are:

275

Name of Polygon	Number of Sides
triangle (equilateral)	3
tetragon (square)	4
pentagon	5
hexagon	6
heptagon	7
octagon	8
nonagon	9
decagon	10
undecagon	11
dodecagon	12

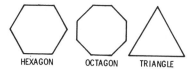

HEXAGON   OCTAGON   TRIANGLE

Constructing a Regular Polygon With a Given Number of Sides

The construction of triangles and squares has been explained previously. To construct any of the polygons, these steps must be followed:

Problem: Construct a regular heptagon (seven sides) with the sides equal to the given side or line *AB*.

Solution:

1. With point *A* as the center and a radius equal to line *AB,* draw a semicircle. Extend the line *AB* beyond the semicircle.

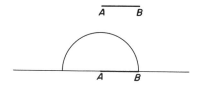

2. By trial and error (plus a protractor), divide the semicircle into seven equal parts.

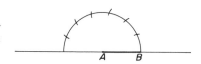

3. Extend lines from point *A* through the first five marks that divide the semicircle into seven parts. Be sure to extend the lines far enough. The lines are 1, 2, 3, 4, and 5. The number of marks used is equal to the number of sides minus 2 or (n — 2).

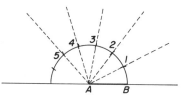

4. With point *A* as the center, measure the distance from point *A* to point *B*. Using this radius and point *B* as the center, make an arc on line *1*. Label this point *C*.

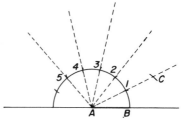

5. With point *C* as the center and the same radius, make an arc crossing line *2*. Continue until an arc has been marked on line *4*.

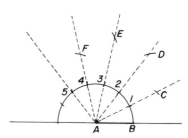

6. Connect these arcs. The arc on line *5* is the previously drawn semicircle.

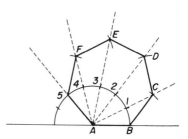

7. The completed diagram is a heptagon (seven equal sides and seven equal angles).

The radius of the semicircle is always equal to the required length of a side. The number of equal divisions required on the semicircle is always equal to the desired number of sides.

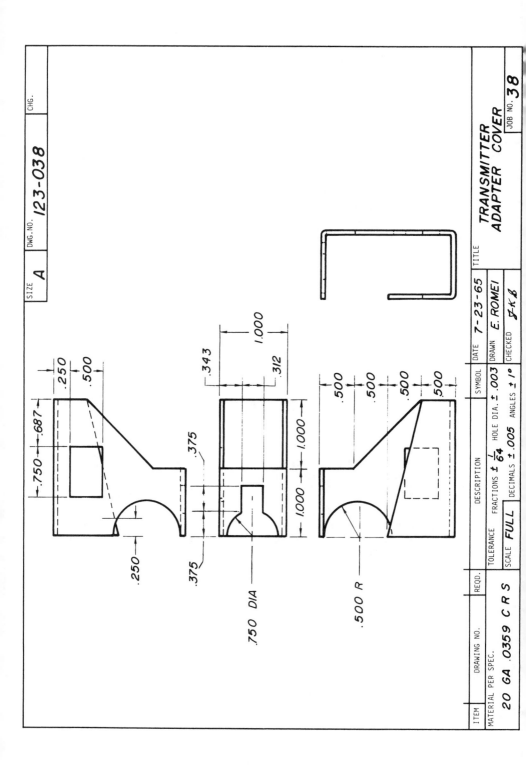

SIZE **A**   DWG. NO. **123-038**   CHG.

.250
.500
.750 — .687

.375

.250

.343

1.000

.312

1.000
1.000
.375

.750 DIA

.500
.500
.500
.500

.500 R

ITEM	REQD.	DRAWING NO.		

MATERIAL PER SPEC.
20 GA .0359 C R S

TOLERANCE	DESCRIPTION	SYMBOL	DATE **7-23-65**	TITLE
FRACTIONS $\pm \frac{1}{64}$ HOLE DIA. $\pm$ .003			DRAWN **E. ROMEI**	**TRANSMITTER**
SCALE **FULL**	DECIMALS $\pm$ .005 ANGLES $\pm 1°$		CHECKED $\mathcal{FKB}$	**ADAPTER COVER**

JOB NO. **38**

Introduction to
Area Measure

The area of a plane figure is the number of equal square units (inches, feet, etc.) that the part contains (Fig. 68-1). Calculation of a square area is useful to the precision sheet metalworker in determining the total material needed to complete a job.

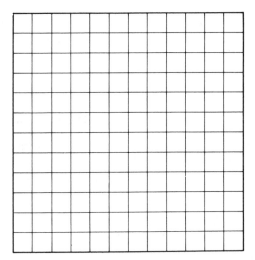

1 Sq Ft = 144 Sq In.

Fig. 68-1

279

The square is *1 square inch,* since each side is 1 inch. A *square foot* is a square in which each side is 1 foot. The abbreviations are *sq in.* and *sq ft* for square inch(es) and square foot (feet), respectively.

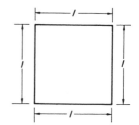

The drawing (Fig. 68-1) illustrates the number of square inches in 1 square foot. There are 12 inches in 1 foot; so there are 12 squares along each side of the square foot. By counting the total number of squares in the diagram, you will find that there are 144 square inches in 1 square foot and 9 square feet in 1 square yard:

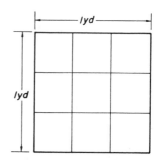

$$144 \text{ sq in.} = 1 \text{ sq ft}$$

$$9 \text{ sq ft} = 1 \text{ sq yd}$$

In determining the units of square measure, the formula will contain exponents. An *exponent* is a small numeral placed slightly above and at the right of a number or symbol. For example, in 4^2, the small number *2* is the exponent; the small numeral *2* means that the number *4* is to be multiplied by itself, as $4 \times 4 = 16$. The exponent indicates the number of times the number is to be multiplied by itself; for example:

$$4^2 \text{ (squared, or to the second power)} = 4 \times 4 = 16$$

$$2^3 \text{ (cubed, or to the third power)} = 2 \times 2 \times 2 = 8$$

$$5^4 \text{ (to the fourth power)} = 5 \times 5 \times 5 \times 5 = 625$$

When an exponent appears with a fraction, the presence of parentheses affects the meaning of the problem; for example:

$$\frac{3^2}{4} = \frac{3 \times 3}{4} = \frac{9}{4} = 2\frac{1}{4}$$

$$\left(\frac{3}{4}\right)^2 = \frac{3 \times 3}{4 \times 4} = \frac{9}{16}$$

An exponent used with a letter means that the letter is taken that many times:

$$b^3 = b \times b \times b$$

The problem cannot be solved further, unless the value b is known.

Numbers that contain exponents cannot be added, subtracted, multiplied, or divided, until the exponents have been eliminated:

$$3^2 + 3^2 \text{ is } not \text{ equal to } 6^2$$

$$3^2 + 3^2 = 9 + 9$$

$$= 18$$

Letters with exponents can be added, subtracted, multiplied, or divided with the exponents treated as follows:

1. *Adding.* The numerical factors are added; the exponents remain the *same.* $\qquad b^2 + 3b^2 = 4b^2$

2. *Subtracting.* The numerical factors are subtracted; the exponents remain the *same.* $\qquad 3a^3 - a^3 = 2a^3$

3. *Multiplying.* The numerical factors are multiplied; the exponents are *added.* $\qquad 2b^2 \times 5b^2 = 10b^4$

4. *Dividing.* The numerical factors are divided; the exponents are *subtracted.* $\qquad 6a^3 \div 3a^2 = 2a$

A letter or a number without an exponent is understood to have the exponent *1,* meaning to the first power or as it presently is:

$$a^1 = a; \text{ and } 3^1 = 3$$

Trade Problem

Problem 1: Find the weight of 3 sq ft of 16-ga. copper.

Solution:

1. Determine the chart to use (see Table 10 in Appendix).
2. Find the weight per sq ft of 16-ga. copper from the chart. It is 3.020 lb per sq ft.
3. The weight per sq ft, as indicated in the chart, is 3.020 lb. Multiply by the number of square feet required (3).

$$\begin{array}{r} 3.020 \\ \times \quad 3 \\ \hline 9.060 \end{array}$$

4. The *weight* of 3 sq ft of 16-ga. copper is *9.060 lb.*

Problem 2:   Find the weight of a 36″ ×
96″ sheet of 18-gauge stainless steel.

Solution:

1. Determine the chart to use (see
   Table 11 in Appendix).

2. Find the total number of square feet, $3 \times 8 = 24$
   since the chart gives weight per sq
   ft.

3. The weight per sq ft, as indicated in   2.1000
   the chart, is 2.1000. Multiply this   ×   24
   weight by the number of sq ft (24).   ‾‾‾‾‾‾
                                                                    84000
                                                                    42000
                                                                  ‾‾‾‾‾‾
                                                                  50.4000

4. A 36″ × 96″ sheet of 18-ga. stainless
   steel weighs *50.4 lb.*

Area of a Square

It is necessary for the precision sheet metalworker to be able to determine the area of a square if he is to determine the total material used to complete a job that is square in shape (Fig. 69-1).

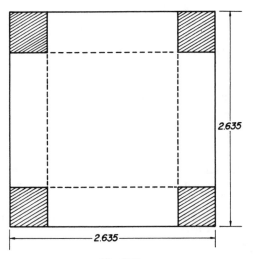

Fig. 69-1

To find the area of a square, multiply the dimensions of two sides. Since all the sides of a square are equal, a formula can be used with an exponent:

283

$A = s^2$ $A = $ area $s = $ length of a side

Examination of the square shows why $A = s^2$. The square is divided into equal units, each side containing four units. If we count the squares, the result is *16*. If we use the formula, we find:

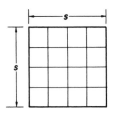

$$A = s^2$$
$$= 4^2$$
$$= 4 \times 4$$
$$= 16 \text{ square units}$$

If the length of a side is given in inches, the area will be in square inches; if the length is given in feet, the area will be in square feet.

Problem: Find the area of a square with 2¼″ sides.

Solution:

1. Select the formula. $A = s^2$
2. Substitute the known dimensions. $= (2¼)^2$, or 2.25^2
3. Solve. $= 2.25 \times 2.25$
                                                                          $= 5.0625$

4. The *area* of the square is *5.06 sq in.*

Trade Problem

Problem: Find the area of the total material to be used for the part in Fig. 69-1 (including waste).

Solution:

1. Select the formula. $A = s^2$
2. Substitute the known dimensions. $= 2.635^2$
3. Solve. $= 2.635 \times 2.635$
                                                                          $= 6.943225$

4. The *area* is *6.943 sq in.*

Area of a Rectangle
or a Parallelogram

The area of a rectangle or a parallelogram is needed by the precision sheet metalworker to determine the total material used to complete jobs that are rectangular or in the shape of a parallelogram (Fig. 70-1).

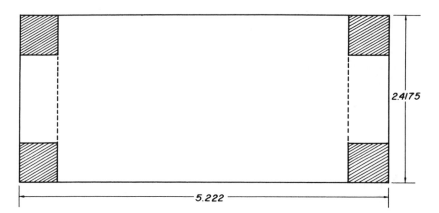

Fig. 70-1

The area of a rectangle is determined in a manner similar to that of a square, except that there are two dimensions to be considered. The longer dimension is

285

called the length l and the shorter dimension is called the width w. The area of a rectangle is the product of its length and its width. The formula is:

$$A = lw$$

in which

    A is the area.
    l is the length of the longer side.
    w is the length of shorter side.

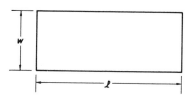

The rectangle shows how the formula is applied. The length of the rectangle is divided into five equal units, and its width is divided into two equal units. If we count the units, the result is 10 units. Using the formula:

$$A = lw$$
$$= 5 \times 2$$
$$= 10 \text{ square units}$$

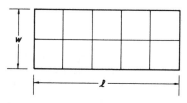

If the lengths of both sides are given in inches, the area will be in square inches; however, if one dimension is given in inches and one dimension in feet, the feet must be converted to inches before multiplying.

The area of a parallelogram can be determined in a similar manner. The illustration shows a parallelogram being converted into a rectangle. Therefore, the same formula is used; however, the length is called the base b and the width is called the height h. The formula is:

$$A = bh$$

in which
    b is the base.
    h is the height.

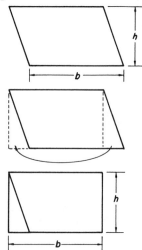

Trade Problem

Problem: Find the area of the total material (including waste) required for the part in Fig. 70-1.

Solution:

1. Select the formula.
2. Substitute.
3. Solve.
4. The *area* of the total material required is 12.624 sq in.

$A = lw$

$= 5.222 \times 2.4175$

$= 12.6241850$

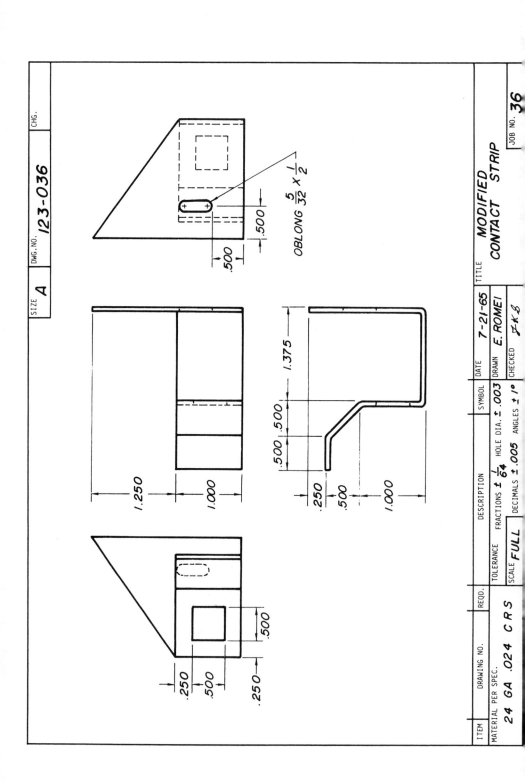

OBLONG $\frac{5}{32} \times \frac{1}{2}$

.500

.500

1.375

.500 .500

.250

.500

1.000

1.250

1.000

.500

.250 .500

.250

SIZE	DWG. NO.	CHG.
A	123-036	

ITEM	DRAWING NO.	REQD.	DESCRIPTION	SYMBOL	DATE 7-21-65	TITLE

MATERIAL PER SPEC.

24 GA .024 CRS

TOLERANCE FRACTIONS ± $\frac{1}{64}$ HOLE DIA. ± .003

SCALE FULL DECIMALS ± .005 ANGLES ± 1°

DRAWN E. ROMEI

CHECKED E.K.B.

MODIFIED
CONTACT STRIP

JOB NO. 36

Area of a Triangle

The precision sheet metalworker must determine the area of a triangle in determining the total material required to complete a job that contains a triangular shape (Fig. 71-1).

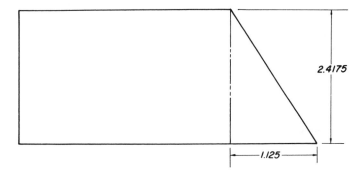

Fig. 71-1

The area of a triangle is equal to one-half the product of its base and its altitude. If lines are drawn parallel to the sides of a triangle, it will become a square, a rectangle, or a parallelogram. As shown in the diagrams, the area of the triangle is one-half the area of its corresponding square, rectangle, or parallelogram.

289

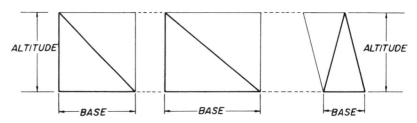

Therefore, the formula is:

$$A = \frac{ab}{2} \text{ or } \frac{1}{2} \, ab$$

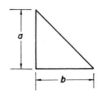

in which

    A is the area.
    a is the altitude.
    b is the base.

Problem: Find the area of a triangle in
    which the base is 5½″ and the alti-
    tude is 2¼″.

Solution:

  1. Select the formula. $A = \dfrac{ab}{2}$

  2. Substitute. $= \dfrac{5.5 \times 2.25}{2}$

  3. Solve. $= \dfrac{12.375}{2}$

                                         $= 6.1875$

  4. The *area* of the triangle is *6.1875 sq*
    in.

Trade Problem

Problem: Find the area of the triangular
    portion of the sheet of metal in Fig.
    71-1.

Solution:

1. Select the formula.

$$A = \frac{ab}{2}$$

2. Substitute.

$$= \frac{2.4175 \times 1.125}{2}$$

3. Solve.

$$= \frac{2.7096875}{2}$$

$$= 1.35488375$$

4. The *area* of the triangular portion of the sheet is *1.355 sq in.*

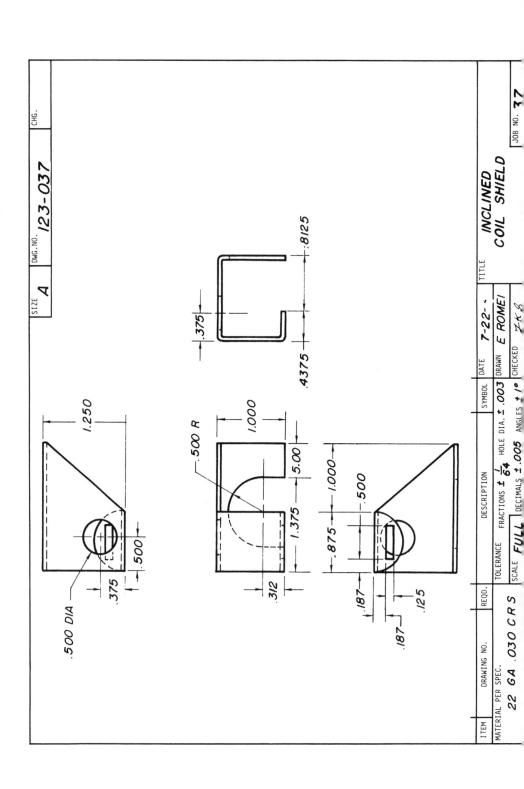

SIZE A   DWG. NO. 123-037   CHG.

1.250

.500 DIA

.375

.500

.500 R

1.000

1.375

5.00

.312

.375

.4375

.8125

1.000

.875

.500

.187

.187

.125

22 GA .030 CRS

ITEM	DRAWING NO.	REQD.	DESCRIPTION	SYMBOL	DATE 7-22-	TITLE

MATERIAL PER SPEC.

TOLERANCE   FRACTIONS ± 1/64   HOLE DIA. ± .003

DECIMALS ± .005   ANGLES ± 1°

SCALE FULL

DRAWN E ROMEI

CHECKED EK B

INCLINED COIL SHIELD

JOB NO. 37

Area of a Trapezoid

A metal part with the overall shape of a trapezoid is sometimes required in precision sheet metalwork; therefore, it is necessary that the worker be able to compute its area (Fig. 72-1).

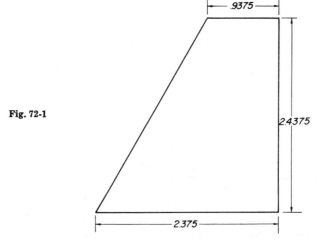

Fig. 72-1

The area of a trapezoid is equal to the sum of the lengths of the two bases divided by two, then multiplied by the altitude. The formula is:

$$A = \frac{(B + b)a}{2}$$

in which

    A is the area.

    a is the altitude.

    B is the length of the larger base.

    b is the length of the smaller base.

The statement that: "The sum of the lengths of the bases divided by two," which is used in the formula, is identical to the *average* of the two bases. By means of this equality, it can be shown that the formula also applies to trapezoids:

1. The line drawn through the trapezoid is equally distant from the two bases, and it results in the average length of the two bases.

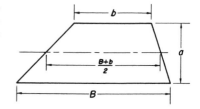

2. Next, a rectangle is formed, using the length of the line, which is the average length of the two bases.

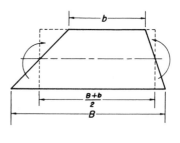

3. The two parts of the trapezoid which remain outside the formed rectangle fit exactly into the two blank spaces inside the rectangle.

4. Thus, the average length of the two bases, (B + b) ÷ 2, is equal to an equivalent rectangle. The altitude remains the same.

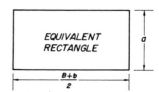

Problem: The bases of a trapezoid are 3.5″ and 1.25″. The altitude is 3″. Find the area, to the nearest 1000th.

Solution:

1. Select the formula.

$$A = \frac{(B + b)a}{2}$$

2. Substitute.

$$= \frac{(3.5 + 1.25)\,3}{2}$$

$$= \frac{4.75 \times 3}{2}$$

3. Solve.

$$= 7.125$$

4. The *area* of the trapezoid is *7.125 sq in.*

Trade Problem

Problem. Find the area of the part in Fig. 72-1.

Solution:

1. Select the formula.

$$A = \frac{(B + b)a}{2}$$

2. Substitute.

$$= \frac{(2.375 + .9375)\,2.4375}{2}$$

3. Solve.

$$= \frac{3.3125 \times 2.4375}{2}$$

$$= \frac{8.07421875}{2}$$

$$= 4.037109375$$

4. The *area* of the trapezoid is *4.037 sq in.*

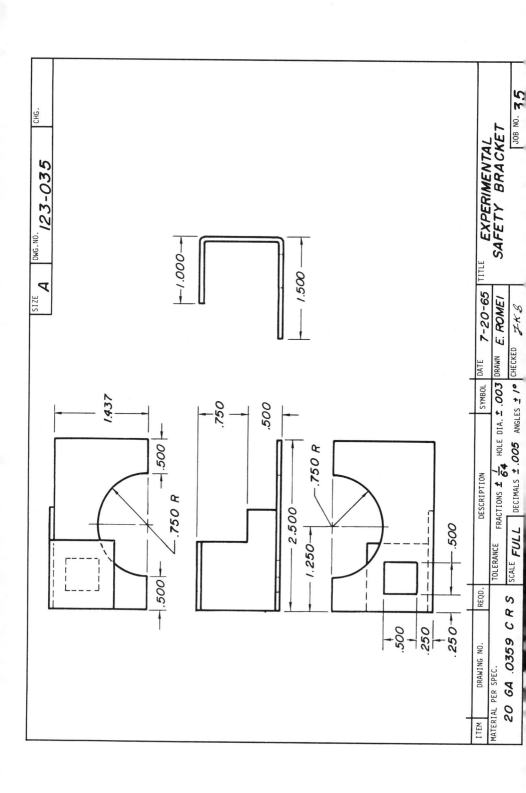

SIZE A DWG. NO. 123-035 CHG.

1.000
1.500

1.437
.500
.750 R
.500
.750
.500
2.500
.750 R
1.250
.500
.500
.250
.250

ITEM DRAWING NO. REQD. DESCRIPTION SYMBOL

MATERIAL PER SPEC.
20 GA .0359 C R S

TOLERANCE FRACTIONS ± 1/64 HOLE DIA. ± .003
SCALE FULL DECIMALS ± .005 ANGLES ± 1°

DATE 7-20-65 TITLE EXPERIMENTAL
DRAWN E. ROMEI SAFETY BRACKET
CHECKED ℐℋℬ JOB NO. 35

Area of a Circle

A flat circular part or plate is sometimes found in precision sheet metal-work. Therefore, it is essential to be able to determine its area (Fig. 73-1).

Fig. 73-1

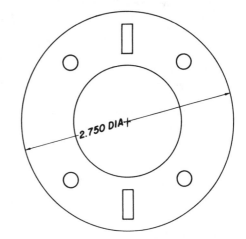

The area of a circle is equal to the product of pi (π) and the radius squared. The formula is:

$$A = \pi\, r^2$$

in which

A is the area.
r is the radius.

In some situations, the value *3.14* provides sufficient accuracy for the symbol π, but we will use the value *3.1416* for more accuracy. To demonstrate the formula, a circle is divided into an equal number of parts. Then these parts are arranged lengthwise.

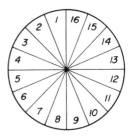

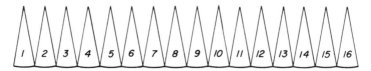

After spreading out the parts, they are arranged to fit together, as shown in the diagram. The diagram formed is approximately a parallelogram. The base of the formed parallelogram is equal to one-half the circumference of the circle (π d/2, or πr). The height of the newly formed

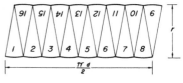

parallelogram is equal to the radius of the circle. Therefore, the area of the parallelogram is lw, in which l is eual to πr and w is equal to r. Therefore, the formula for the area of a circle is: $\pi r \times r$, or πr^2.

Problem: Find the area of a circle with
       a diameter of 4″.

Solution:

 1. Select the formula. $A = \pi r^2$
 2. Substitute. $= 3.1416 \times 2^2$
 3. Solve. $= 3.1416 \times 4$
                                             $= 12.5664$

 4. The *area* of the circle is
     12.566 sq in.

Trade Problem

Problem: Find the area of the part in
       Fig. 73-1.

Solution:

 1. Select the formula. $A = \pi r^2$

2. Substitute. $= 3.1416 \times 1.375^2$

3. Solve. $= 3.1416 \times 1.8906$

$= 5.93950896$

4. The *area* of the circular
   part is *5.9395 sq in.*

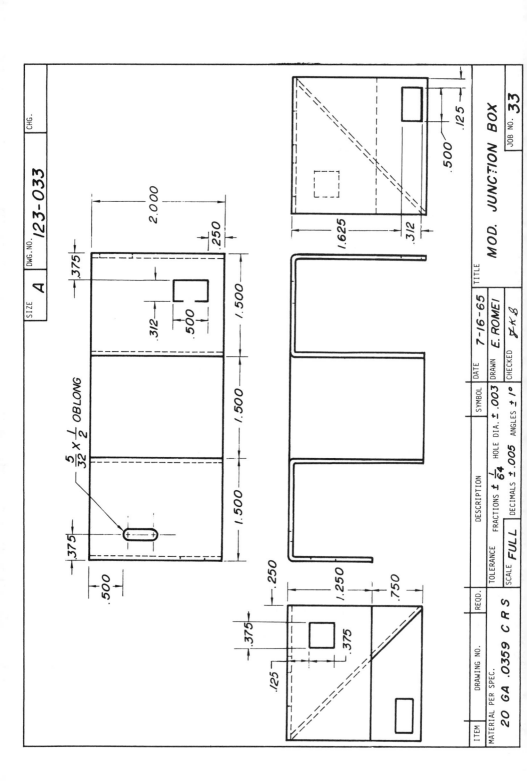

SIZE **A** | DWG. NO. **123-033** | CHG.

2.000
.250
.375
.312
.500
1.500
1.500
1.500
1.500
$\frac{5}{32} \times \frac{1}{2}$ OBLONG
.375
.500

1.625
.312
.500
.125

.250
1.250
.750
.375
.375
.125

MATERIAL PER SPEC.
20 GA .0359 C R S

ITEM | REQD. | DRAWING NO. | DESCRIPTION | SYMBOL | DATE **7-16-65** | TITLE

MOD. JUNCTION BOX

TOLERANCE FRACTIONS $\pm \frac{1}{64}$ HOLE DIA. $\pm$ .003
DECIMALS $\pm$ .005 ANGLES $\pm 1°$

SCALE **FULL**

DRAWN **E. ROMEI**
CHECKED

JOB NO. **33**

Addition and Subtraction of Square Areas

An object or metal part may consist of several plane figures. To find the total area of the part, the square areas of the various plane figures must be added. On the other hand, a part may contain one or more holes (Fig. 74-1). In this type of object, subtraction of the square areas from the total area is used to find the square area of the metal in the part.

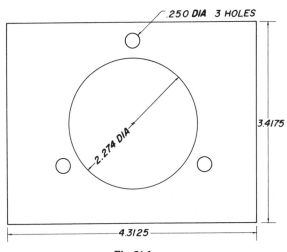

.250 *DIA* 3 HOLES

2.274 DIA

3.4175

4.3125

Fig. 74-1

301

Only like units can be added or subtracted. If one dimension is in square inches and the other is in square feet, the square feet must be converted to square inches, remembering that 144 sq in. = 1 sq ft. Then, the dimensions are either added or subtracted with the attached units (sq ft, sq in., etc.). For example:

$$\begin{array}{r} 3.145 \text{ sq in.} \\ + \underline{4.134 \text{ sq in.}} \\ 7.279 \text{ sq in.} \end{array}$$

Trade Problem

Problem: Find the area of the metal, in square inches, in the metal part in Fig. 74-1.

Solution:

1. The overall area of the part must be determined.

$$A = lw$$
$$= 4.3125 \times 3.4175$$
$$= 14.7380$$

2. The overall area is *14.7380 sq in.*
3. The area of the larger hole must be determined.

$$A = \pi r^2$$
$$= 3.1416 \times 1.137^2$$
$$= 3.1416 \times 1.2928$$
$$= 1.4759$$

4. The area of the *larger* circle is *1.4759 sq in.*
5. The area of one of the smaller circles must be determined.

$$A = \pi r^2$$
$$= 3.1416 \times .125^2$$
$$= 3.1416 \times .0156$$
$$= .0490$$

6. The area of each of the *smaller* circles is *.0490 sq in.*
7. The areas of the four circles are added.

$$\begin{array}{r} 1.4759 \text{ sq in.} \\ .0490 \text{ sq in.} \\ .0490 \text{ sq in.} \\ \underline{.0490 \text{ sq in.}} \\ 1.6229 \text{ sq in.} \end{array}$$

8. The *total area* of the four circles is *1.6229 sq in.*
9. The total area of the four circles must be subtracted from the area of the overall part.

$$\begin{array}{r} 14.7380 \text{ sq in.} \\ - \underline{1.6229 \text{ sq in.}} \\ 13.1151 \text{ sq in.} \end{array}$$

10. The *square area* of the metal in the part is *13.1151 sq in.*

Area of a
Semicircular-Sided Part

A flat part or plate may be square or rectangular in shape with a semicircle on each end. The precision sheet metalworker must be able to determine its area (Fig. 75-1).

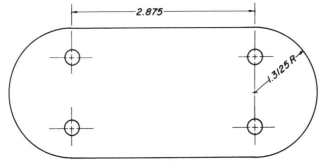

Fig. 75-1

Since a semicircular-sided plane figure consists of two half circles and a rectangle or square, finding its area involves finding the area of a circle and the area of a rectangle or square; then the two sums are added. Therefore, the formula is:

$$A = \pi r^2 + 2rw$$

303

in which

A is the area of the semicircular-sided
plane figure.
r is the radius.
w is the distance between the centers of
the semicircles.

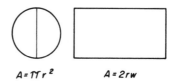

$A = \pi r^2$ $A = 2rw$

For the area of the rectangular or square part, 2r is used, rather than the
length symbol. Since there is a circular part at each end, the height is twice
the radius.

Problem: If the radius of each semicircle
is 2¼" and the distance between the
centers of the semicircles is 1¾",
find the total area of the plane
figure.

Solution:

1. Determine the formula. $A = \pi r^2 + 2rw$
2. Substitute the known dimensions. $= 3.1416 \times 2.25^2 +$
                                                  $2 (2.25 \times 1.75)$
3. Solve. $= 3.1416 \times 5.0625 +$
                                                  4.50×1.75
                                             $= 15.904 + 7.875$
                                             $= 23.779$

4. The *total area* of the plane figure is
   23.779 sq in.

Trade Problem

Problem: Find the total area of the semicircular-sided part in Fig. 75-1,
disregarding the holes in the part.

Solution:

1. Determine the formula. $A = \pi r^2 + 2rw$
2. Substitute the known dimensions. $= 3.1416 \times 1.3125^2 +$
                                                  $2 (1.3125 \times 2.875)$
3. Solve. $= 3.1416 \times 1.7227 +$
                                                  2.625×2.875
                                             $= 5.4120 + 7.5469$
                                             $= 12.9589$

4. The *total area* of the part is
   12.9589 sq in.

Area of a
Regular Polygon

The precision sheet metalworker may find it necessary to determine the area of a polygon with many sides (Fig. 76-1), especially when finding the volume of a part; this is explained later.

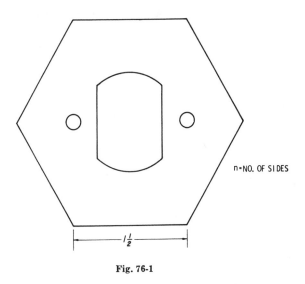

n = NO. OF SIDES

$1\frac{1}{2}$

Fig. 76-1

Definitions

1. An *inscribed circle* is the circle drawn inside a regular polygon; it barely touches a single point on each side.

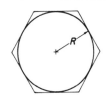

2. A *circumscribed circle* barely touches the vertex of each of the angles of a regular polygon.

In addition to determining the area of the polygons, we can use similar formulas to determine the area of both an inscribed circle and a circumscribed circle, when the length of a side is known.

Areas of Regular Polygons

The table (Table 76-1) gives the formulas for the area, the radius of an inscribed circle, and the radius of a circumscribed circle of a regular polygon. If the radius of the circle is known, the area can be found.

Table 76-1. Areas of Regular Polygons

Name of Regular Polygon	Number of sides (s)	Area of polygon	Radius of inscribed circle	Radius of circumscribed circle
Triangle	3	$0.433s^2$	$0.289s$	$0.577s$
Tetragon	4	$1.000s^2$	$0.500s$	$0.707s$
Pentagon	5	$1.720s^2$	$0.688s$	$0.851s$
Hexagon	6	$2.598s^2$	$0.866s$	$1.000s$
Heptagon	7	$3.634s^2$	$1.038s$	$1.152s$
Octagon	8	$4.828s^2$	$1.207s$	$1.307s$
Nonagon	9	$6.182s^2$	$1.374s$	$1.462s$
Decagon	10	$7.694s^2$	$1.539s$	$1.618s$
Undecagon	11	$9.366s^2$	$1.703s$	$1.775s$
Dodecagon	12	$11.196s^2$	$1.866s$	$1.932s$

Problem 1: Find the area of a nonagon with sides that are 1.2″.

Solution:

1. Determine the formula. $A = 6.182s^2$
2. Substitute the known dimensions. $= 6.182 \times 1.2^2$

3. Solve. $= 6.182 \times 1.44$

4. The *area* of the nonagon is $= 8.90208$
8.902 sq in.

Problem 2: Find the radius of the circumscribed circle of a pentagon, if a side is 1.2".

Solution:

1. Determine the formula. $r = .851s$
2. Substitute the known dimensions. $= .851 \times 1.2$
3. Solve. $= 1.0212$
4. The *radius* of the circumscribed circle is *1.02 in.*

Trade Problem

Problem: Find the area of the part in Fig. 76-1, disregarding the holes.

Solution:

1. Determine the formula. Since there are six sides, it is: $A = 2.598s^2$

2. Substitute the known dimensions. $= 2.598 \times 1.5^2$
3. Solve. $= 2.598 \times 2.25$
$= 5.84550$

4. The *area* of the part is *5.85 sq in.*

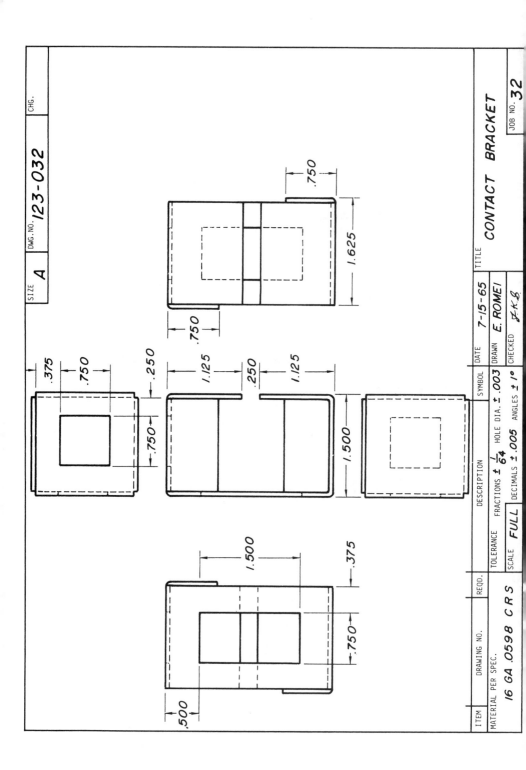

SIZE **A** | DWG. NO. **123-032** | CHG.

.375
.750
.250

.750

1.125
.250
1.125

1.500

.750

1.625

.750

1.500

.375

.750

.500

ITEM	DRAWING NO.	REQD.	DESCRIPTION	SYMBOL	DATE 7-15-65	TITLE *CONTACT BRACKET*
					DRAWN *E. ROMEI*	
					CHECKED *J.K.B.*	JOB NO. **32**

MATERIAL PER SPEC.
16 GA .0598 CRS

TOLERANCE   FRACTIONS ± $\frac{1}{64}$ HOLE DIA. ± .003
DECIMALS ± .005   ANGLES ± 1°

SCALE *FULL*

Units and Conversion
of Volume Measurements

Length is measured in units of *linear* measure; *area* is measured in units of *square* measure; and *volume* is measured in units of *cubic* measure. The measurement of the enclosed space is the volume. A precision sheet metalworker occasionally may be required to determine the volume of a part or container, then convert it to either liquid or dry measure to determine the volume of liquid or dry quantity that fits into it (Fig. 77-1).

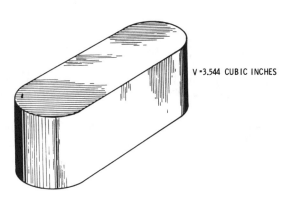

V =3.544 CUBIC INCHES

Fig. 77-1

309

A *cube* is a solid enclosed by six squares, all of the same size. The volume of an object or container is measured by the number of equal cubes it can contain, usually in *cubic inches*. In 1 cubic inch, all the dimensions are equal to 1 inch. There are three dimensions: length, width, and height. *Cubic feet* (cu ft) and *cubic yards* (cu yd) are used to measure the volumes of the larger objects or containers.

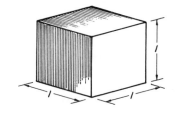

To find the number of cubic inches contained in 1 cubic foot, multiply: 12 in. × 12 in. × 12 in. = 1728 cu in. To prove this equation, you can count 12 layers in the diagram, and in the top layer you can count (12 × 12), or 144 units. Since there are 12 layers with 144 units, there are (144 units × 12) or 1728 units. Therefore, there are 1728 cu in. in 1 cu ft.

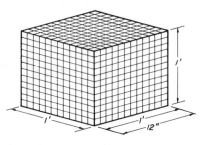

In a cube, all three measurements (length, width, and height) are identical. A rectangular solid shows the three dimensions.

A *cylindrical* solid has two dimensions: the altitude and either the diameter or the radius.

Dry Measure

To convert volume into dry measure, use the following:

Table	*Conversion Units*
2 pints = 1 quart (qt)	1 bu = 2150.42 cu in.
6 quarts = 1 peck (pk)	
4 pecks = 1 bushel (bu)	1 bu = 1.24446 cu ft

To convert:	*Do the following:*
cu in. to bu	divide cu in. by 2150.42
cu ft to bu	divide cu ft by 1.24446
bu to cu in.	multiply bu by 2150.42
bu to cu ft	multiply bu by 1.24446

Problem 1: Convert 5000 cu in. to bushels.

Solution:

1. From the conversion table, it is necessary to divide the cu in. (5000) by 2150.42.

$$2150.42 \overline{)5000.00000} \quad 2.325$$

2. The result is *2.325 bu.*

Problem 2:   Convert 2.5 bushels to cu ft.

Solution:

1. From the conversion table, it is necessary to multiply the bu (2.5) by 1.24446

$$\begin{array}{r} 1.24446 \\ \times\quad 2.5 \\ \hline 622230 \\ 248892 \\ \hline 3.111150 \end{array}$$

2. The result is *3.111 cu ft.*

Liquid Measure

To convert volume measure to liquid measure, use the following:

Table	*Conversion Units*
4 gills = 1 pint (pt)	1 cu ft = 7.48 U.S. gal
2 pints = 1 quart (qt)	231 cu in. = 1 U.S. gal
4 quarts = 1 gallon (gal)	31½ gal = 1 barrel (bbl)

To convert:	*Do the following:*
cu in. to gal	divide cu in. by 231
cu ft to gal	multiply cu ft by 7.48
gal to cu in.	multiply gal by 231
gal to cu ft	divide gal by 7.48

Problem 1:   Convert 200 cu in. to gallons.

Solution:

1. From the conversion table, it is necessary to divide the cu in. (200) by 231.

$$231\overline{\smash{\big)}\,200.0000}^{.8658}$$

2. The result is *.8658 gal.*

Problem 2:   Convert 200 cu ft to gallons.

Solution:

1. From the conversion table, it is necessary to multiply the given cu ft (200) by 7.48

$$\begin{array}{r} 7.48 \\ \times\ 200 \\ \hline 1496.00 \end{array}$$

2. The result is *1496 gal.*

Trade Problem

Problem: How many gallons of liquid are
        required to fill the container in Fig.
        77-1?

Solution

1. From the conversion table, it is
   necessary to divide the volume (3.544
   cu in.) by 231.
2. The number of *gallons* required is
   0.0153 gal.

$$231\ \overline{\smash{\big)}\ 3.5440} \quad {.0153}$$

Volume of a Square or Rectangular Part

A precision sheet metalworker must be able to determine the volume of a square or rectangular part to determine the volume of liquid or dry-measure units that it can hold (Fig. 78-1).

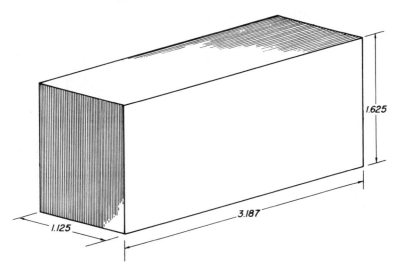

Fig. 78-1

313

Volume of a Cube

In a cube, all the sides are equal. Therefore, its volume is the length of one side cubed (to the third power). The formula is:

$$V = s^3$$

in which
  V is the volume.
  s is a side.

Problem: If a side of a cube is 2¼ in., find its volume.

Solution:

1. Determine the formula.
2. Substitute the known dimensions.
3. Solve.

4. The *volume* is *11.391 cu in.*

$V = s^3$
  $= 2.25^3$
  $= 2.25 \times 2.25 \times 2.25$
  $= 11.390625$

Volume of a Square Prism

In a *square* prism, the two ends are square and the four sides are rectangular. Therefore, the volume is the area of the square multiplied by the height. The formula is:

$$V = s^2h$$

in which
  V is the volume.
  s is a side of the square.
  h is the height of the rectangular part.

Problem: Find the volume of a square container in which each side is 2.5″ and the height is 4″.

Solution:

1. Determine the formula.
2. Substitute the known dimensions.
3. Solve.
4. The *volume* is *25 cu in.*

$V = s^2h$
  $= 2.5 \times 2.5 \times 4$
  $= 6.25 \times 4$
  $= 25$

Volume of a Rectangular Part

In a rectangular part, there are three different dimensions—length, width, and height. The *volume* is equal to the area of the base times the height. The *area* of the base is equal to the length times the width. The formula is:

$$V = lwh$$

in which
- V is the volume.
- l is the length of base.
- w is the width of base.
- h is the height of the part.

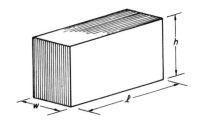

Problem: Find the volume of a rectangular container with length 4.5″, width 2″, and height 2.25″.

Solution:

1. Determine the formula.	V = lwh
2. Substitute the known dimensions.	= 4.5 × 2 × 2.25
3. Solve.	= 9.0 × 2.25
	= 20.25
4. The *volume* is *20.25 cu in.*	

Trade Problem

Problem: Find the volume of the part in Fig. 78-1.

Solution:

1. Determine the formula.	V = lwh
2. Substitute the known dimensions.	= 3.187 × 1.125 × 1.625
3. Solve.	= 3.585 × 1.625
	= 5.826
4. The *volume* is *5.826 cu in.*	

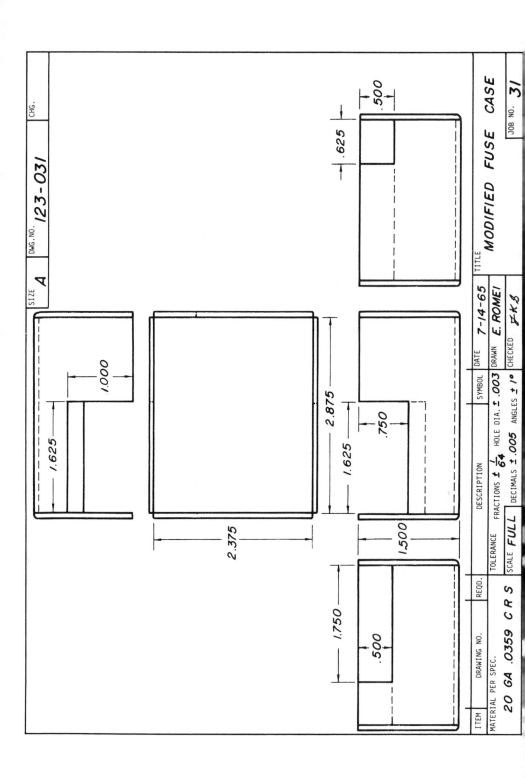

.500

.625

.500

1.000

1.625

2.875

2.375

.750

1.625

1.500

1.750

SIZE A | DWG. NO. 123-031 | CHG.

TITLE MODIFIED FUSE CASE

JOB NO. 31

DATE 7-14-65 | DRAWN E. ROMEI | CHECKED FKB

SYMBOL | DESCRIPTION

TOLERANCE FRACTIONS $\pm \frac{1}{64}$ HOLE DIA. $\pm$ .003

DECIMALS $\pm$ .005 ANGLES $\pm$ 1°

SCALE FULL

REQD.

DRAWING NO.

MATERIAL PER SPEC.
20 GA .0359 C R S

ITEM

Volume of
a Cylindrical or
Semicircular-Sided Part

A precision sheet metalworker may be required to determine the volume of liquid or dry measure units that a cylindrical or semicircular-sided part can hold (Fig. 79-1). Therefore, he is required to determine its volume first.

Fig. 79-1

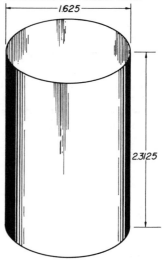

317

Volume of a Cylinder

In a cylinder, two dimensions are involved: The length and the diameter or radius. The *volume* is equal to the area of the circle times the length of the cylinder. The formula can be written in either of two ways:

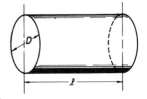

$$V = Al; \text{ or } V = \pi r^2 l$$

in which
  V is the volume.
  A is the area of the circle.
  l is the length.
  r is the radius of the circle.

Problem: If the diameter of a cylinder is 3″ and its height (or length) is 4¾″, find its volume.

Solution:

1. Determine the formula.
2. Substitute the known values.
3. Solve.

$\begin{aligned}
V &= \pi r^2 l \\
&= 3.1416 \times 1.5^2 \times 4.75 \\
&= 3.1416 \times 2.25 \times 4.75 \\
&= 3.1416 \times 10.6875 \\
&= 33.576
\end{aligned}$

4. The *volume* is *33.576 cu in.*

Volume of a Semicircular-Sided Part

In a semicircular-sided part, there are three dimensions: the radius of the semicircles, the width between the centers of the semicircles, and the height of the part. The volume is found by multiplying the area of the base by the height of the part. The formula is:

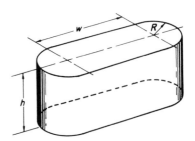

$$V = Ah; \text{ or } V = (\pi r^2 + 2rw)\, h$$

in which
  V is the volume.
  A is the area of the base.

r is the radius of the semicircle.
w is the distance between the semi-
    circles.
h is the height of the part.

Problem: Find the volume of a semicircu-
    lar-sided part with a radius of $1\frac{1}{2}''$,
    a width of $2''$, and a height of $2\frac{1}{2}''$.

Solution:

1. Determine the formula.

2. Substitute the known dimensions.

3. Solve.

$$V = (\pi\, r^2 + 2rw)\, h$$
$$= (3.1416 \times 1.5^2) + 2\,(1.5 \times 2) \times 2.5$$
$$= (7.0686 + 6.0)\, 2.25$$
$$= 13.0686 \times 2.25$$
$$= 29.404350$$

4. The *volume* is *29.4 cu in.*

Trade Problem

Problem: Find the volume of the part in
    Fig. 79-1.

Solution:

1. Determine the formula.

2. Substitute the known values.

3. Solve.

$$V = \pi\, r^2 l$$
$$= 3.1416 \times .8125^2 \times 2.3125$$
$$= 3.1416 \times .6602 \times 2.3125$$
$$= 2.0741 \times 2.3125$$
$$= 4.79635625$$

4. The *volume* of the part is *4.796 cu
    in.*

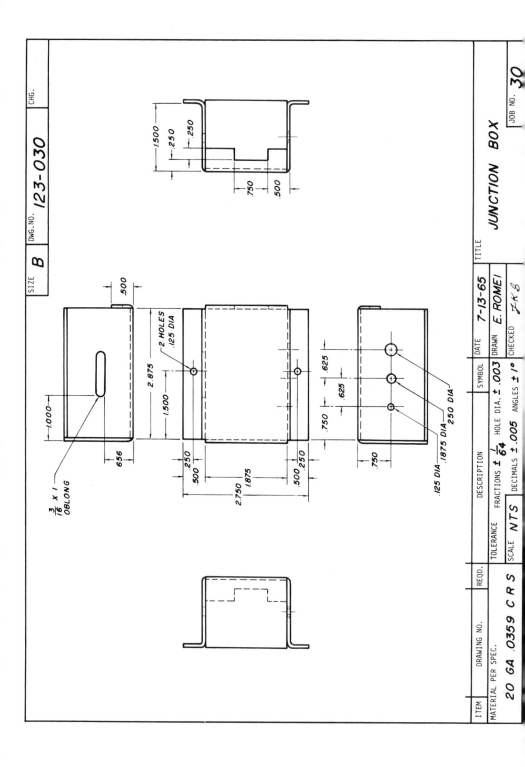

SIZE **B** DWG. NO. **123-030** CHG.

.500

2 HOLES
.125 DIA

2.875

1.500

.250
.500

2.750
1.875

1.000

.656

$\frac{3}{16} \times 1$
OBLONG

.625

.625

.750

.750

.125 DIA
.1875 DIA
.250 DIA

.500 .250

1.500
.250
.250
.750
.500

JUNCTION BOX

ITEM	DRAWING NO.	REQD.	DESCRIPTION	SYMBOL	DATE **7-13-65**	TITLE

MATERIAL PER SPEC.

20 GA .0359 CRS

TOLERANCE   FRACTIONS $\pm \frac{1}{64}$ HOLE DIA. $\pm$ .003
SCALE **NTS**   DECIMALS $\pm$ .005   ANGLES $\pm$ 1°

DRAWN **E. ROMEI**
CHECKED *J.K.B.*

JOB NO. **30**

Volume of a Sphere

In a sphere, every point on its surface is equidistant from an inside point. This inside point is the *center* of the sphere. The sphere is a round object. A precision sheet metalworker occasionally may deal with an object or part of this shape; therefore, it may be necessary to determine its volume. The object or part made by the precision sheet metalworker is usually a half sphere or hemisphere, as illustrated in Fig. 80-1.

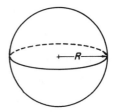

Fig. 80-1

The radius is the distance from the center of the sphere to its surface. The diameter is twice the radius. The diameter passes through the center of the sphere. If the sphere is cut into two parts along any diameter, the result is two hemispheres or two half spheres.

Before determining the volume of a sphere, we must be able to determine the surface area of the sphere. The *surface area* is equal to four times the area of a circle with the same radius. The formula is:

$$A_s = 4 \pi r^2$$

Problem: If the radius of a sphere is 2.5″,
        find its surface area.

Solution:

1. Determine the formula. $A_s = 4 \pi r^2$
2. Substitute the known values. $= 4 \times 3.1416 \times 2.5^2$
3. Solve. $= 12.5664 \times 6.25$
                                             $= 78.5400$

4. The *surface area* is *78.54 sq in.*

The volume of a sphere is equal to one-third the product of its surface area
and the radius. The formula is:

$$V = \frac{1}{3} A_s r; \text{ or } V = \frac{3}{4} \pi r^3$$

Problem: Find the volume of the above
        sphere with 2.5″ radius.

Solution:

1. Determine the formula. $V = \frac{1}{3} A_s r$

2. Substitute the known values. $= \frac{1}{3} \times 78.54 \times 2.5$

3. Solve. $= 26.18 \times 2.5$
                                             $= 65.450$

4. The *volume* of the sphere is *65.45
   cu in.*

Solution:

1. Determine the formula to use when $V = \frac{4}{3} \pi r^3$
   the surface area has not been deter-
   mined previously.

2. Substitute the known values. $= \frac{4}{3} \times 3.1416 \times 2.5^3$

3. Solve. $= 4.1888 \times 15.625$
                                             $= 65.450$

4. The *volume* of the sphere is *65.45
   cu in.*

Trade Problem

Problem: Find the volume of the hemisphere (half sphere) in Fig. 80-1.

Solution:

1. Determine the formula.

$$V = \frac{4}{3}\,\pi\, r^3 \div 2$$

2. Substitute the known values.

$$= \frac{4}{3} \times 3.1416 \times 1.5^3 \div 2$$

3. Solve.

$$= 4.1888 \times 3.375 \div 2$$
$$= 14.13720 \div 2$$
$$= 7.0686$$

4. The *volume* of the hemisphere is
7.07 cu in.

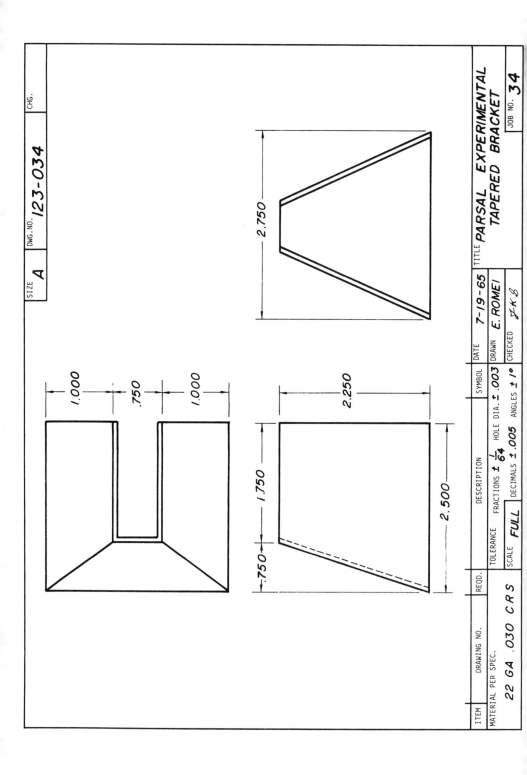

SIZE **A** | DWG. NO. **123-034** | CHG.

1.000   .750   1.000

2.750

2.250

1.750   .750

2.500

| ITEM | DRAWING NO. | REQD. | DESCRIPTION | SYMBOL | DATE 7-19-65 | TITLE *PARSAL EXPERIMENTAL* |
| | | | | | | *TAPERED BRACKET* |

MATERIAL PER SPEC.

22 GA .030 CRS

TOLERANCE   FRACTIONS $\pm \frac{1}{64}$ HOLE DIA. $\pm$ .003

SCALE **FULL**   DECIMALS $\pm$ .005   ANGLES $\pm 1°$

DRAWN E. ROMEI

CHECKED *J K B*

JOB NO. **34**

Volume of a
Tapered Part

The precision sheet metalworker occasionally may make a part with a taper. Therefore, it may be necessary for him to calculate the volume of a tapered part (Fig. 81-1).

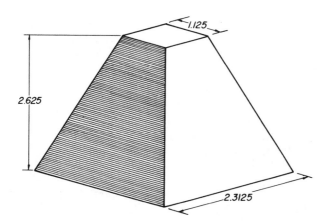

Fig. 81-1

Volume of a Pyramid or Cone

In a pyramid or cone, the height and the necessary dimension or dimensions for determining the area of a base are known. The volume is one-third the product of the height and the area of the base. The formula is:

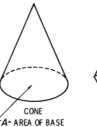 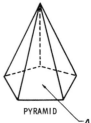

CONE

PYRAMID

A = AREA OF BASE

A

$$V = \frac{1}{3} A_b h$$

Problem: The base of a cone has a radius of 1.5″ and the height is 3.25″. Find its volume.

Solution:

1. Determine the formula.

    $$V = \frac{1}{3} A_b h$$

2. Substitute the formula for the area of the base, which is $A = \pi r^2$.

    $$= \frac{1}{3} \pi r^2 h$$

3. Substitute the known values.

    $$= \frac{1}{3} \times 3.1416 \times 1.5^2 \times 3.25$$

4. Solve.

    $$= 1.0472 \times 2.25 \times 3.25$$
    $$= 2.3562 \times 3.25$$
    $$= 7.657650$$

5. The *volume* is *7.658 cu in.*

Volume of a Portion of a Right Regular Pyramid or Cone

The volume of a portion of a pyramid or cone with the end or point removed is sometimes required. A regular pyramid or cone means that an imaginary line drawn from the center of the lower base to the center of the upper base is perpendicular to both bases. The formula for the volume is:

$$V = \frac{1}{3} h \left(A_b + A_t + \sqrt{A_b A_t} \right)$$

in which
  A_b is the area of lower base.
  A_t is the area of upper base.

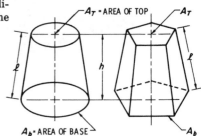

A_T = AREA OF TOP

A_T

A_b = AREA OF BASE

A_b

Problem: Find the volume of a portion of
a right regular cone with a lower
base having a 2″ radius and an upper
base having a 1″ radius. The height
is 2.5″.

Solution:

1. Determine the formula.

$$V = \frac{1}{3} h(A_b + A_t + \sqrt{A_b A_t})$$

2. Substitute the known values.

$$= \frac{1}{3} \times 2.5(3.1416 \times 2^2)$$
$$+ (3.1416 \times 1^2) + \sqrt{A_b A_t}$$

3. Solve.

$$= .833(12.5664 + 3.1416 +$$
$$\sqrt{12.5664 \times 3.1415})$$
$$= .833(12.5664 + 3.1416 +$$
$$\sqrt{39.4766})$$
$$= .833(12.5664 + 3.1416$$
$$+ 6.285)$$
$$= .883 \times 21.993$$
$$= 18.320169$$

4. The *volume* of the cone is *18.32 cu in.*

Trade Problem

Problem: Find the volume of the tapered
part in Fig. 81-1.

Solution:

1. Determine the formula:

$$V = \frac{1}{3} h(A_b + A_t + \sqrt{A_b A_t})$$

2. Substitute the known values.

$$= \frac{1}{3} \times 2.625(2.3125 \times 2.3125)$$
$$+ (1.125 \times 1.125) + \sqrt{A_b A_t}$$

3. Solve.

$$= .875(5.3477 + 1.2656 +$$
$$\sqrt{6.77})$$
$$= .875(5.3477 + 1.2656$$
$$+ 2.602)$$
$$= .875 \times 9.2153$$
$$= 8.0633875$$

4. The *volume* of the tapered part
is *8.06 cu in.*

Appendix

Table 1. Decimal Equivalents of Number Size Drills

No.	Size of Drill (inches)	No.	Size of Drill (inches)	No.	Size of Drill (inches)	No.	Size of Drill (inches)
1	.2280	21	.1590	41	.0960	61	.0390
2	.2210	22	.1570	42	.0935	62	.0380
3	.2130	23	.1540	43	.0890	63	.0370
4	.2090	24	.1520	44	.0860	64	.0360
5	.2055	25	.1495	45	.0820	65	.0350
6	.2040	26	.1470	46	.0810	66	.0330
7	.2010	27	.1440	47	.0785	67	.0320
8	.1990	28	.1405	48	.0760	68	.0310
9	.1960	29	.1360	49	.0730	69	.0292
10	.1935	30	.1285	50	.0700	70	.0280
11	.1910	31	.1200	51	.0670	71	.0260
12	.1890	32	.1160	52	.0635	72	.0250
13	.1850	33	.1130	53	.0595	73	.0240
14	.1820	34	.1110	54	.0550	74	.0225
15	.1800	35	.1100	55	.0520	75	.0210
16	.1770	36	.1065	56	.0465	76	.0200
17	.1730	37	.1040	57	.0430	77	.0180
18	.1695	38	.1015	58	.0420	78	.0160
19	.1660	39	.0995	59	.0410	79	.0145
20	.1610	40	.0980	60	.0400	80	.0135

Table 2. Decimal Equivalents of Letter Size Drills

Letter	Size of Drill (inches)	Letter	Size of Drill (inches)
A	.234	N	.302
B	.238	O	.316
C	.242	P	.323
D	.246	Q	.332
E	.250	R	.339
F	.257	S	.348
G	.261	T	.358
H	.266	U	.368
I	.272	V	.377
J	.277	W	.386
K	.281	X	.397
L	.290	Y	.404
M	.295	Z	.413

Table 3. American National Thread Dimensions

Size	NC	Threads Per Inch NF	NS	Decimal Equivalent of Tap Drill
0	....	80	....	.0469
1	....	....	56	.0550
1	64	....	....	.0595
1	....	72	....	.0595
2	56	....	....	.0700
2	....	64	....	.0700
3	48	....	....	.0785
3	....	56	....	.0820
4	....	....	32	.0820
4	....	....	36	.0860
4	40	....	....	.0890
4	....	48	....	.0935
5	....	....	36	.0980
5	40	....	....	.1015
5	....	44	....	.1040
6	32	....	....	.1065
6	....	....	36	.1110
6	....	40	....	.1130
8	....	....	30	.1285
8	32	....	....	.1360
8	....	36	....	.1360
8	....	....	40	.1405
10	24	....	....	.1495
10	....	....	28	.1540
10	....	....	30	.1570
10	....	32	....	.1590
12	24	....	....	.1770
12	....	28	....	.1820
12	....	....	32	.1850
1/4	20	....	....	.2010
1/4	....	28	....	.2130
5/16	18	....	....	.2570
5/16	....	24	....	.2720
3/8	16	....	....	.3125
3/8	....	24	....	.3320
7/16	14	....	....	.3680
7/16	....	20	....	.3906
1/2	13	....	....	.4219
1/2	....	20	....	.4531
9/16	12	....	....	.4844
9/16	....	18	....	.5156
5/8	11	....	....	.5312
5/8	....	18	....	.5781
3/4	10	....	....	.6562
3/4	....	16	....	.6875
7/8	9	....	....	.7656
7/8	....	14	....	.8125
7/8	....	....	18	.8281
1	8	....	....	.8750
1	....	14	....	.9375

Table 4. Tap Drill Sizes for Machine Screw Threads
(75% Depth of Thread)

Tap Size	Threads per Inch	Diameter Hole	Drill	Tap Size	Threads per Inch	Diameter Hole	Drill
0	80	.048	3/64	10	32	.160	21
1	72	.060	53	10	30	.158	22
1	64	.058	53	10	28	.155	23
2	64	.071	50	10	24	.149	25
2	56	.069	50	12	28	.181	14
3	56	.082	45	12	24	.175	16
3	48	.079	47	14	24	.201	7
4	48	.092	42	14	20	.193	10
4	40	.088	43	16	22	.224	2
4	36	.085	44	16	20	.219	7/32
5	44	.103	37	16	18	.214	3
5	40	.101	38	18	20	.245	D
5	36	.098	40	18	18	.240	B
6	40	.114	33	20	20	.271	I
6	36	.111	34	20	18	.266	17/64
6	32	.108	36	22	18	.292	L
7	36	.124	1/8	22	16	.285	9/32
7	32	.121	31	24	18	.318	O
7	30	.119	31	24	16	.311	5/16
8	36	.137	29	26	16	.337	R
8	32	.134	29	26	14	.328	21/64
8	30	.132	30	28	16	.363	23/64
9	32	.147	26	28	14	.354	T
9	30	.145	27	30	16	.289	25/64
9	24	.136	29	30	14	.380	V

Table 5. Tap Drill Sizes for Fractional Size Threads
(75% Depth Thread)
(American National Thread Form)

Tap Size	Threads per Inch	Diam. Hole	Drill	Tap Size	Threads per Inch	Diam. Hole	Drill
1/16	72	.049	3/64	1/2	20	.451	29/64
1/16	64	.047	3/64	1/2	13	.425	27/64
1/16	60	.046	56	1/2	12	.419	27/64
5/64	72	.065	52	9/16	27	.526	17/32
5/64	64	.063	1/16	9/16	18	.508	33/64
5/64	60	.062	1/16	9/16	12	.481	31/64
5/64	56	.061	53	5/8	27	.589	19/32
3/32	60	.077	5/64	5/8	18	.571	37/64
3/32	56	.076	48	5/8	12	.544	35/64
3/32	50	.074	49	5/8	11	.536	17/32
3/32	48	.073	49	11/16	16	.627	5/8
7/64	56	.092	42	11/16	11	.599	19/32
7/64	50	.090	43	3/4	27	.714	23/32
7/64	48	.089	43	3/4	16	.689	11/16
1/8	48	.105	36	3/4	12	.669	43/64
1/8	40	.101	38	3/4	10	.653	21/32
1/8	36	.098	40	13/16	12	.731	47/64
1/8	32	.095	3/32	13/16	10	.715	23/32
9/64	40	.116	32	7/8	27	.839	27/32
9/64	36	.114	33	7/8	18	.821	53/64
9/64	32	.110	35	7/8	14	.805	13/16
5/32	40	.132	30	7/8	12	.794	51/64
5/32	36	.129	30	7/8	9	.767	49/64
5/32	32	.126	1/8	15/16	12	.856	55/64
11/64	36	.145	27	15/16	9	.829	53/64
11/64	32	.141	9/64	1	27	.964	31/32
3/16	36	.161	20	1	14	.930	15/16
3/16	32	.157	22	1	12	.919	59/64
3/16	30	.155	23	1	8	.878	7/8
3/16	24	.147	26	1 1/16	8	.941	15/16
13/64	32	.173	17	1 1/8	12	1.044	1 3/64
13/64	30	.171	11/64	1 1/8	7	.986	63/64
13/64	24	.163	20	1 3/16	7	1.048	1 3/64
7/32	32	.188	12	1 1/4	12	1.169	1 11/64
7/32	28	.184	13	1 1/4	7	1.111	1 7/64
7/32	24	.178	16	1 5/16	7	1.173	1 11/64
15/64	32	.204	6	1 3/8	12	1.294	1 19/64
15/64	28	.200	8	1 3/8	6	1.213	1 7/32
15/64	24	.194	10	1 1/2	12	1.419	1 27/64
1/4	32	.220	7/32	1 1/2	6	1.338	1 11/32
1/4	28	.215	3	1 5/8	5 1/2	1.448	1 29/64
1/4	27	.214	3	1 3/4	5	1.555	1 9/16
1/4	24	.209	4	1 7/8	5	1.680	1 11/16
1/4	20	.201	7	2	4 1/2	1.783	1 25/32
5/16	32	.282	9/32	2 1/8	4 1/2	1.909	1 29/32
5/16	27	.276	J	2 1/4	4 1/2	2.034	2 1/2
5/16	24	.272	I	2 3/8	4	2.131	2 1/8
5/16	20	.264	17/64	2 1/2	4	2.256	2 1/4

Table 5. Tap Drill Sizes for Fractional Size Threads (Cont'd)
(75% Depth Thread)
(American National Thread Form)

Tap Size	Threads per Inch	Diam. Hole	Drill	Tap Size	Threads per Inch	Diam. Hole	Drill
5/16	18	.258	F	2 5/8	4	2.381	2 3/8
3/8	27	.339	R	2 3/4	4	2.506	2 1/2
3/8	24	.334	Q	2 7/8	3½	2.597	2 19/32
3/8	20	.326	21/64	3	3½	2.722	2 23/32
3/8	16	.314	5/16	3 1/8	3½	2.847	2 27/32
7/16	27	.401	Y	3 1/4	3½	2.972	2 31/32
7/16	24	.397	X	3 3/8	3¼	3.075	3 1/16
7/16	20	.389	25/64	3 1/2	3½	3.200	3 3/16
7/16	14	.368	U	3 5/8	3¼	3.325	3 5/16
1/2	27	.464	15/32	3 3/4	3	3.425	3 7/16
1/2	24	.460	29/64	4	3	3.675	3 11/16

Table 6. Approximate Pressures Required for Punching
Round Holes in Mild Sheet Steel

Gauge	28	26	24	22	20	18	16	14	12	10	5/32	3/16	1/4
Material Thickness	.0149	.0179	.0239	.0299	.0359	.0478	.0598	.0747	.1046	.1345	.1562	.1875	.250
Hole Diameter	Pressure in Tons												
.125	.2	.2	.2	.3	.4	.5	.6	.7	1.0	1.3	1.5	1.8	2.5
.1875	.2	.3	.4	.4	.5	.7	.9	1.1	1.5	2.0	2.3	2.8	3.7
.250	.3	.4	.5	.6	.7	.9	1.2	1.5	2.1	2.6	3.1	3.7	4.9
.3125	.4	.4	.6	.7	.9	1.2	1.5	1.8	2.6	3.3	3.8	4.6	6.1
.375	.4	.5	.7	.9	1.1	1.4	1.8	2.2	3.1	4.0	4.6	5.5	7.4
.4375	.5	.6	.8	1.0	1.2	1.6	2.1	2.6	3.6	4.6	5.4	6.4	8.6
.500	.6	.7	.9	1.2	1.4	1.9	2.3	2.9	4.1	5.3	6.1	7.4	9.8
.5625	.7	.8	1.1	1.3	1.6	2.1	2.6	3.3	4.6	5.9	6.9	8.3	11.1
.625	.7	.9	1.2	1.5	1.8	2.4	2.9	3.7	5.1	6.6	7.7	9.2	12.3
.6875	.8	1.0	1.3	1.6	1.9	2.6	3.2	4.0	5.7	7.3	8.4	10.1	13.5
.750	.9	1.1	1.4	1.8	2.1	2.8	3.5	4.4	6.2	7.9	9.2	11.0	14.7
.8125	1.0	1.1	1.5	1.9	2.3	3.1	3.8	4.8	6.7	8.6	10.0	12.0	16.0
.875	1.1	1.2	1.6	2.1	2.5	3.3	4.1	5.1	7.2	9.2	10.7	12.9	17.2
.9375	1.2	1.3	1.8	2.2	2.6	3.5	4.4	5.5	7.7	9.9	11.5	13.8	18.4
1.0000	1.3	1.4	1.9	2.4	2.8	3.8	4.7	5.9	8.2	10.6	12.3	14.7	19.6

Table 7.　Standard Gauges and Equivalents in Decimals of an Inch

Ga. No.	Aluminum & Brass Brown & Sharpe	Steel Sheets Mfrs. Std.
6.0's	.5800	....
5-0's	.5165	....
4-0's	.4600	....
3-0's	.4096	....
2-0's	.3648	....
0	.3249	....
1	.2893	....
2	.2576	....
3	.2294	.2391
4	.2043	.2242
5	.1819	.2092
6	.1620	.1943
7	.1443	.1793
8	.1285	.1644
9	.1144	.1495
10	.1019	.1345
11	.0907	.1196
12	.0808	.1046
13	.0720	.0897
14	.0641	.0747
15	.0571	.0673
16	.0508	.0598
17	.0453	.0538
18	.0403	.0478
19	.0359	.0418
20	.0320	.0359
21	.0285	.0329
22	.0253	.0299
23	.0226	.0269
24	.0201	.0239
25	.0179	.0209
26	.0159	.0179
27	.0142	.0164
28	.0126	.0149
29	.0113	.0135
30	.0100	.0120
31	.0089	.0105
32	.0080	.0097
33	.0071	.0090
34	.0063	.0082

Table 8. Galvanized Carbon Steel Sheets

Galv. Sheet Ga. No.	Approx. Lb Per Sq Ft	Thick. Equiv., Galv. Sht. Ga. No.	Thick. Range (inches)
8	7.03125	0.1681	.1756-.1607
9	6.40625	0.1532	.1606-.1458
10	5.78125	0.1832	.1457-1308
11	5.15625	0.1233	.1307-.1159
12	4.53125	0.1084	.1158-.1009
13	3.90625	0.0934	.1008-.0860
14	3.28125	0.0785	.0859-.0748
15	2.96875	0.0710	.0747-.0673
16	2.65625	0.0635	.0672-.0606
17	2.40625	0.0575	.0605-.0546
18	2.15625	0.0516	.0545-.0486
19	1.90625	0.0456	.0485-.0426
20	1.65625	0.0396	.0425-.0382
21	1.53125	0.0366	.0381-0352
22	1.40625	0.0336	.0351-.0322
23	1.28125	0.0306	.0321-.0292
24	1.15625	0.0276	.0291-.0262
25	1.03125	0.0247	.0261-.0232
26	0.90625	0.0217	.0231-.0210
27	0.84375	0.0202	.0209-.0195
28	0.78125	0.0187	.0194-.0180
29	0.71875	0.0172	.0179-.0165
30	0.65625	0.0157	.0164-.0150
31	0.59375	0.0142	.0149-.0138
32	0.56250	0.0134	.0137-.0131

Table 9. Sheet Gauges and Weights
(Steel and Nonferrous Metals)

Carbon Steel			Brass		
USS Ga. No.	Revised Mfrs. Thickness for Steel	Approx. Wt. per sq ft (lb)	B & S Ga. No.	Dec. Thickness	Approx. Wt. per sq ft (lb)
1	.28125	11.250	1	.2893	12.75
2	.26562	10.620	2	.2576	11.35
3	.2391	10.000	3	.2294	10.11
4	.2242	9.375	4	.2043	9.002
5	.2092	8.750	5	.1819	8.015
6	.1943	8.125	6	.1620	7.138
7	.1793	7.500	7	.1443	6.358
8	.1644	6.875	8	.1285	5.662
9	.1494	6.250	9	.1144	5.041
10	.1345	5.625	10	.1019	4.490
11	.1196	5.000	11	.1907	3.997
12	.1046	4.375	12	.0808	3.560
13	.0897	3.750	13	.0720	3.173
14	.0747	3.125	14	.0641	2.825
15	.0673	2.812	15	.0571	2.516
16	.0598	2.500	16	.0508	2.238
17	.0538	2.250	17	.0453	1.996
18	.0478	2.000	18	.0403	1.776
19	.0418	1.750	19	.0359	1.582
20	.0359	1.500	20	.0320	1.410
21	.0329	1.375	21	.0285	1.256
22	.0299	1.250	22	.0254	1.119
23	.0269	1.125	23	.0226	.9958
24	.0239	1.000	24	.0201	.8857
25	.0209	.875	25	.0179	.7887
26	.0179	.750	26	.0159	.7006
27	.0164	.687	27	.0142	.6257
28	.0149	.625	28	.0126	.5552
29	.0135	.562	29	.0113	.4979
30	.0120	.500	30	.0100	.4406

Table 10. Sheet Gauges and Weights
(Steel and Nonferrous Metals)

Copper			Zinc		
Stubs Ga. No.	Dec. Thickness	Approx. Wt. per sq ft (lb)	Zinc Ga. No.	Dec. Thickness	Approx. Wt. per sq ft (lb)
1	.300	13.94	24	.125	4.70
2	.284	13.20	23	.100	3.75
3	.259	12.04	22	.090	3.37
4	.238	11.07	21	.080	3.00
5	.220	10.22	20	.070	2.62
6	.203	9.420	19	.060	2.25
7	.180	8.360	18	.055	2.06
8	.165	7.660	17	.050	1.87
9	.148	6.875	16	.045	1.68
10	.134	6.225	15	.040	1.50
11	.120	5.575	14	.036	1.35
12	.109	5.065	13	.032	1.20
13	.095	4.410	12	.028	1.05
14	.083	3.860	11	.024	.90
15	.072	3.338	10	.020	.75
16	.065	3.020	9	.018	.67
17	.058	2.695	8	.016	.60
18	.049	2.280	7	.014	.52
19	.042	1.952	6	.012	.45
20	.035	1.627	5	.010	.37
21	.032	1.484	4	.008	.30
22	.028	1.302	3	.006	.22
23	.025	1.162	....	....	....
24	.022	1.022	....	....	....
25	.020	.928	....	....	....

Table 11. Stainless Steel Sheets
(Approximate Weights and Thicknesses)

Thickness Ordering Range (inches)			Gauge No.	Approximate Decimal Parts of an Inch	Av. Wt. per sq ft (in lb) for Chrome Nickel— Cold-Rolled Alloys
.161	to	.176	8	.17187	7.2187
.146	to	.160	9	.15625	6.5625
.131	to	.145	10	.140625	5.9062
.115	to	.130	11	.125	5.5200
.009	to	.114	12	.109375	4.5937
.084	to	.098	13	.09375	3.9374
.073	to	.083	14	.078125	3.2812
.066	to	.072	15	.0703125	2.9521
.059	to	.065	16	.0625	2.6250
.053	to	.058	17	.05625	2.3625
.047	to	.052	18	.050	2.1000
.041	to	.046	19	.04375	1.8375
.036	to	.040	20	.0375	1.5750
.033	to	.035	21	.034375	1.4437
.030	to	.032	22	.03125	1.3125
.027	to	.029	23	.028125	1.1813
.024	to	.026	24	.025	1.0500
.0199	to	.023	25	.021875	0.9187
.0178	to	.0198	26	.01875	0.7875
.0161	to	.0177	27	.0171875	0.7218
.0146	to	.0160	28	.015625	0.6562
.0131	to	.0145	29	.0140625	0.5906
.0115	to	.0130	30	.0125	0.5250
.0105	to	.0114	31	.0109375	0.4594
.0095	to	.0104	32	.01015625	0.4265

Table 12. Square Root Table (for numbers 1.0 to 9.99)

No.	0	1	2	3	4	5	6	7	8	9
1.0	1.000	1.005	1.010	1.015	1.020	1.025	1.030	1.034	1.039	1.044
1.1	1.049	1.054	1.058	1.063	1.068	1.072	1.077	1.082	1.086	1.091
1.2	1.095	1.100	1.105	1.109	1.114	1.118	1.122	1.127	1.131	1.136
1.3	1.140	1.145	1.149	1.153	1.158	1.162	1.166	1.170	1.175	1.179
1.4	1.183	1.187	1.192	1.196	1.200	1.204	1.208	1.212	1.217	1.221
1.5	1.225	1.229	1.233	1.237	1.241	1.245	1.249	1.253	1.257	1.261
1.6	1.265	1.269	1.273	1.277	1.281	1.285	1.288	1.292	1.296	1.300
1.7	1.304	1.308	1.311	1.315	1.319	1.323	1.327	1.330	1.334	1.338
1.8	1.342	1.345	1.349	1.353	1.356	1.360	1.364	1.367	1.371	1.375
1.9	1.378	1.382	1.386	1.389	1.393	1.396	1.400	1.404	1.407	1.411
2.0	1.414	1.418	1.421	1.425	1.428	1.432	1.435	1.439	1.442	1.446
2.1	1.449	1.453	1.456	1.459	1.463	1.466	1.470	1.473	1.476	1.480
2.2	1.483	1.487	1.490	1.493	1.497	1.500	1.503	1.507	1.510	1.513
2.3	1.517	1.520	1.523	1.526	1.530	1.533	1.536	1.539	1.543	1.546
2.4	1.549	1.552	1.556	1.559	1.562	1.565	1.568	1.572	1.575	1.578
2.5	1.581	1.584	1.587	1.591	1.594	1.597	1.600	1.603	1.606	1.609
2.6	1.612	1.616	1.619	1.622	1.625	1.628	1.631	1.634	1.637	1.640
2.7	1.643	1.646	1.649	1.652	1.655	1.658	1.661	1.664	1.667	1.670
2.8	1.673	1.676	1.679	1.682	1.685	1.688	1.691	1.694	1.697	1.700
2.9	1.703	1.706	1.709	1.712	1.715	1.718	1.720	1.723	1.726	1.729
3.0	1.732	1.735	1.738	1.741	1.744	1.746	1.749	1.752	1.755	1.758
3.1	1.761	1.764	1.766	1.769	1.772	1.775	1.778	1.780	1.783	1.786
3.2	1.789	1.792	1.794	1.797	1.800	1.803	1.806	1.808	1.811	1.814
3.3	1.817	1.819	1.822	1.825	1.828	1.830	1.833	1.836	1.838	1.841
3.4	1.844	1.847	1.849	1.852	1.855	1.857	1.860	1.863	1.865	1.868
3.5	1.871	1.873	1.876	1.879	1.881	1.884	1.887	1.889	1.892	1.895
3.6	1.897	1.900	1.903	1.905	1.908	1.910	1.913	1.916	1.918	1.921
3.7	1.924	1.926	1.929	1.931	1.934	1.936	1.939	1.942	1.944	1.947
3.8	1.949	1.952	1.954	1.957	1.960	1.962	1.965	1.967	1.970	1.972
3.9	1.975	1.977	1.980	1.982	1.985	1.987	1.990	1.992	1.996	1.997
4.0	2.000	2.002	2.005	2.007	2.010	2.012	2.015	2.107	2.020	2.022
4.1	2.025	2.027	2.030	2.032	2.035	2.037	2.040	2.042	2.045	2.047
4.2	2.049	2.052	2.054	2.057	2.059	2.062	2.064	2.066	2.069	2.071
4.3	2.074	2.076	2.078	2.081	2.083	2.086	2.088	2.090	2.093	2.095
4.4	2.098	2.100	2.102	2.105	2.107	2.110	2.112	2.114	2.117	2.119
4.5	2.121	2.124	2.126	2.128	2.131	2.133	2.135	2.138	2.140	2.142
4.6	2.145	2.147	2.149	2.152	2.154	2.156	2.159	2.161	2.163	2.166
4.7	2.168	2.170	2.173	2.175	2.177	2.179	2.182	2.184	2.186	2.189
4.8	2.191	2.193	2.195	2.198	2.200	2.202	2.205	2.207	2.209	2.211
4.9	2.214	2.216	2.218	2.220	2.223	2.225	2.227	2.229	2.232	2.334
5.0	2.236	2.238	2.241	2.243	2.245	2.247	2.249	2.252	2.254	2.256
5.1	2.258	2.261	2.263	2.265	2.267	2.269	2.272	2.274	2.276	2.278
5.2	2.280	2.283	2.285	2.287	2.289	2.291	2.293	2.296	2.298	2.300
5.3	2.302	2.304	2.307	2.309	2.311	2.313	2.315	2.317	2.319	2.322
5.4	2.324	2.326	2.328	2.330	2.332	2.335	2.337	2.339	2.341	2.343
No.	0	1	2	3	4	5	6	7	8	9

Table 12. (Cont'd) Square Root Table (for numbers 1.0 to 9.99)

No.	0	1	2	3	4	5	6	7	8	9
5.5	2.345	2.347	2.349	2.352	2.354	2.356	2.358	2.360	2.363	2.364
5.6	2.366	2.369	2.371	2.373	2.375	2.377	2.379	2.381	2.383	2.385
5.7	2.387	2.390	2.392	2.394	2.396	2.398	2.400	2.402	2.404	2.406
5.8	2.408	2.410	2.412	2.415	2.417	2.419	2.421	2.423	2.425	2.427
5.9	2.429	2.431	2.433	2.435	2.437	2.439	2.441	2.443	2.445	2.447
6.0	2.449	2.452	2.454	2.456	2.458	2.460	2.462	2.464	2.466	2.468
6.1	2.470	2.472	2.474	2.476	2.478	2.480	2.482	2.484	2.486	2.488
6.2	2.490	2.492	2.494	2.496	2.498	2.500	2.502	2.504	2.506	2.508
6.3	2.510	2.512	2.514	2.516	2.518	2.520	2.522	2.524	2.526	2.528
6.4	2.530	2.532	2.534	2.536	2.538	2.540	2.542	2.544	2.546	2.548
6.5	2.550	2.551	2.553	2.555	2.557	2.559	2.561	2.563	2.565	2.567
6.6	2.569	2.571	2.573	2.575	2.577	2.579	2.581	2.583	2.585	2.587
6.7	2.588	2.590	2.592	2.594	2.596	2.598	2.600	2.602	2.604	2.606
6.8	2.608	2.610	2.612	2.613	2.615	2.617	2.619	2.621	2.623	2.626
6.9	2.627	2.629	2.631	2.632	2.634	2.636	2.638	2.640	2.642	2.644
7.0	2.646	2.648	2.650	2.651	2.653	2.655	2.657	2.659	2.661	2.663
7.1	2.665	2.666	2.668	2.670	2.672	2.674	2.676	2.678	2.680	2.681
7.2	2.683	2.685	2.687	2.689	2.691	2.693	2.694	2.696	2.698	2.700
7.3	2.702	2.704	2.706	2.707	2.709	2.711	2.713	2.715	2.717	2.718
7.4	2.720	2.722	2.724	2.726	2.728	2.729	2.731	2.733	2.735	2.737
7.5	2.793	2.740	2.742	2.744	2.746	2.748	2.750	2.751	2.753	2.755
7.6	2.757	2.759	2.760	2.762	2.764	2.766	2.768	2.769	2.771	2.773
7.7	2.775	2.777	2.778	2.780	2.782	2.784	2.786	2.787	2.789	2.791
7.8	2.793	2.795	2.796	2.798	2.800	2.802	2.804	2.805	2.807	2.809
7.9	2.811	2.812	2.814	2.816	2.818	2.820	2.821	2.823	2.825	2.827
8.0	2.828	2.830	2.832	2.834	2.835	2.837	2.839	2.841	2.843	2.844
8.1	2.846	2.848	2.850	2.851	2.853	2.855	2.857	2.858	2.860	2.862
8.2	2.864	2.865	2.867	2.869	2.871	2.872	2.874	2.876	2.877	2.879
8.3	2.881	2.883	2.884	2.886	2.888	2.890	2.891	2.893	2.895	2.897
8.4	2.898	2.900	2.902	2.903	2.905	2.907	2.909	2.910	2.912	2.914
8.5	2.915	2.917	2.919	2.921	2.922	2.924	2.926	2.927	2.929	2.931
8.6	2.933	2.934	2.936	2.938	2.939	2.941	2.943	2.944	2.946	2.948
8.7	2.950	2.951	2.953	2.955	2.956	2.958	2.960	2.961	2.963	2.965
8.8	2.966	2.968	2.970	2.972	2.973	2.975	2.977	2.978	2.980	2.982
8.9	2.983	2.985	2.987	2.988	2.990	2.992	2.993	2.995	2.997	2.998
9.0	3.000	3.002	3.003	3.005	3.007	3.008	3.010	3.012	3.013	3.015
9.1	3.017	3.018	3.020	3.022	3.023	3.025	3.027	3.028	3.030	3.032
9.2	3.033	3.035	3.036	3.038	3.040	3.041	3.043	3.045	3.046	3.048
9.3	3.050	3.051	3.053	3.055	3.056	3.058	3.059	3.061	3.063	3.064
9.4	3.066	3.068	3.069	3.071	3.072	3.074	3.076	3.077	3.079	3.081
9.5	3.082	3.084	3.085	3.087	3.089	3.090	3.092	3.094	3.095	3.097
9.6	3.098	3.100	3.102	3.103	3.105	3.106	3.108	3.110	3.111	3.113
9.7	3.114	3.116	3.118	3.119	3.121	3.122	3.124	3.126	3.127	3.129
9.8	3.130	3.132	3.134	3.135	3.137	3.138	3.140	3.142	3.143	3.145
9.9	3.146	3.148	3.150	3.151	3.153	3.154	3.156	3.158	3.159	3.161
No.	0	1	2	3	4	5	6	7	8	9

Table 13. Square Root Table (for numbers 10 to 54.9)

No.	0	1	2	3	4	5	6	7	8	9
10	3.162	3.178	3.194	3.209	3.225	3.240	3.256	3.271	3.286	3.302
11	3.317	3.332	3.347	3.362	3.376	3.391	3.406	3.421	3.435	3.450
12	3.464	3.479	3.493	3.507	3.521	3.536	3.550	3.564	3.578	3.592
13	3.606	3.619	3.633	3.647	3.661	3.674	3.688	3.701	3.715	3.728
14	3.742	3.755	3.768	3.782	3.795	3.808	3.821	3.834	3.847	3.860
15	3.873	3.886	3.899	3.912	3.924	3.937	3.950	3.962	3.975	3.987
16	4.000	4.012	4.025	4.037	4.050	4.062	4.074	4.087	4.099	4.111
17	4.123	4.135	4.147	4.159	4.171	4.183	3.195	4.207	4.219	4.231
18	4.243	4.254	4.266	4.278	4.290	4.301	4.313	4.324	4.336	4.347
19	4.359	4.370	4.383	4.393	4.405	4.416	4.427	4.438	4.450	4.461
20	4.472	4.483	4.494	4.506	4.517	4.528	4.539	4.550	4.561	4.572
21	4.583	4.593	4.604	4.615	4.626	4.637	4.648	4.658	4.669	4.680
22	4.690	4.701	4.712	4.722	4.733	4.743	4.754	4.764	4.775	4.785
23	4.796	4.806	4.817	4.827	4.837	4.848	4.858	4.868	4.879	4.889
24	4.899	4.909	4.919	4.930	4.940	4.950	4.960	4.970	4.980	4.990
25	5.000	5.010	5.020	5.030	5.040	5.050	5.060	5.070	5.079	5.089
26	5.099	5.109	5.119	5.128	5.138	5.148	5.158	5.167	5.177	5.187
27	5.196	5.206	5.215	5.225	5.235	5.244	5.254	5.263	5.273	5.282
28	5.292	5.301	5.310	5.320	5.329	5.339	5.348	5.357	5.367	5.376
29	5.385	5.394	5.404	5.413	5.422	5.431	5.441	5.450	5.459	5.468
30	5.477	5.486	5.495	5.505	5.514	5.523	5.532	5.541	5.550	5.559
31	5.568	5.577	5.586	5.595	5.604	5.612	5.621	5.630	5.639	5.648
32	5.657	5.666	5.675	5.683	5.692	5.701	5.710	5.718	5.727	5.736
33	5.745	5.573	5.762	5.771	5.779	5.788	5.797	5.805	5.814	5.822
34	5.831	5.840	5.848	5.857	5.865	5.875	5.882	5.891	5.899	5.908
35	5.916	5.925	5.933	5.941	5.950	5.958	5.967	5.975	5.983	5.992
36	6.000	6.008	6.017	6.025	6.033	6.042	6.050	6.058	6.066	6.075
37	6.083	6.091	6.099	6.107	6.116	6.124	6.132	6.140	6.148	6.156
38	6.164	6.173	6.181	6.189	6.197	6.205	6.213	6.221	6.229	6.237
39	6.245	6.253	6.261	6.269	6.277	6.285	6.293	6.301	6.309	6.317
40	6.325	6.332	6.340	6.348	6.356	6.364	6.372	6.380	6.387	6.395
41	6.403	6.411	6.419	6.427	6.434	6.442	6.450	6.458	6.465	6.473
42	6.481	6.488	6.496	6.504	6.512	6.519	6.527	6.535	6.542	6.550
43	6.557	6.565	6.573	6.580	6.588	6.595	6.603	6.611	6.618	6.626
44	6.633	6.641	6.648	6.656	6.663	6.671	6.678	6.686	6.693	6.701
45	6.708	6.716	6.723	6.731	6.738	6.745	6.753	6.760	6.768	6.775
46	6.782	6.790	6.797	6.804	6.812	6.819	6.826	6.834	6.841	6.848
47	6.856	6.863	6.870	6.877	6.885	6.892	6.899	6.907	6.914	6.921
48	6.928	6.935	6.943	6.950	6.957	6.964	6.971	6.979	6.986	6.993
49	7.000	7.007	7.014	7.021	7.029	7.036	7.043	7.050	7.057	7.064
50	7.071	7.078	7.085	7.092	7.099	7.106	7.113	7.120	7.127	7.134
51	7.141	7.148	7.155	7.162	7.169	7.176	7.183	7.190	7.197	7.204
52	7.211	7.218	7.225	7.232	7.239	7.246	7.253	7.259	7.266	7.273
53	7.280	7.287	7.294	7.301	7.308	7.314	7.321	7.328	7.335	7.342
54	7.348	7.355	7.362	7.369	7.376	7.382	7.389	7.396	7.403	7.409
No.	0	1	2	3	4	5	6	7	8	9

Unit **82**

Using the Hand-Held Calculator
to Solve Sheet Metal Problems

A calculator is a computing machine that performs either basic arithmetic or advanced mathematical processes, depending on the complexity of the calculator. All calculators can compute the four basic processes of addition, subtraction, multiplication and division. More complex calculators are frequently identified as engineering and scientific calculators, advanced business calculators or electronic slide rules.

Basic Characteristics and Terminology

Small calculators are classified as "hand-held" or "pocket calculators." Larger calculators are called "desk-top" models. Some calculators are battery-operated; others depend on electric power, some use solar power, or a combination.

Calculators are modern and compact with integrated electronic circuits that perform the mathematical operations; they are also called electronic calculators. They have many advantages over the older forms of calculators, slide rules and other business machines. These advantages include:

- Portable, lightweight, small size

- High calculating speed and great accuracy

- Relatively inexpensive

Every calculator has a keyboard. The keyboard consists of ten keys for the basic numerals 0 through 9, a decimal point, and a set of keys for instructions relating to mathematical processes (+, -, x, etc.) that are to be performed.

The mechanical operations of the keys provide the input. The internal computer component performs the mathematical processes. The answer appears as a numerical value in the display.

Four-Function Calculator

The electronic calculator that performs the four basic processes is identified as a four-function type. This four-function calculator can also be used to perform higher mathematical processes, by breaking down the problem into a series of steps using the four basic processes. The four-function calculator usually includes a percent (%) key.

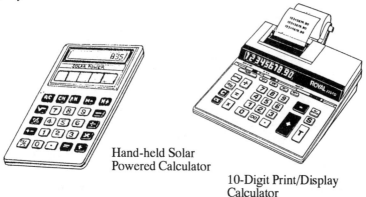

Hand-held Solar
Powered Calculator

10-Digit Print/Display
Calculator

Programmable Calculator

Programmable (scientific/engineering) calculators contain a memory for storing numbers and instructions to perform a sequence of operations. The sequence in which the instructions are to be executed forms a program for solving the problem.

The program can be stored in the calculator. Problems are entered and all mathematical processes are performed according to the specified sequence. The program may be repeated any number of times using different numerical values. At the completion of the problem, the correct answer is displayed. There is no further operator input into the problem. This type of hand-held calculator is not discussed further in this section, as it is not generally needed in sheet metal work.

On-Off

Some calculators have a combined on-off key to depress, some have a small lever on the side to push back and forth, and some are "solar" powered. Solar calculators need to be exposed to bright enough sunlight or electric light.

Calculator Display

The numerical readout on a calculator is provided in a lighted display. The display serves three main purposes:

- Answers to problems presented as a series of numerical digits in the readout display.

- Intermediate numbers used in a calculation; as they are entered on the keyboard, they are displayed as a visual check.

- Information is fed back to a calculator operator through the display.

The number of digits in a calculator display varies. Six-digit displays are found in the less expensive models. Twenty or more digits are used in scientific calculators where greater precision is required. A practical common electronic calculator has an eight-digit display.

Some accounting, scientific and other business applications require a printed record. Printing calculators are either designed with impact ribbon, heat-sensitive mechanical printers, ink injectors or other mechanisms to produce a record tape.

Clear Functions

Use these keys to clear or erase the results of previous calculations and to reset the calculator to 0. Press the clear C key on many calculators to reset the entire contents. The circuitry of the calculator is then set to start a new calculation.

Use the clear-entry CE or clear-display CD key to correct number-entry errors without losing any previous part of the problem. Press the CE key to erase an error and to enter a correct value.

On some models, you use the same key C/CE to perform the clear-error and total-erase processes. Correct an entry mistake by pressing the C/CE key once and entering the correct value. This does not disturb any previously recorded data or calculations. Press the C/CE twice to erase all previous data and to clear the machine completely, ready to start a new calculation.

Basic Mathematical Processes Using a Four-Function Calculator

You can use any calculator for the four basic arithmetical processes of addition, subtraction, multiplication, and division. To do this, you must know the basic arithmetic principles and their application. The calculator simplifies all of the basic processes, ensures accurate results, and saves time.

Addition - The following are two basic methods of addition, the second being quicker and recommended.

Method #1 for addition:

Step 1 -   Turn the calculator on.

Step 2 -   Press the numbered key or keys to enter the first numerical value. Read
           the visual display to check that the correct number is entered.

Step 3 -   Press the + key.

Step 4 -   Press the numbered keys to enter the second numerical value. Read the
           visual display for accuracy.

Step 5 -   Press the = key. This value is the sum of the two numbers entered.

Step 6 -   Press the + key. If you do not, you will lose the previous result and be
           starting a new problem.

Step 7 -   Press the numbered keys to enter the third value. Read the visual display
           to check the entry.

Step 8 -   Press the = key. This is the sum of all three numbers. The display
           shows this sum.

Method #2 for addition:

This eliminates pressing both the = and + keys after each entry. Pushing just the
+ key serves the function of displaying the accumulated answer when adding.
Follow these steps (for adding three numbers):

Step 1 -   Turn the calculator on.

Step 2 -   Press the numbered keys to enter the first numerical value. Check this
           number on the display.

Step 3 -   Press the + key.

Step 4 -   Press the numbered keys to enter the second numerical value. Check the
           display.

Step 5 -   Press the + key. The sum appears on display now.

Step 6 -   Enter the third value. Again, check this entry on the display.

Step 7 -   Press the + key or the = key. Read the answer.

Decimal Values

If whole numbers and decimal values are involved, use the decimal key to enter the value. The floating-decimal point within the calculator automatically indicates the position of the decimal point in the answer.

Checking Your Answers

The best way to check your answers is to do the same problem again. If you get the same answer, it is probably correct. If not, do the problem another time or two. If you have a printing calculator, check the printout to see that you entered the correct numbers.

Subtraction - You can also use the same two methods just described for addition for problems involving subtraction. Instead of pressing the + key, press the - key.

Correcting an Error

If you have entered a wrong numerical value, follow these two steps to correct the error:

1. Press the C or CE/C key once. This removes the last entry.

2. Enter the correct value on the keyboard. Check this value on the display. Then proceed with the remaining part of the problem. If you have already pushed a function key (such as + or -) after the wrong numeric entry, you cannot clear just the wrong entry; you must clear the entire problem and start the problem again.

Multiplication and Division

To multiply 14 x 2 x 14 follow these steps:

        Step 1 - press the keys for the number 14.
        Step 2 - press the multiply key (x).
        Step 3 - press the number 2 key.
        Step 4 - press the equal key (=). The answer 28 will display.
        Step 5 - press the multiply key again.*
        Step 5 - press the keys for the number 14.
        Step 6 - press the equal key (=) again. The answer 392 will display.

        *To do repeat multiplication, merely press the = key again and it will automatically multiply the current answer by 14 again, and keep on doing this.

To divide, follow these steps with the problem 48 ÷ 2 ÷ 2.

Step 1 - press the keys for the number 48.
Step 2 - press the ÷ key.
Step 3 - press the number 2 key.
Step 4 - press the = key. The answer 24 will display.
Step 5 - press the ÷ key again. *
Step 6 - press the number 2 key again.
Step 7 - press the = key again. The answer 12 will appear.

* to do repeat division (since we are continuing to divide by 2), you can just depress the = key again. Each time you use the = key, it will automatically divide by 2 again.

Combination or Series of Arithmetic Processes

Many practical problems require a series of mathematical processes. These series are generally called chain calculations. They may involve addition, subtraction, multiplication and division in varying combinations. In a chain process, one of the goals is to solve the problem without having to store or write down any more intermediate values than necessary. Another goal is to keep the number of key strokes to a minimum, especially significant if you are doing a large volume of calculations.

These are the rules of order to follow in carrying out chain calculations.

1. Complete multiplication and division calculations before addition and subtraction. For example, solve the problem:

$7 + 9 \times 5 - 8 \div 4$

Do the multiplication(9 x 5 = 45) and division (8 ÷ 4 = 2) processes first. Then add 7 + 45 - 2 = 50.

If the rules of order were not followed and you put the numbers in the calculator in sequence, an incorrect answer is obtained. For example:

$7 + 9 \times 5 \div 4 = 20$

2. Group portions of the problem before starting any mathematical processes. In the previous example, group the values and use parentheses to show it more clearly.

$7 + (9 \times 5) - (8 \div 4) = 50$

Conversions of Fractions and Decimals

You need to use calculators with whole numbers or decimal parts. Therefore, it is necessary to convert a fractional quantity to its equivalent decimal value in order to use a calculator. Do this easily by dividing the numerator by the denominator. For example, to convert the fraction 7/64 to its equivalent decimal value, divide the numerator 7 by the denominator 64 = .109375.

To convert a decimal quantity to its fractional value, determine the number of decimal digits in the fractional part. A quantity like 1.104 indicates that there are 104 thousandths in the fractional part. So, the 1.104 quantity, written as a mixed number is 1 104/1000.

You can reduce this fraction by dividing by the greatest common divisor which is 8 in this example. Expressed in its lowest terms, the 104/1000 = 13/125 since 8 goes into 104 evenly 13 times; and 8 goes into 1000 evenly 125 times.

The Memory Function

Many calculators have registers (memories) that store values to be used in a problem. The registers are fixed because they are permanently tied into the calculator circuitry.

More complex calculators have greater capacity with long multi-digit numbers that normally require complex calculations. Auxiliary memory is provided in such calculators to permit the storage and later recall of intermediate calculation results.

You use separate keys to control the auxiliary memory features on the calculator demonstrated here. A CM key (clear memory) is sometimes labeled MC; it clears all numbers from the memory register, returning to zero. Pressing the RM key (sometimes labeled as MR) recalls and transfers the value in memory to the accumulator register. The numerical value is displayed and is ready to be used in the next calculation without clearing or disturbing the memory accumulation.

You can calculate the sum or difference of the memory content and the content of the accumulator register by pressing the appropriate M+ or M- key. The sum or difference calculation then remains in the memory. To store a number in memory, first clear the memory with the CM key; then press the M+ key to transfer the accumulator contents to the memory. Use the M- key to subtract numbers in display from memory. On some calculators, when using memory, a decimal place appears in the furthest left ("left-most") digit space.

1. **Problem:** Convert 3/16" to a decimal to the nearest thousandth.

    Solution:

    Enter the number 3 in the calculator.

    Depress the divide key.

    Enter the number 16 in the calculator.

    Depress the equal = key.

    The answer is .1875

    Rounded to the nearest thousandth (3 decimal places), the answer is .188"

2. **Problem:** Find the surface area of a speaker face plate that is 3.25 by 4.625" to the nearest hundredth.

    Solution:

    Formula: length x width   l x w

    Enter the number 3.25 in the calculator.

    Depress the multiply x key

    Enter the number 4.625

    Depress the equal = key

    The answer is 15.031 or 15.03 sq. in.

3. **Problem:** Find the surface area of an 18" round tube with a diameter of 6".

    Solution:

    Formula: π DL   (3.1416 x diameter x length)

    Enter the number 3.1416 then the multiply key x.

    Enter the number that represents the diameter (6") and then the multiply key again.

    Enter the number that represents the length (18").

Then depress the equal sign = to get 339.2928

The answer is 339.2928 sq. in.

If you need the answer in sq. ft., as is needed in problem 4, divide the answer by 144 (the number of square inches in a square foot).

The answer is 2.356 sq. ft.

4. **Problem:** Find the weight of the metal for Problem #3 using 22 gauge galvanized iron.

Solution:

Formula: A x pounds per square foot

Enter the answer from problem #3 which is 2.356 sq. ft., then depress the multiply key.

Then enter the pounds per square foot for galvanized iron (1.40625 from the chart).

Depress the equal key =

The answer is 3.313125 pounds or 3.31 lb.

5. **Problem:** Find the area of a triangle in which the base is 5 1/2" and the altitude is 2 1/4".

Solution:

Formula $A = \dfrac{ab}{2}$

Insert the correct numbers $A = \dfrac{5.5 \times 2.25}{2}$

Multiply 5.5 x 2.25 = 12.375

Divide 12.275 by 2 = 6.1875

answer = 6.1875 sq. in. is the area of the triangle

6. **Problem:** Find the total length of the metal required for the part illustrated.

   Solution:

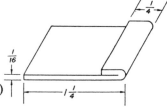

   The formula is   length = l + h - 1/2 t

                   t = metal thickness

                   l = length of metal

                   h = hem length (single hem)

   Substitute dimensions: 1 1/4 + 1/4 - (1/2 x 1/16)

   Convert the fractions to decimals: 1.25 + .25 - (.5 x .0625)

   Solve the problem in parentheses first   .5 x .0626 = .031

   Continue the problem entering each number and function. 1.25 + .25 - .031

   The answer is 1.469   or 1.47 inches or 1 15/32"

Index

BACKGROUND OF AUTHOR

Since 1964 Dick has been a teacher at Prosser Vocational School in Chicago. Here he has trained hundreds of students, apprentices and mechanics in sheet metal work.

He conducts both day and evening classes. The day sessions are for high school vocational students readying themselves to enter the trade when they graduate. At night, he holds classes for apprentices and also for mechanics wanting to brush-up, advance themselves or simply keep pace with a changing industry.

Also, he has periodically served as a curriculum consultant for the Chicago public school system. And he has conducted company training programs for several industrial firms.

In his spare time, he has authored a total of twenty-three books on various phases of sheet metal work, making him one of the most published, if not the most published, authors in this field. Nineteen of these books are published by Practical Publications.

Four of these books published by Practical Publications are "Today's 40 Most Frequently-Used Fittings", "Round Fittings Used Today Including Methods and Techniques of Fabricating Round Work", "Fittings Used Today That Require Triangulation Including The Theory of Triangulation", and "Specialty Items Used Today". These volumes cover the sheet metal fittings that are used today, as well as many important facts pertaining to the layout and fabrication of fittings.

Also published by Practical Publications is a 12 volume set containing a textbook, workbook and an instructor's guide on each of the following subjects: blueprint reading, shop math, shop theory and shop practices. All of these are geared to precision sheet metal (close tolerance) work. The additional titles include "Short Courses in Sheet Metal Shop Theory", "Practical Sheet Metal Projects", and "Sheet Metal Shop Fabrication Problems".

The three books published by Howard W. Sams include a textbook entitled "Sheet Metal Technology" containing 22 chapters which encompass all facets of the sheet metal industry. To accompany this book, he wrote a complete spiritmaster test package and a separate instructor's guide. He also wrote "Careers in Air Conditioning and Refrigeration" published by National Textbook Company.

Before becoming a trade teacher, Dick worked for 10 years as a sheet metal apprentice and mechanic for both large and small shops in the Chicago area. Today he still enjoys returning to the sheet metal trade during each summer to keep abreast of the latest methods and techniques.

Aside from his vast trade experience, Dick holds a Bachelor of Science degree in Industrial Education from Chicago State University. He attended evening classes for 14 years, fit into his already busy schedule, to obtain this degree.

Dick formerly was Technical Editor of AMERICAN ARTISAN, and currently is Shop and Job Tips Editor of HAC, a heating, air conditioning, air handling and sheet metal monthly magazine. He writes monthly articles concerning problems facing the sheet metal contractor today. The articles consist of methods and techniques for doing work in the shop and on the job. Dick covers many aspects of design, fabrication and installation of residential, commercial and industrial ductrun systems. Each article is profusely illustrated and easily understood.

FMA and THE FABRICATOR®

When you need reliable technical information on today's most productive metal forming and fabricating processes, join the Fabricators & Manufacturers Association, International (FMA). This not-for-profit organization serves industry as a resource for metal forming and fabricating technology, as well as management information. FMA serves members in over 25 countries on five continents.

The most important reason to join FMA or one of its technology associations is to receive vital technical and management information that will improve the productivity of your operations. When you join FMA, you automatically receive many informative publications that will keep you up-to-date on the newest techniques, equipment and industry activities.

As a member of FMA, you also have access to the most complete technical library in the fabricating industry. This library is your premier source for useful information that can help you work with suppliers, distributors and potential customers worldwide.

These pages tell you more about FMA's educational benefits and membership services. To receive more information or to join FMA, call the FMA Membership Department at (815) 399-8700.

The FMA staff and educational resources are ready to help you achieve your goals for high quality and productivity in your manufacturing operations.

TECHNICAL DIVISIONS/TECHNOLOGY ASSOCIATIONS

FMA membership allows you to enroll in either the Technical Division or Technology Association of your choice. This member benefit allows FMA to serve your interests more effectively by providing you with specialized technical information in your specific area of activity:

FMA Technical Divisions . . .

FMA Sheet Metal Fabricating Division
FMA Roll Forming Division
FMA Technical Divisions (contd.) . . .
FMA Pressworking Division   (contd.)

METAL *Fabricating* INSTITUTE

Metal Fabricating Institute was founded in the late 1960's as a full-time educational and service organization for the metal fabricating industry. The educational arm of the Institute was established as "a self-sustaining educational program devoted to basic education and new techniques in metal fabricating ... and is recognized for its practical approach to everyday fabricating problems."

The Institute sponsored its first fabricating seminar in June, 1968, at Rockford College, Rockford, Illinois. That seminar, which drew 230 attendees, marked a notable beginning of higher education in the metal fabricating industry. Since that first seminar, the Institute has sponsored well-over 100 fabricating, manufacturing, and management seminars all over the continental United States and Canada.

Seminars are conducted at various universities throughout the country and only through the permission of the engineering departments of the cooperating universities. Some of the colleges and universities utilized as training centers, past and present, have included Rockford College (Illinois), Purdue University, University of Cincinnati, California State College at Long Beach, San Jose State College, Texas Christian University, Southern Methodist University, Texas A & M University, University of South Florida at Tampa, North Carolina State University, Spring Garden College (Philadelphia), and McMasters University in Ontario, Canada. With an "alumni association" exceeding six thousand in number, Metal Fabricating Institute attracts attendees from a broad cross-section of both the metal fabricating industry as well as geographical regions. From the small job shops to the Fortune 500's, participants come from all over the United States, as well as from many parts of Canada and Europe. A typical seminar averages a representation of thirty-three states and one or two foreign countries.

If you would like more information about our seminars, please write to:

Metal Fabricating Institute
710 South Main Street
Rockford, Illinois 61101

The ASM of today . . . and the future . . . is an organization as dynamic as the promise of technology.

As the need of ASM's constituencies for reliable technical information has expanded beyond metals alone to include other engineered materials, such as composites, ceramics, and polymers as well as electronic materials, so has the responsibility for the Society to broaden its technical scope to develop services within these areas.

Similarly, ASM's sphere of influence is international in nature as the Society seeks technical information wherever developed and distributes it wherever needed.

A prime example of ASM's technical and international involvement is the Society's leadership role in the **International Data Program for Alloy Phase Diagrams,** a large and important worldwide program to compile, evaluate, and disseminate phase diagram information.

Educational courses on videotape, problem-solving computer software, new computerized informational databases, leading-edge technical conferences, new handbooks and periodical publications . . . all are the results of a plan with the objective of enhancing ASM's reputation as the world's leading society for engineered materials.

There are nearly 200 **Chapters** located in North America and, internationally, in many other countries. Some Chapters are dedicated to a particular technical area, such as electronic materials or extractive metallurgy. Nearly 100 **Student Chapters** are functioning at colleges, universities, trade schools, and high schools, aiding young people contemplating careers in metallurgy and materials technology.

Keeping people abreast of technology requires that information gathered be disseminated as rapidly as possible. One of ASM's major means of accomplishing this is through periodically-issued magazines and journals.

The monthly *Metal Progress* magazine has been one of the leading sources of metals technology since 1930. *Metal Progress* provides a concise coverage of metals and metalworking and covers new developments in processing and fabrication.

Advanced Materials & Processes, a new ASM monthly magazine, focuses on materials for high-performance applications, addressing the technical issues involved in selecting polymers, composites, and ceramics.

Members are updated on all Society activities through *ASM News,* a monthly tabloid newspaper.

ASM publishes three respected engineering journals, issued on a quarterly or semi-annual basis: *Journal of Heat Treating, Journal of Materials for Energy Systems,* and *Journal of Applied Metalworking.* The Society co-publishes (with the Institute of Metals, London) *International Metals Reviews* and (TMS-AIME) *Metallurgical Transactions.*

The bi-monthly *Bulletin of Alloy Phase Diagrams* provides rapid dissemination of evaluated phase diagrams developed in the International Data Program for Alloy Phase Diagrams.

AMERICAN SOCIETY FOR METALS • METALS PARK, OHIO 44073

SNIPS MAGAZINE

SNIPS is published monthly and is a journal of constructive help for the air conditioning, warm air heating, sheet metal and ventilation trades, and those who do roofing work in connection.

SNIPS is a friendly, close-to-the-reader, newsy periodical, long established as the "Bible" of the industry. Stories feature work done by readers, plus numerous new product reviews and reports of local, state and national trade association activities on an almost exclusive basis.

In addition to the feature articles, **SNIPS** regular "Department News" sections include:

Advertisers Index
Book News
Coming Conventions
Computer News
Editor's Page
Estimating, Credits and
    Collections
HVACR Service Information
Heating Problem Discussions
Hydronics News
Industry Educational News
Insurance and Safety Matters
Letters From Readers
Little Journeys to Interesting
    Places
Machine, Tool and Shop News
Management Matters

Market Matters
National Association News
Obituaries
Rambling With Reps
Refrigeration News
Roofing, Siding and Insulation
    News
Solar Heating News
Solid Fuel Heating News
Successful Sales Ideas
Supply Trade and New Product
    News
Supply Trade Personnel News
Truck News
Ventilation News
Want Ads

SNIPS features local and regional events in the "Sectional News" including the US in 14 sections, Canada and other foreign countries.

A special service provided by **SNIPS** is its Book Department which carries a wide selection of trade and related books.

Write for subscription information and for a Book Catalog:

SNIPS Magazine
1949 Cornell
Melrose Park, IL 60160   FAX 708-544-3884

FMA and THE FABRICATOR®

FMA Coil Processing Division
FMA Plate and Structural Fabricating Division

FMA Technology Associations . . .

1. American Tube Association/FMA
2. Tube & Pipe Fabricators Association, International/FMA
3. Society for Computer-Aided Engineering/FMA

Educational benefits include:

1. Technical Information Center
2. Technology Conferences, Seminars and Workshops

EXPOSITIONS include:

1. FABTECH Expositions and Conferences
2. PRESSTECH Expositions and Conferences
3. Tube & Pipe International Expositions

PUBLICATIONS include:

1. The **FABRICATOR®**
2. **STAMPING Quarterly®**
3. **TPQ--The Tube & Pipe Quarterly**
4. Quarterly Technology Updates
5. FMA News
6. Member Resource Directory

The **FABRICATOR®** is published 10 times a year. Subscriptions are free to anyone in the metal forming and fabricating industry, and may be obtained by calling the Circulation Department, phone below. You may also write or call for details regarding membership and services available.

Fabricators & Manufacturers Association, Intl.
833 Featherstone Road
Rockford, IL 61107-6302

Phone 815-399-8700   FAX 815-399-7279

PRACTICAL PUBLICATIONS
DIVISION OF PRACTICAL PRODUCTS — ESTABLISHED 1969

PRECISION SHEET METAL — 2nd Edition
Shop Theory (Text) - 736 pages - $49.95
Student's Workbook - 206 pages - $21.95
Instructor's Guide - 206 pages - $29.95

PRECISION SHEET METAL
Shop Practice (Text) - 88 pages - $15.95
Student's Workbook - 86 pages - $21.95
Instructor's Guide - 86 pages - $29.95

SHEET METAL TECHNOLOGY
3rd Edition
360 Pages 7" x 9" - $19.95

SPECIALTY ITEMS USED TODAY
2nd Edition
Including Methods of Design
and Fabrication and
Important Trade Topics
670 pages
407 pages of trade information
$54.95

**INSTRUCTOR'S ANSWERS
GUIDE FOR PRACTICAL
SHEET METAL LAYOUT SERIES**
$24.95

**SHEET METAL SHOP
FABRICATION PROBLEMS**
Including Over 350
Graded Parts
136 Pages - $19.95

**PRACTICAL SHEET METAL
PROJECTS**
2nd Edition
130 Graded Projects
With Drawings, Forming
Information and Sequences
213 Pages - $26.95

**SHEET METAL LAYOUT TABLES
FOR THE HEATING, VENTILATING
AND AIR CONDITIONING INDUSTRY**
Over 205 Pages Consisting of
Over 31,000 Mathematical
Solutions - $29.95

**PRACTICAL GUIDE FOR
IMPROVING YOUR
SHEET METAL SHOP LAYOUT**
With Easy-To-Use
Suggestions and Aids
212 pages - $29.95

ORDER FORM
PLEASE PRINT

We Use
United Parcel Service

ORDER BY: _____
_____ Date

SHIP TO: (If Different Than Ordered By)

_____
Name

_____
Address

_____
City

_____
State   Zip

Phone Number (in the event of any problem with
your order)

____ — ____ - _____
Area Code

_____
Name

_____
Address

_____
City

_____
State   Zip

☐ **Payment Enclosed**
(we pay postage and handling)

☐ **Bill School**
(includes postage and small fee for packaging)

*10% Educational Discount — School, Union or Association letterhead or invoice must accompany order.

Qty.	Title	Price
_____	Practical Sheet Metal Projects	29.95
_____	Sheet Metal Shop Fabrication Problems including over 350 Graded Parts	21.95
_____	Today's 40 Most Frequently-Used Fittings	
	---Volume 1 ----------	29.95
	---Volume 2 ----------	39.95
_____	Round Fittings Used Today including Methods and Techniques of Fabricating Round Work 3rd Edn.	21.95
_____	Fittings Used Today that Require Triangulation including the Theory of Triangulation 3rd Edn.	21.95
_____	Specialty Items Used Today including Methods of Design and Fabrication and Important Trade Topics 3rd Edn.	54.95
_____	Instructor's Answer Guide For Practical Sheet Metal Layout Series	29.95
_____	Today's Practical Guide To Increasing Profits For Contractors	49.95
_____	Sheet Metal Layout Tables for the Heating, Ventilation and Air Conditioning Industry including over 31,000 Practical, Usable, Accurate Mathematical Solutions	29.95
_____	Practical Guide For Improving Your Sheet Metal Shop Layout with easy to use Suggestions and Aids	29.95
_____	Precision Sheet Metal Shop Theory textbook	21.95
_____	Student's Workbook	21.95
_____	Instructor's Guide	26.95
_____	Precision Sheet Metal Blueprint Reading textbook	18.95
_____	Student's Workbook	21.95
_____	Instructor's Guide	26.95
_____	Precision Sheet Metal Mathematics textbook	21.95
_____	Student's Workbook	21.95
_____	Instructor's Guide	26.95
_____	Precision Sheet Metal Shop Practice textbook	15.95
_____	Student's Workbook	21.95
_____	Instructor's Guide	26.95
_____	Sheet Metal Technology textbook 3RD Edn.	24.95
_____	Student's Workbook	9.95
	Instructor's Guide	9.95
_____	Opportunities in Refrigeration and Air Conditioning (order from VGM Career Horizons, 8259 Niles Center Road, Skokie, IL 60077)	Hard 9.95
_____		Soft 7.95

PRACTICAL PUBLICATIONS
DIVISION OF PRACTICAL PRODUCTS — ESTABLISHED 1969
6272 W. North Avenue • Chicago, Illinois 60639 - 9990 • (312) 237-2986

_____ Practical Cost Estimating for Metal Fabrication	$64.95